Torpedo Squadron Four
A Cockpit View of World War II

Third Edition

Gerald W. Thomas

Contents

Dedication

To my wife, Jean Ellis Thomas.

Acknowledgements

I want to recognize and thank the pilots and crewmen of Air Group 4. So many of them are now gone. These men have been called *"the Greatest Generation."* It was the most honored privilege of my life to serve with them.

I want to thank my son David for editing this extensively revised version of the book, preparing the photos for publication, for establishing the web site airgroup4.com, and for his continued pursuit of World War II history.

I want to thank Steinbjorn Mentzoni, of Sandnessjøen, Norway, who has worked tirelessly to research the history of OPERATION LEADER, and who is responsible for the remains of my comrades who lost their lives on that strike being found and returned to their families, and for the extraordinary memorial to them in Fagervika.

Front Cover

Torpedo 4 Executive Officer Lt Lee L. Hamrick takes off as waves break 80 feet over the flight deck of the *USS ESSEX*. February 22, 1945. Inset: Gerald Thomas, *ESSEX*.

Back Cover

Torpedo 4 Avenger flown by Lt(jg) Ralph R. Anderson lying on *USS RANGER* stacks after rolling over side upon landing, Unidentified crewman works to remove torpedo. March 2, 1943.

Air Group 4 Web Site

For additional research on Air Group 4, visit the web site:

www.AirGroup4.com

Preface

This document presents a view of WWII as seen from the cockpit of a torpedo plane and later rehashed in the Ready Rooms of three aircraft carriers. The focus is on the activities of one squadron, Torpedo Four (VT-4).

There were no identifiable heroes or aces in our squadron -- just ordinary young men caught in an extraordinary World War, taking orders from a high command that we recognized by name but never met on a personal basis. The squadron lost many pilots and crew members during operations and combat duty. Others were rescued from water landings or flight deck crashes.

VT-4 was commissioned January 10, 1942, aboard the original *USS RANGER* while at anchor off Bermuda. It was the Navy's first torpedo squadron commissioned at sea. Serving in both the Atlantic and the Pacific theaters of operation, VT-4 was credited with destruction of more than 160,000 tons of enemy shipping and numerous shore-based military installations.

Torpedo 4 was assigned to three different aircraft carriers during World War II. On the *RANGER*, the squadron was commissioned with six Douglas "Devastators". Later, VT-4 became a nine-plane unit flying some of the first Grumman TBF Avengers. Aboard the *USS BUNKER HILL* and *USS ESSEX* in the Pacific, the squadron operated with 15-18 TBMs. Some highlights of the VT-4 record include:

Supporting the Allied invasion of North Africa and conducting antisubmarine patrols in escort of Navy convoys in the North Atlantic.

Operating from the *RANGER* to participate with the British Home Fleet in a major strike against German shipping and port facilities near Bodø, Norway (this was six months after a German

submarine commander had been wrongly credited with sinking the *RANGER*).

Supporting the Allied invasions of several of the Philippine Islands, Iwo Jima, and Okinawa.

Participating in the first U.S. carrier air attacks against Formosa.

Conducting torpedo and glide-bombing attacks on Saigon (French Indo-China), and Hainan (China), as well as attacking many Japanese ships and shore installations in the Pacific.

Participating in the first carrier-based naval strikes on Tokyo and other targets on the Japanese Mainland.

Planes from Torpedo 4 were on the flight deck ready for launch on November 25, 1944, when a Kamikaze flew through heavy flak and exploded on the port bow of the *ESSEX*.

Torpedo 4 (VT-4) operated with Bombing 4 (VB-4) and Fighting 4 (VF-4) as a coordinated strike group, designated as Air Group 4. In late December 1944, the dive-bombers, because of heavy combat losses, were replaced on the *ESSEX* with two Marine fighter squadrons (VMF-124 and VMF-213). Thus, this historical account must include a part of the combat records of these additional squadrons who played an essential role in the effectiveness of all air group operations.

This brief history of our Torpedo Squadron was compiled from declassified records in the Naval archives, from personal journals, from interviews with pilots and flight crew, and from selected historical documents. The extensive quotes used, drawn directly from the debriefings after each mission, serve as a base for the factual history of strikes on the enemy. As one pilot in the squadron, I have inserted personal accounts which reflect part of the emotion, tension, frustration, and sense of humor of squadron members.

I have purposely shown the tactical organization of the squadron, listing the pilots and flight crew assigned to each strike. It was these individuals, coming from various backgrounds, who made our squadron an effective fighting unit. Some of us stayed together for almost four years -- much of the time confined to a Ready Room or the small living quarters on an aircraft carrier. We were almost like a family unit. When we lost a squadron member, we did not have time to properly mourn the loss because of the continual pressures of the next combat operation. This historical record, compiled 35 years after the end of WWII, is one way to recall and acknowledge those who made the sacrifice.

Gerald W. Thomas

Thomas flying a North American SNJ over Massachusetts. April, 1943.

Note: Ebook versions of **Torpedo Squadron Four: A Cockpit View of World War II** are available for the Kindle, Android, and others.

Chapter 1 | Operation Leader: Initiation Over Norway

"Tracers circled the cockpit and my engine took a direct hit."

The first US carrier-based attack on Nazi-held Norway during World War II was assigned the code name OPERATION LEADER and was carried out by aircraft from the *USS RANGER*, on October 4, 1943. Prior to this operation, German news releases stated that the *RANGER* had been torpedoed and sunk by a German submarine. The captain of the sub (U-404), Lt Otto Von Bulow, who had been decorated by Hitler with Oak Leaves to the Knight's Cross, was credited with this kill.[1] Thus, the Norway strike was an embarrassment to both Hitler and Von Bulow.

At the time of the Norway strike, the *RANGER* was operating as a part of the British Home Fleet under the overall command of Admiral Sir Bruce Fraser. In addition to the Admiral's flagship, *HMS DUKE OF YORK*, the command consisted of the *HMS ANSON*, three British cruisers, six British destroyers, a US contingent of several destroyers supporting the cruiser *USS TUSCALOOSA*, and the *USS RANGER*. Rear Admiral Hustvedt was in command of the *RANGER* Task Force.[2]

A Pilot's View

The boatswain's whistle shrieked through the loud speaker in the passageway. The announcement came:

> Now hear this! Now hear this! The *RANGER* has just crossed the Arctic Circle. The captain congratulates all those on board for attaining membership in the Bluenose Society. With Neptune's permission and the blessings of Aurora Borealis, Bluenose certificates will be issued to all hands.

It was the evening of October 3, 1943, and the *RANGER* had just crossed the Arctic Circle. We had completed a busy day of inspecting planes, loading bombs, and studying maps. A big engagement against the Nazis lay ahead. Everything was in readiness for a predawn takeoff. All pilots could draw from memory a rough sketch of the coastline and adjacent islands of Norway from Sandnessjoen to the Bodø airport. A description of the fjords and mountains had been furnished by former members of the Royal Norwegian Air Force. Pictures of German ships that might be encountered were examined, and pinpoints on the map indicated the gun emplacements that were established before the German occupation.

Rough seas on the North Atlantic always made me seasick. That night aboard the *RANGER* was no exception. I was unable to eat supper, so I climbed into my bunk early with a bad headache. I felt better lying down. Even though it was bitter cold outside, it was too warm in the Officers' Quarters. It was always warm and stuffy, with bad odors everywhere, when the sea was rough. Cigarette smoke was especially bad. Fortunately my bunk was against an outside steel bulkhead that was cool from contact with the water. I often turned aside the covers and rolled against the cold steel. It made me feel better. My stomach settled and I finally fell asleep -- perhaps about midnight. I slept fitfully and tried not to think about the briefing the previous afternoon -- or the prospect of tomorrow.

Reveille was sounded about 2 a.m. It was hard to get up! I was still groggy, sick, and uneasy. I put on heavy clothes including my green wool Red Cross sweater. The word had spread among the pilots that these hand-knit sweaters, donated by the Red Cross, were flak-proof. It couldn't hurt to have extra protection from both flak and the Arctic cold.

The **USS RANGER**, CV-4, was the first US Naval vessel designed and constructed as an aircraft carrier. Authorized February 13, 1929, her keel was laid September 26, 1931 by the Newport News Shipbuilding and Dry Dock Company, Newport News, Virginia. She was launched February 25, 1933, and commissioned June 4, 1934.

RANGER in Hampton Roads, Virginia, August 1942. Note the 6 stacks, which were folded down during air operations.

Bluenose Certificate issued to Gerald Thomas on crossing the Arctic Circle, October 3, 1943.
Signed by Captain Gordon Rowe, Commanding Officer, *USS RANGER*.

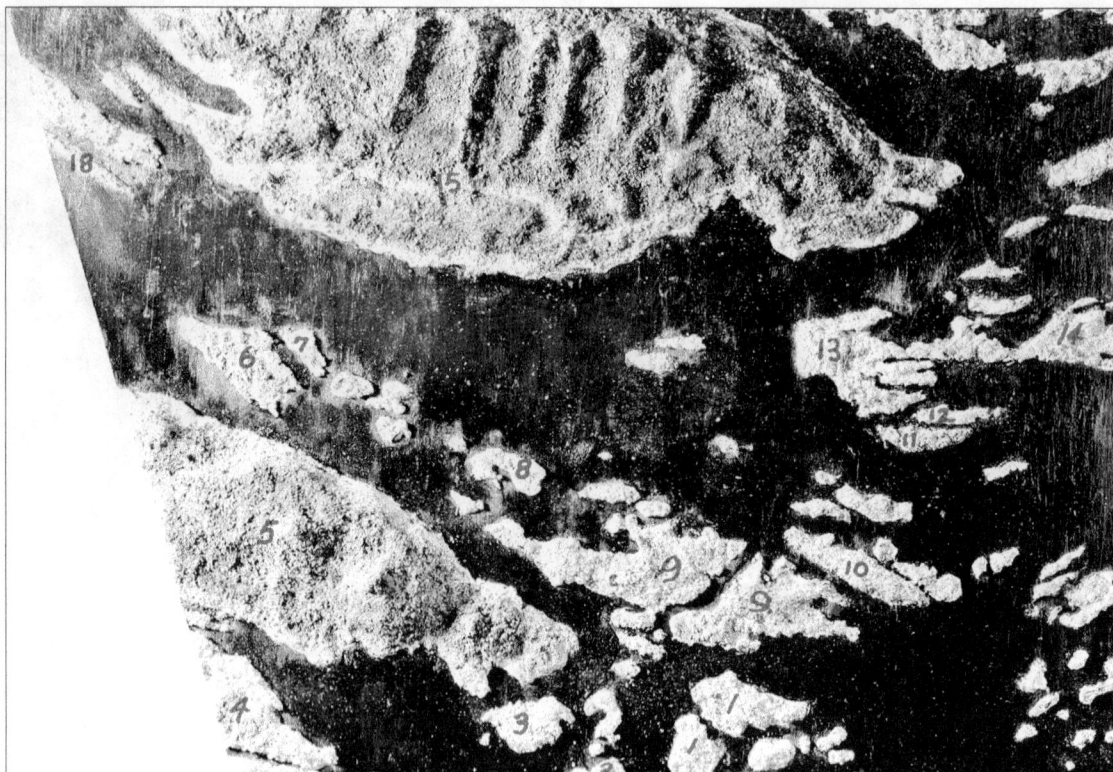

One of several table-top models made prior to OPERATION LEADER to familiarize the pilots with the area of their air operations. This model shows Bodo and surrounding territory.

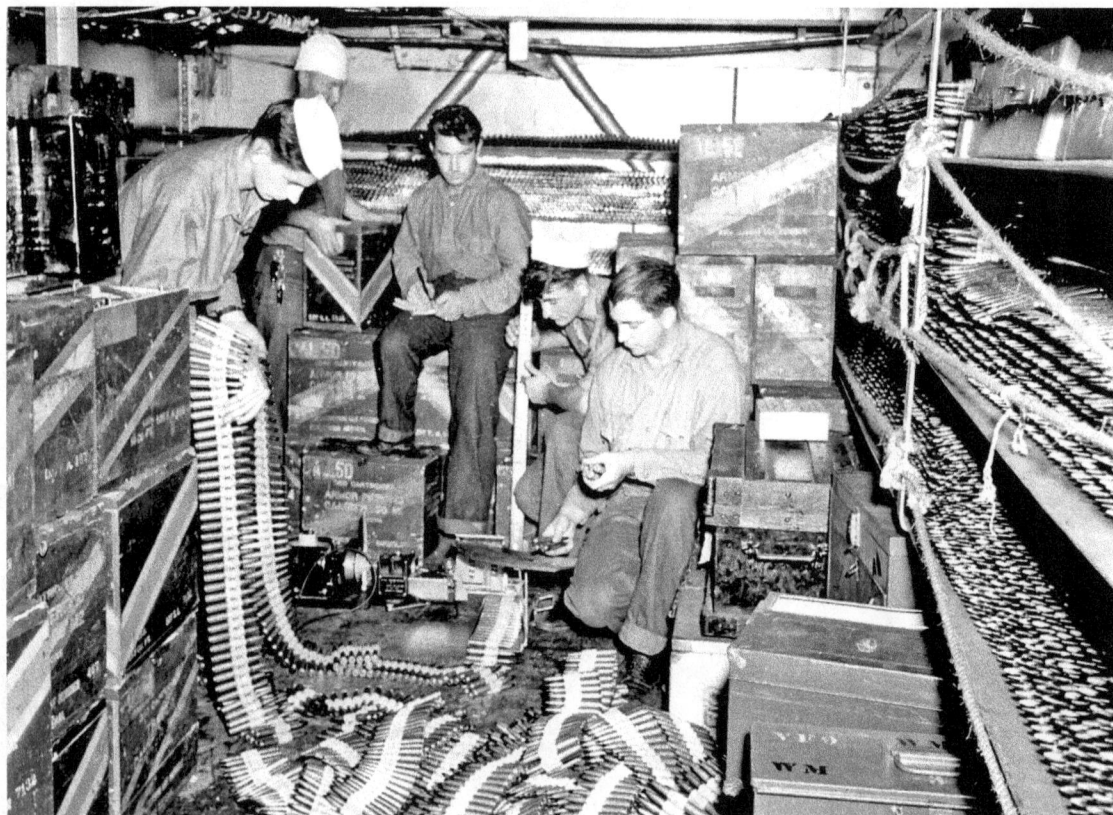

Ship's Armory, *RANGER*. Crewmen unidentified.

In preparation for OPERATION LEADER, Lt Keene R. Hammond checks for faulty ammunition being loaded into the mid-ammunition can of his F4F "Wildcat" fighter by W. Q. Hase, S2/c and G. H. Hampton, AOM3/c. Hammond commanded the F4F's that accompanied VT-4 on the strike. Hammond was killed January 6, 1945 on a strike on Laoag, Philippines when his plane was hit by AA fire and exploded during an attempted water landing. *RANGER*, October 2, 1943.

Torpedo Squadron 4 aboard *RANGER*. Front Row: Ens George D. Walker, Ens Robert F. Ruth, Lt(jg) Page P. Stephens, Ens Felix E. Ward, Ens Wilbur S. Souza, Ens Gerald M. Barnett. Second Row: Lt(jg) Louis G. Gardemal, Lt J. Welsh Harriss, Lt Richard Claytor, Lt Cdr D. Woot Taylor, Lt Cdr Homer H. Hutcheson, Lt(jg) George W. Bolt. Back Row: Lt(jg) John H. Palmer, Lt(jg) Lee L. Hamrick, Lt(jg) Ralph R. Anderson, Lt(jg) Robert E. Trexler, Ens Gerald W. Thomas. September, 1943.

At 0430, "Flight Quarters" was sounded and pilots and crew lay up to their respective Ready Rooms. Preliminary flight instructions were already coming over the teletype, and there was a feeling of anxiety in the air as most of us faced our first mission over enemy territory.

Will Souza, Bob Ruth, and I were all new ensigns in Torpedo Squadron 4. A couple of months earlier we had been enjoying "good duty" as test pilots for CASU-22 (Carrier Aircraft Service Unit 22) at Quonset Point, Rhode Island. The three of us had been together through most of flight training at Corpus Christi, Texas, and dive-bomber training at Opa Locka, Florida. We were not trained as torpedo pilots, although we were carrier-qualified. I had completed my 8 required qualification landings aboard the British carrier *HMS ATTACKER* off Norfolk, Virginia. On the final qualification landing, as my SNJ trainer hit the flight deck, the tail hook caught a tie-down iron instead of a cable because the wooden flight deck was worn down to expose the iron strips. The tail hook snapped off, and I crashed forward into the barrier. I walked away from the damaged plane, and the landing counted toward the necessary 8 required for carrier qualification.

My reflections on this incident were interrupted when our Squadron Commander, D. W. "Woot" Taylor, took charge of the briefing. It went something like this:

We are to launch planes from 100 miles out to sea. Our target is German shipping and shore installations in the vicinity of Bodø, Norway. The dive-bombers will hit the Port of Bodø almost due east of the launch site. The torpedo planes will attack shipping along the fjords south of Bodø. Fighter cover will be split, part for the dive-bombers, part for us. All torpedo planes are loaded with four 500-pound bombs with armor-piercing, 10-second-delay fuses. Stay close, follow the signals. Since only CRAG (Commander Ranger Air Group) and the VT-4 skippers have planes

equipped with VHF (Very High Frequency), we will all maintain radio silence. Do not use your radios! We must not reveal the location of the task force or the nature of our mission! We will operate in two-plane sections. When we spot a ship, the leader of the two-plane section will wobble his wings violently. This maneuver will be spotted by the fighters flying overhead. Four fighter planes will then split off and dive to strafe the ship -- hopefully reducing AA fire. The first two torpedo planes will follow the strafing fighters and drop their bombs at masthead level on the ship. Only two TBFs will go down at a time. When we spot the next ship, the next two torpedo planes will follow the same procedure -- four fighters will strafe, two torpedo planes will go in for masthead bombing runs. Is that clear? Stay close in formation! Follow the signals! Do not break radio silence!

Torpedo Squadron 4 consisted of 14 pilots, about 35 crewmen, but only 9 Grumman Avengers (TBFs). A tenth TBF on board was assigned to Cdr Joseph A. Ruddy, which meant that five VT-4 pilots with crews would not fly. Homer H. Hutcheson, the Exec, knew I was seasick, so he originally assigned Ensign Souza to the flight. However, at the last minute he told me to pilot Four-Tare-Nine (4-T-9), the last plane on the flight deck.

I hurriedly copied the Point Option Data (ship's location, speed, wind direction, velocity, etc.) on my plotting board and strapped on my parachute harness. The parachute straps did not fit very well over the .38 shoulder holster -- I was sure I would break a rib if I bailed out. I took the gun off, put it back on, took it off again, and finally decided to leave it in the Ready Room. I wouldn't be likely to use it anyway if I went down in occupied territory.

At 0618, the *northern attack group* and a small combat air patrol were launched. The attack group consisted of 20 Dauntless dive-bombers, escorted by 8 Wildcat fighters, with Lt Cdr George O. Klinsmann as the leader in one of the SBDs. This group

SBD "Dauntless" dive-bomber off the **RANGER** drops a practice bomb, June, 1943.

TBF "Avenger" torpedo bomber. Undated photo.

was sent toward Bodø.

As the last SBD cleared the flight deck, plane handlers spotted the deck with the TBFs and fighter escort planes.

"Pilots, man your planes." The orders came over the squawk box to man our planes before I could recalculate the ship's position or do any more sophisticated navigation. As pilots and crew rushed up to the flight deck in the dark, a below-freezing wind blew across the deck and helped relieve my nausea. I found Four-Tare-Nine near the fantail on the flight deck.

I climbed onto the wing of the huge Avenger, and the plane captain helped me fasten my seat-pack chute, safety belt, and shoulder straps. He produced the yellow sheet, which I signed, and we went over the ordinance data.

"Check your wheel chocks, propeller clearance, and all loose gear about the decks. Stand by to start engines!" "Stand clear of propellers!" The loudspeaker broke the predawn silence as the expectant pilots checked switches, the gas mixture, and went through the check-off list. With the word to *"Start engines,"* all engines turned over simultaneously. With the exception of a couple of cold, balky engines, the flight deck suddenly came alive.

I admired the plane handlers who stood among the tightly packed planes and were able to guide them into launch position without getting chopped up by a propeller.

I taxied into the takeoff spot, received the rev-up signal, and checked out all instruments. The engine sounded good; so I nodded my head to the launching officer, and he dropped his flag directing the takeoff. I popped the flaps about halfway down the flight deck and took off into the semidarkness of the North Atlantic. As I raised the wheels, I made the usual right turn to clear my slipstream from the flight path of the next plane. With all 9 torpedo planes now in formation, we turned toward the coast of Norway -- German territory!

As I settled down for the 100-mile flight to Norway, I wondered how in the world a country boy from Idaho had gotten into this kind of situation! My obsession with flying started when I was 14.

The bay mare picked up her ears. Almost immediately, the horse on the right followed suit. The team heard something above the sound of the wagon wheels crunching on the rocky road leading to the abandoned dry farm. My Dad was driving the wagon, and I was in the seat beside him. I looked to see if the horses had spotted something on the open range -- perhaps an antelope or a herd of horses. I scanned the rolling sagebrush-covered hills that we called the Medicine Lodge Bench. Only a few seconds after the horses picked up their ears, Dad and I heard the sound. *"By golly, it's one of those flying machines!"* my Dad said. *"Probably a barnstormer from Butte or Pocatello."* It was the first real airplane either of us had ever seen. The horses became very excited as the plane flew by. But the team was not nearly as excited as I was! What a thrill to see a real airplane out here in Southern Idaho! Dad and I talked a lot about the flying machine as we rolled up barbed wire from the abandoned dry farm and headed home. I resolved then and there to someday take a ride in an airplane and maybe even learn to fly. It didn't seem too likely with all the problems we had out here on the ranch during the Depression. The year was 1933.

But this was no time to dream about the past. Our Torpedo 4 *southern attack group* made landfall between Sandnessjoen and Kunna Head just as dawn was breaking. The rugged mountains along the coast were covered with snow, and no German fighters had flown out to intercept us. The attack was indeed a surprise.

The skipper turned the formation north to follow the shipping lanes along the coast. About this time, the Germans were alerted and scattered AA fire developed. In a few minutes we spotted our first large enemy ship -- a transport. Taylor wobbled his wings, the fighters went in to strafe, and the first two torpedo planes made a masthead run

VT-4 Avengers 4-T-22 and 4-T-5 pass Skomver Lighthouse on way to Bodø strike.
Detail shows lighthouse. October 3, 1943. Norway.

Passenger vessel sighted by Northern Attack Group (VB-4).

on the ship. After the attack, the two torpedo planes rejoined our group where we were now flying at about 1500-2000 feet. The AA fire intensified as we continued our flight toward Bodø.

Suddenly, the Avenger flown by Lt(jg) John Palmer exploded just in front of me and started a gradual spiral toward the sea. The skipper broke radio silence and told the plane crew to bail out, but only one parachute popped into sight before the plane plunged into the sea. I drew myself into the center of my own cockpit under the protection of the armor plate, making myself as small as possible as the bursts of AA fire spotted the sky. We continued the flight down the fjords.

A few minutes later a second strike group attacked another ship. Another successful run and the ship was left burning.

Then, before it was our turn, I suddenly realized that Lt(jg) Trexler, my section leader, was wobbling his wings. He must have received a hand signal, which meant that our attack section was next. I had been watching a tanker-like ship chugging down the shipping lanes just ahead of us (the American records identify this ship as **MFS 231**, a oil tanker, but German records show the ship was a freight barge carrying 40 tons of ammunition.) By the time Trex gave the signal to attack, we were almost directly over the ship -- still at about 1500 feet. That meant more of a dive-bombing run than a glide-bombing run as planned. Trex turned his plane sharply into a dive.

I had been lagging too far behind in formation, so I knew I would reach the ship just in time to get in Trex's bomb blast -- remembering the 5-second delay fuse. Consequently, I rolled the plane violently to shortcut the distance down and pushed into the dive. As I rolled, my right wing blocked my view of Trex's plane. In the dive, I realized that he wasn't in front of me. I learned later that he had pulled out of the dive for two reasons: first, the fighter planes flying above didn't get the signal in time to strafe; second, the dive was too steep for a torpedo plane.

As I put more and more pressure on the stick to hold down the nose of the huge Avenger, I rapidly went through the switching procedure to arm the bombs, open the bomb bay, and turn the guns on for strafing. I didn't have time to roll the tabs forward to reduce the pressure on the stick. I fired a couple of bursts from the machine guns, pushed the "pickle," and dropped two 500-pounders. It was a tight pull to get out of the dive just above water level. Because of the steep dive, I could not hold the nose on target, so the two bombs straddled the bow of the ship -- at least 50 feet too far forward splashing water on the deck of the tanker.

My belly gunner, Jackson, who also served as bombardier, called on the intercom to tell me that we had a clean miss, but two bombs were left in the bomb bay. At that point, I threw caution to the wind. I guess I almost forgot that I was in combat -- rather, I automatically followed the pattern of a practice mission. I was flying about 50 feet above the water, moving rapidly toward a small, rocky island that outlined the seaward boundary of the shipping lanes. As I pulled the plane into a steep wingover and passed over one of the islands, someone shouted over the radio, *"Watch that shore battery!"* I didn't realize that I had turned just above a gun emplacement or that my wings were perforated with bullet holes. Anyway, I turned back for a masthead run on the German tanker which was now headed toward the shore where I could quarter its wake -- an ideal attack position.

As I approached the ship, I became conscious of -- almost surprised to see -- tracers floating toward me from about three locations on the tanker. And I was moving so darned slow -- even at full throttle!

I didn't have the time or the presence of mind to strafe on this second approach. As I got closer and closer to the tanker, all the ship's gunners stopped firing except one. The tracers that flashed by made a complete circle of the cockpit. Then, just before I pushed the bomb release over the ship, my engine took a direct hit. There was a small explosion

Northbound freight barge *MFS 231* sighted by Southern Attack Group (VT-4).

Attack on *MFS 231* by Lt(jg) Hamrick (4-T-3). The top gun-camera photo was taken as Hamrick releases his bombs -- the second shows the freighter being straffed as Hamrick pulls out of his dive.

Hamrick's bomb drop on *MFS 231* overshoots the freighter.

The top gun-photo shows *MFS 231* just as Thomas (4-T-9) drops his first two bombs on the freighter. Note the oil slick caused by Hamrick's missed bombs. The bottom photo shows Thomas' second bomb drop on the freighter. In his second strike Thomas hit the freighter amidships.

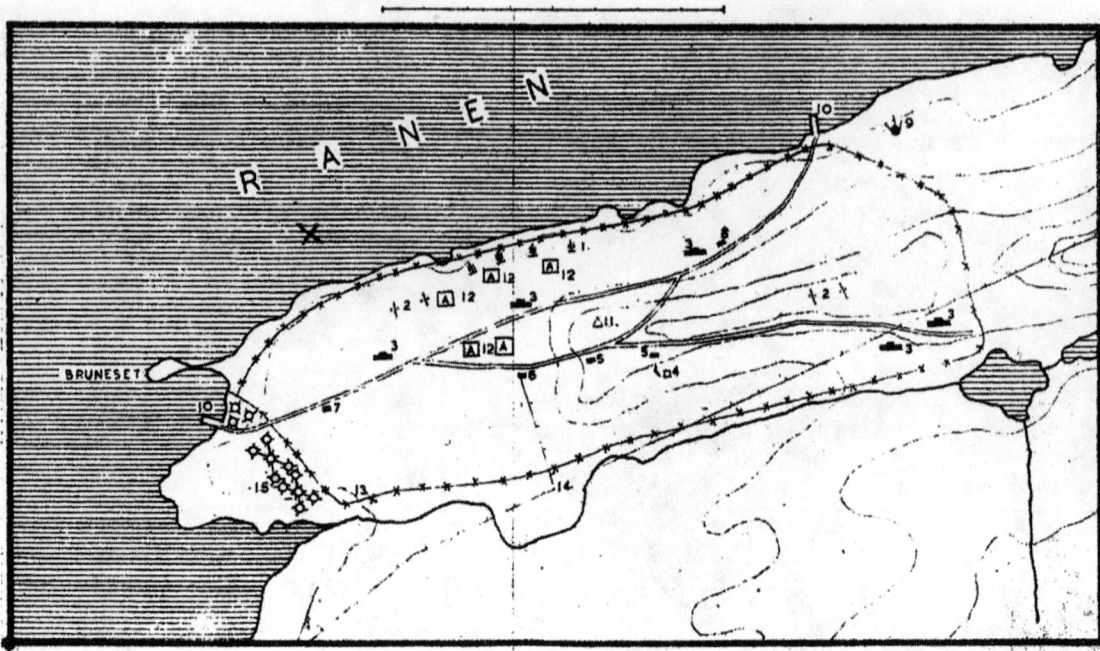

1945 German map of the AA emplacements encountered by VT-4. **Legend**:
(1) Four sets of 10.5 cm AA guns; (2) light AA guns; (3) Barracks; (4) Power plant;
(5) Officer billets; (6) Commanding officer residence; (7) Guards hut; (8) Canteen;
(9) Searchlight; (10) Quays; (11) Guard tower; (12) Ammunition shelters;
(13) Barbed wire; (14) Telephone wire; (15) Landmines
The X marks the spot where Lt(jg) John H. Palmer's plane was shot down.

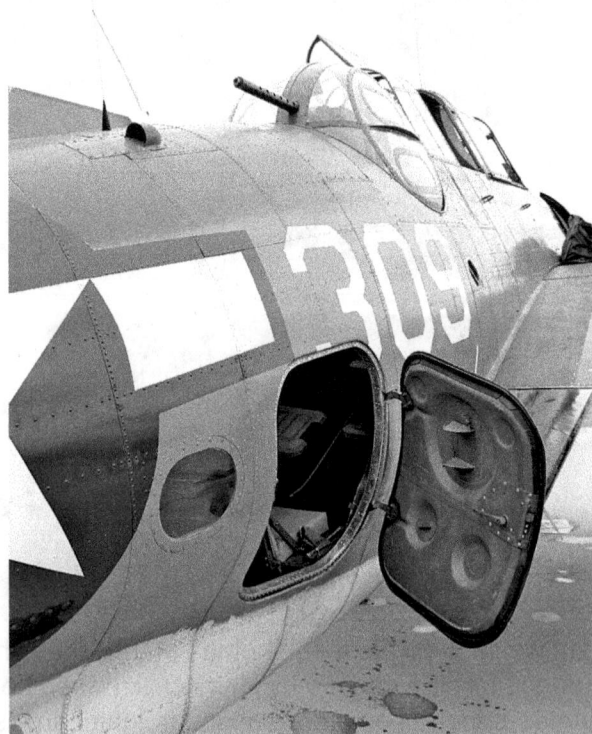

The crew escape hatch of an TBF Avenger. It was extremely difficult to bail out
of an Avenger, which is why many crewmen lost their lives in a downed plane
while the pilot survived. Restored Avenger. Scottsdale, Arizona. May 27, 2005.

with a brief flash of fire and smoke over the cockpit as I pushed the pickle releasing the two remaining bombs. One 500-pounder landed on the deck of the tanker. The ship exploded and ran aground as it burned.

Garner, my turret gunner, shouted, *"We're on fire!"* I hauled back on the stick to gain altitude, then picked up the mike and shouted over the intercom, *"Bail Out!"*

At about 800 feet, I opened the hatch, sprung my safety belt, and started to climb out of the cockpit. I had never bailed out of a plane before and in the confusion forgot to pull the radio cord from my helmet. Consequently, I heard a call from Garner. *"Don't jump, don't jump. Jackson's popped his chute in the plane and he can't get out!"* It seems that Jackson, in his excitement, had accidentally pulled his ripcord inside the belly of the TBF. The spring-loaded silk had let loose all over the place. He tried several times to bundle the slippery silk in his arms and work his way through the narrow door, but no such luck -- he was trapped.

As I settled back into the cockpit, I picked up the mike and gave instructions to Jackson and Garner to fasten their safety belts and prepare for a crash landing. Our plane was still over the shipping lanes -- not far from the burning tanker. The engine was smoking but there was no active fire.

There was no way I could land on that rough, rocky shore of Norway, so I chose to make a water landing. I started letting down toward one of the small islands to make a wheels-up, full-stall water landing.

About then I realized that I was the lone target of concentrated AA fire. It got hotter as I lost altitude. I began to think I would never make it all the way down, so I shoved the throttle forward and headed toward the open sea, taking some violent evasive action to shake the gunners off my tail. It was a miracle that I wasn't hit again.

At about two miles out I started climbing to gain altitude. The plane was still laying down a stream of smoke. I checked the cockpit instruments expecting to see several red warning lights, but there were none. Oil pressure, OK; cylinder head temperature, OK; tachometer and throttle, working. I was carrying about 30 inches of mercury -- what a relief!

Now, to do some quick planning. The *RANGER* was 100 miles out in a sea that was rough and cold. We were told at the briefing that we could expect to live about 15-20 minutes in the icy North Atlantic -- an hour at the most. The distance to neutral Sweden was only 90 miles. Scuttlebutt was that there was good duty in neutral Sweden for Americans. Ten miles may make the difference in a damaged plane, so I called the crew and said that we would head for Sweden.

I watched the instruments carefully as I climbed to 3000, then 5000 feet. Turning toward shore, I looked at the snow-covered mountain range that characterized Norway -- not a pleasant sight for a pilot with a damaged plane. As we flew toward the shoreline, another hazard developed. All my fellow squadron buddies had left the area and flown toward Bodø. I was alone. Every Nazi AA gun on shore started shooting at us -- it became mighty uncomfortable!

OK, forget Sweden -- I'll head for the carrier! I turned back toward the sea.

Instruments still OK -- I cut back on the throttle. I must save the engine, if possible. I pulled the plotting board out of the instrument panel into my lap and suddenly realized that I didn't know precisely where the carrier was located. What heading should I take to find the *RANGER*? I looked around to check for other planes and saw an Avenger to the south. I headed toward it, but it pulled away. Later I found out that the pilot thought I might be a German Focke-Wulf, so he wasn't about to be approached. I decided to guess at a heading and hope for the best because I was restricted to dead reckoning without precise Point Option data. That was a sure formula for disaster.

62 years after he last flew an Avenger, Thomas gets an opportunity to return to the cockpit in a restored WWII Avenger. Rexburg, Idaho. July 19, 2007.

Cockpit, restored Avenger. Rexburg, Idaho. July 19, 2007.

A few minutes later I spotted several torpedo planes and joined them in formation. By now, radio silence had been broken by various distress calls, but I still didn't use the mike. I signaled to one of the pilots and pointed to my engine. He flew around old Four-Tare-Nine and gave me the thumbs up signal, while I wondered how that engine could still run and continue to smoke.

I concentrated on the rest of the 100-mile flight over the cold North Atlantic, watching the instruments carefully and listening for the first change in the sound of the engine. The canopy around the cockpit was now almost completely covered with oil, so I opened the hatch and reached my left hand into the wind stream to wipe away some of the oil. I succeeded only in smearing the oil around and almost broke my arm from the force of the wind. The open hatch gave me some increased visibility, but the cold air made me shiver.

The **RANGER**, alerted to the approach of returning planes, had started turning into the wind when I spotted the task force from about 15 miles out. Breaking away from the other planes, I headed straight for the **RANGER**. I dropped the wheels and tail hook and opened the flaps. Red lights appeared on the instrument panel indicating that my oil pressure was about gone, but the hydraulic system seemed to be functioning.

My first pass over the carrier was almost crosswise to the flight deck because the ship was heeled over from its turn toward the wind. Looking out the side of the cockpit, I spotted the signal officer giving me an emphatic wave-off.

"Hell, I know I'll never make it around again!" I just barely missed a destroyer as I wrapped the plane into a tight turn and started back toward the carrier. There was no possibility of following the signal officer's hand directions through the oil-covered canopy. However, I had some visibility out the right side of the cockpit, so I placed the island of the ship about where I thought it should be to line up with the flight deck. I chopped the throttle, pulled the stick into my lap to stall the plane, and hoped for the best.

Luckily, my tail hook caught a wire just as I hit the barrier. My right wing also hit the ship's island. As the plane crashed, I released my safety harness and jumped out onto the wing. Plane handlers were spraying the smoking plane as I slid off the wing and ran forward on the fight deck. My crew, Garner and Jackson, escaped at the same time.

As I ran toward the hatch that led to the Ready Room, the flight deck officer stepped quickly in my path, grabbed me by the neck, and shouted, *"You son of a bitch! You landed on a wave-off and fouled up the flight deck. Now, how in hell am I going to get the other planes aboard?"*

I shook the air officer's hand loose from my flight suit and went on down to the Ready Room knowing I might face a court martial. To land on a wave-off was a major offense.

A few minutes later we were informed that the flight deck was cleared, and other returning planes were landing. They took my plane, Four Tare Nine, down the elevator for an engine change and wing repairs. I told my story, but no one gave me any assurance that I would not receive a reprimand.

Sometime later (November 22), the **RANGER** raised anchor in Scapa Flow and returned home. Our squadron flew ashore for a short training period before transferring to the Bunker Hill in the Pacific.

One day Ensign Makibbin and I went by the cleaners on the Navy base at Quonset Point to pick up our uniforms. I noticed a surprised look on the face of the young woman at the counter when I gave her my name. As she brought my uniform, she asked if I was the Ensign Thomas of Torpedo Four. When I said yes, she introduced herself as Mrs. Jackson and said, *"My husband thinks you are the best pilot in the Navy!"*

I never saw Mrs. Jackson again, but her husband flew with me until June of 1944. He was a loyal and dedicated crewman.

Mrs. Jackson's statement made me feel good, but for some time I carried the guilt of "fouling up the flight deck." I have the Skipper to thank for helping me tell my story and later recommending the Air Medal. Part of the citation read: "... *Although his plane was struck several times in the engine, he left the enemy beached and badly down by the stern before setting out on a precarious return flight to his carrier with failing power, an oil-covered windscreen, and a damaged wing.*"

The crash landing on the *RANGER* after the Norway strike with 3.2 harrowing hours in the air was recorded in my official pilot's log as Carrier Landing Number 13. I was now, at least in some circles, a "veteran Navy pilot." My initiation into Torpedo 4 was over.

Memorial to the men of Air Group 4 who lost their lives in OPERATION LEADER:
Lt(jg) John H. Palmer with crewmen Joseph L. Zalom and Reginald H. Miller, VT-4 (4-T-4);
Lt(jg) Clyde A. Tucker, Jr. with his turret gunner Stephen D. Bakran, VB-4 (4-B-19);
Lt(jg) Sumner R. Davis with his turret gunner D. W. McCarley, VB-4 (4-B-15).
Fagervika, Norway. December, 2008. Photo by Steinbjørn Mentzoni.

Chapter 2 | OPERATION LEADER: The Historical Record

"Both dive-bombers were brought down by AA fire."

Documents from the US and British archives indicate that OPERATION LEADER was carried out according to plan. There were more target ships in the area than intelligence led us to believe. Both the northern and the southern attack groups inflicted substantial damage to German shipping.

The Northern Attack Group

The first attack group of Dauntless dive-bombers and Wildcat fighters, led by Cdr Klinsmann, made landfall at Myken Light and continued northeastward along the shipping lanes. One section bombed the 8000-ton freighter *LA PLATA*. Another attacked a tanker and a transport accompanied by a German destroyer. The 14,000-ton *SCHLESWIG* was hit with a 500-pounder, forcing the ship to run aground. Other smaller ships were bombed and damaged near the Port of Bodø.

The tactical organization of VB-4 was: [1][10]

Pilot	Gunner
Lt Cdr G. O. Klinsmann	E. M. Rogers
Lt C. F. Weeks	H. C. Meredith
Lt H. J. Stratton	Lt Odd Dahm (Norway)
Lt(jg) R. W. Ross	L. J. Devine
Lt J. L. Bettinger	D. T. Shaw
Lt(jg) J. G. McReynolds	W. C. Parrish
Lt W. H. Longley	L. E. Edens
Lt(jg) C. G. Hendricks	Keefe
Lt H. R. Keller	W. T. Shackelford
Lt(jg) C. R. Breckheimer	Branson
Lt L. M. Boykin	H. H. Reed
Lt(jg) S. R. Davis	D. W. McCarley
Lt C. V. Johnson	S. M. Eardley
Lt(jg) C. A. Tucker	S. D. Bakran
Lt R. W. Phillips	J. J. Lankowicz
Lt(jg) W. E. Dill	L. J. Blier
Lt G. P. Chase	A. W. Lorentzen
Lt(jg) P. H. Gordon	M. S. Waterson
Lt D. K. Weitzenfeld	K. W. Jobe
Lt G. C. Simmons	L. E. Colon

Two additional SBDs were launched for anti-sub patrol and loaded with depth charges:

Pilot	Gunner
Lt(jg) L. R. Norman	J. C. Brilhart
Lt(jg) D. E. Way	G. C. Ellis

Wildcat fighters assigned to the Northern Attack Group were under the command of VF-4 skipper C. L. Moore, Jr. This escort consisted of Lt(jg) G. M. Harris, Jr; Ens L. K. Lepp; Lt E. F. Craig; Ens L. A. Hensley; Lt(jg) B. N. Mayhew; and Lt(jg) C. M. White.

The anticipated German fighter interception did not materialize. The attack was a complete surprise. However, the Germans were able to man anti-aircraft batteries. One of these gun emplacements had not been identified by the Norwegians who provided briefings before the strike. This AA battery was responsible for at least one of the SBD losses.

The *RANGER* log book shows the following persons from VB-4 missing in action: [2]

Lt(jg) Sumner R. Davis and his gunner Donald W. McCarley, ARM 2/c.

Lt(jg) Clyde A. Tucker, Jr. with his gunner, Stephen D. Bakran, ARM 2/c.

Both dive-bombers were brought down by anti-aircraft fire. Tucker failed to pull out of the dive, and the plane exploded as it hit the water. There were no reports of survivors. [3]

The other Dauntless, piloted by Davis, ditched at sea. Returning pilots reported that they saw Davis and his gunner launch a life raft and signal that they were OK. I met Sumner Davis at a *RANGER* reunion in 1989. He and McCarley were picked up

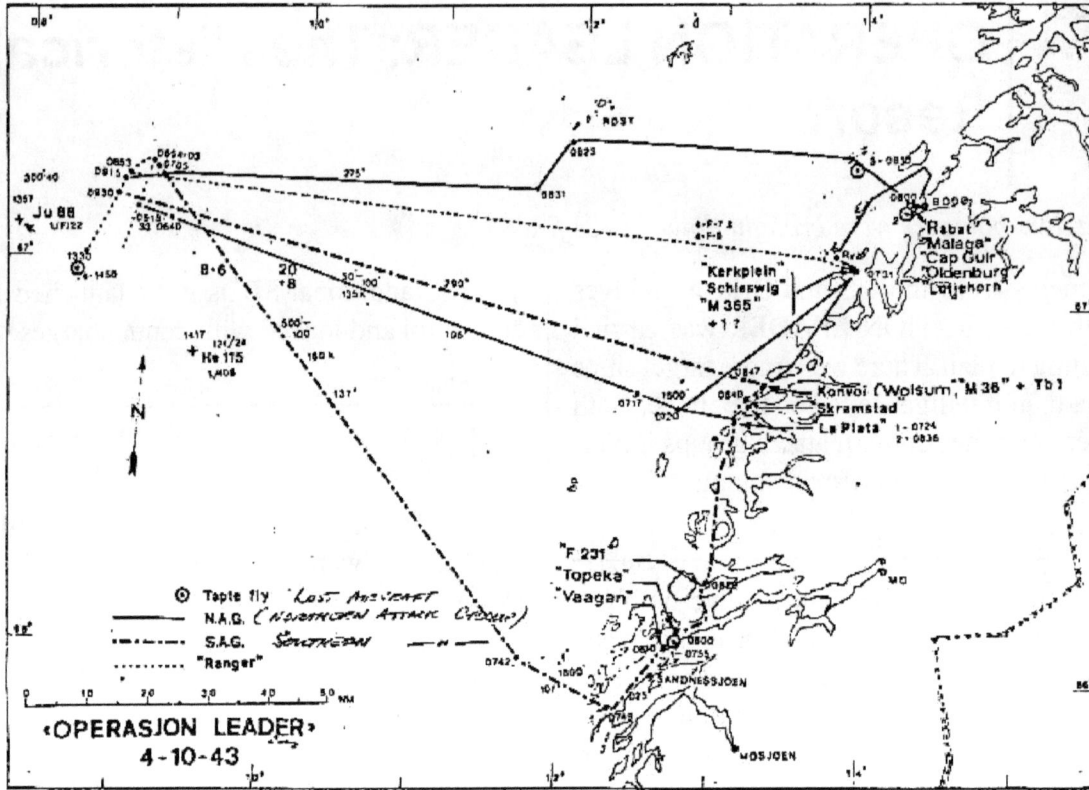

Flight paths of the two strike groups and the locations of the ships struck in the attack. The Northern Group consisted of 20 SBD Dauntless dive-bombers (VB-4) and 8 F4F Wildcat fighters. The Southern Group consisted of 10 TBF Avengers (VT-4) and 6 F4Fs.

SBD 4-B-19 piloted by Lt(jg) Clyde A. Tucker with ARM2c Stephen D. Bakran as gunner passes Kunna Head South of Bodø.

by the Germans, and Davis was sent to Stalag Luft One. McCarley was sent to a different prison camp.

The Southern Attack Group

Air Group Commander Ruddy led the second attack group of torpedo planes with fighter cover along the fjords between Sandnessjoen and Kunna Head.[1]

The tactical organization for VT-4:

Pilot	Crew
Cdr J. A. Ruddy	H. Kirsebom/J. Aday
Lt L. L. Hamrick	C. W. Barr/J. T. Rushing
Lt Cdr D. W. Taylor	H. Karsemeyer/ G. Lightfoot
Lt(jg) F. Ward, Jr.	D. Applegate/D. L. King
Lt(jg) J. Palmer	J. Zalom/ R. Miller
Ens R. F. Ruth	R. G. Walsh/M. Richardson
Lt Cdr H. H. Hutcheson	C. J. Lacy/P. J. Blanos
Lt(jg) G. M. Barnett	C. P. Bowman/B. M. Dalton
Lt B. R. Trexler	R. F. Gray/H. D. Youmans
Ens G. W. Thomas	C. P. Jackson/S. E. Garner

One of Cdr Ruddy's crewmen was Lt Kirsebom from the Royal Norwegian Navy. He was familiar with the area and provided advice to Ruddy as the attack group made landfall.

The VF-4 fighters accompanying VT-4 were Lt Cdr G. H. Carter; Lt(jg) W. W. Taylor; Lt E. M. Seiler; Lt(jg) C. C. Andrews; Lt K. G. Hammond; and Lt(jg) R. C. Cronin.

The torpedo planes under the direction of Cdr Taylor made landfall near Fagervika, Norway. The Avengers were loaded with 500-pound bombs with armor piercing, ten-second delay fuses. When a German ship was spotted the fighters were to go in first for a strafing run followed by a 2-plane section of torpedo planes in a glide bombing attack at near mast-head level. Radio silence was maintained until the first plane (Palmer) was shot down.

The Action Report listed Lt(jg) John H. Palmer with crewmen Joseph L. Zalom, ART/c and Reginald H. Miller, AMM/c as missing in action.

Lt Cdr Taylor had the unpleasant task of writing a follow-up letter to the families of the missing men. He wrote the parents of crewman Reginald Miller that: [4]

"We were engaged by anti-aircraft fire and the plane in which Reginald was the turret gunner was hit and set afire. The pilot jettisoned his bombs and pulled up alongside of me. I called the burning plane by radio and told all hands to jump."

Notification of next of kin was also the responsibility of Father Joseph T. O`Callahan, Chaplain of the *RANGER*. (Father O`Callahan later received the Congressional Medal of Honor for bravery during the Kamikaze attack on the *USS FRANKLIN*. In his memoirs he stated that the *RANGER* was his first and most loved aircraft carrier.)

While no German fighters were encountered during the strike, three snoopers were spotted in and out of the clouds as the task force withdrew. At 1457 hours, the *RANGER*'s combat air patrol intercepted a Junkers 88. The plane was shot down by the combined efforts of Lt(jg) B. N. Mayhew and Lt(jg) D. S. Laird. At 1513 hours, an HE 115 was shot down after several passes by Lt E. F. Craig, Ens L. A. Hensley, Mayhew, and Laird.

As OPERATION LEADER came to an end the *RANGER* tallied up the aircraft damage report. In addition to the three planes brought down by AA fire, the report shows: [1]

- F4F Wildcat piloted by C. P. Hopson returning from Combat Air Patrol made an off-canter landing and splashed in the water. The pilot was rescued by the *HMS SCOURGE*.

- Lt(jg) G. M. Harris, Jr. in Wildcat 4-F-1 was wounded by anti-aircraft fire, made a hard landing on the carrier collapsing his landing gear and was taken to sick bay.

- Avenger 4-T-9, piloted by Ens Thomas, was hit in the engine and crash landed on the carrier as the engine froze from lack of oil.

- SBD 4-B-11, piloted by Lt C. V. Johnson, sustained one AA hit on the starboard wing. No adverse effects on controls.

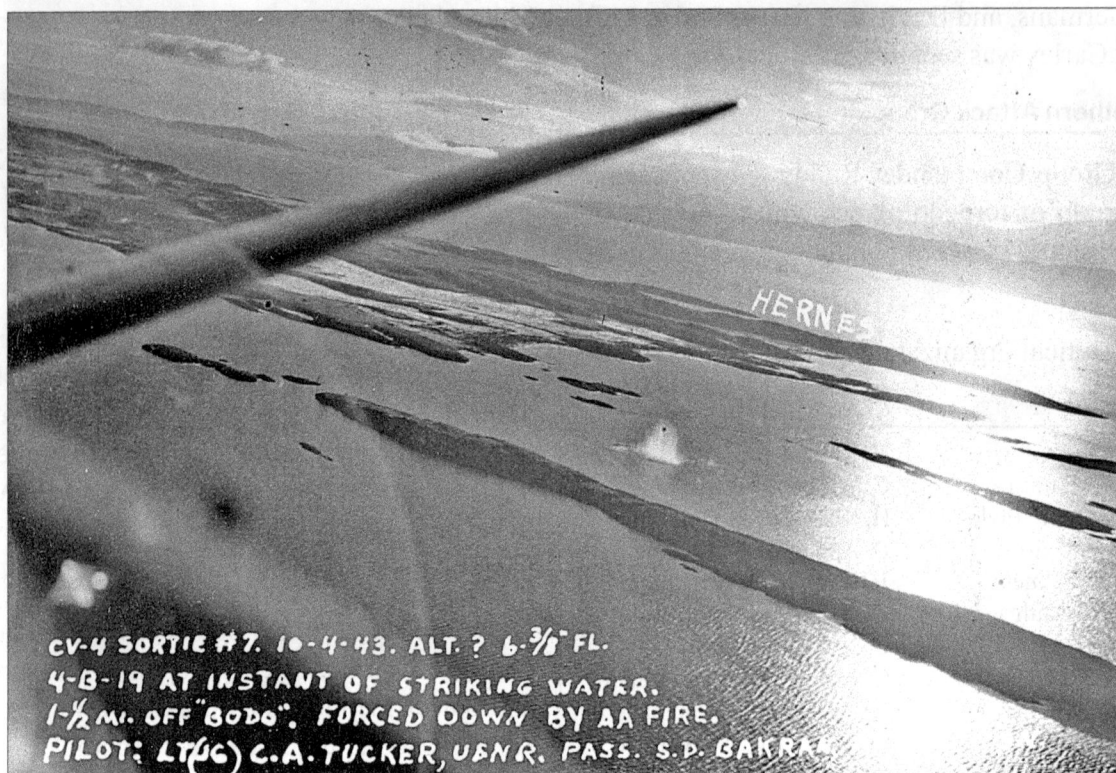

CV-4 SORTIE #7. 10-4-43. ALT. ? 6·3/8" FL.
4-B-19 AT INSTANT OF STRIKING WATER.
1-½ MI. OFF "BODO". FORCED DOWN BY AA FIRE.
PILOT: LT(JG) C.A. TUCKER, USNR. PASS. S.D. BAKRAC

Tucker's SBD 4-B-19 strikes the water after being shot down by AA fire.

"RIGMOR"- NORWEGIAN TANKER- 5486 GT. 381'L. 55'B. 25'D.
BURNING ASTERN ABOUT #9 OR 10 TANK, 20/30 YDS. AHEAD
OF ENGINE, AND HEADED FOR ROCKS WHEN LAST SEEN.

SCHLESWIG, misidentified as "**RIGMOR**," under attack.

- SBD 4-B-23, piloted by Lt R. W. Phillips, was hit, apparently by explosive 40 mm on right stabilizer resulting in holes in fin and rudder, one hit on left wing, apparently same type of shell, fragments nicked the gasoline tank but did not puncture it, fragments also pierced upper skin of wing. No adverse effects on controls.

- SBD 4-B-13, piloted by L. M. Boykin, received three hits on the starboard wing by what appeared to be 20 mm; several hits on port elevator and horizontal stabilizer and one hit on starboard horizontal stabilizer. Controls not affected.

- SBD 4-B-27, piloted by Lt G. C. Simmons, was hit by 40 mm in radio compartment aft of rear gunner, right rudder cable severed, battery, IFF and radar damaged during attack on *RIGMOR*.

Analysis by American and British Commanders

In an analysis of OPERATION LEADER, some debate emerged as to the effectiveness of the glide-bombing attacks and the limitations of the equipment. Rear Admiral Hustvedt stated: [1]

"The inadequacy of the designed speed of the RANGER was keenly felt. It was necessary to reduce the loading of six of the Dauntless dive-bombers. The five-second delay bombs reduced the damage from near-misses.... Greater damage could have been inflicted had at least some of the torpedo planes been loaded with torpedoes."

Hustvedt concluded, *"In this operation with the British Home Fleet, the RANGER and her air group have brought much credit to themselves and to the United States Navy."*

Air Group Commander Ruddy's follow-up report stated that:

"The Avenger is definitely the plane for this type of work.... The best form of attack is a 30-degree jinking-glide with slight pull-out and release at masthead height.... We learned much.... We went in as many

boys and came out as many men."

The "confidential" report of Cdr Gordon Rowe, Commanding Officer of the *RANGER*, dated October 9, to the Commander-in-Chief, US Atlantic Fleet, stated: [1]

"This was the first action for many of the pilots employed (60%). As a result, there was an undue eagerness to over-expend ammunition against the first targets that showed up.... However, the loss of three planes due to antiaircraft fire and the mute testimony of bullet-ridden planes upon return to the ship indicate that the pilots drove home their attacks in accordance with the best traditions of the service and all credit is due to the flight personnel for their splendid work in inflicting so much damage on the enemy."

Admiral Fraser, Commander-in-Chief of the British Home Fleet reported: [1]

"From the results of the operation as observed and photographed, it appears that a damaging blow was struck at enemy shipping.... LEADER was executed essentially as planned."

OPERATION LEADER: The German View

The German version of OPERATION LEADER has been provided by Steinbjørn Mentzoni from the Norwegian Archives of captured German documents. This report, originally in German, was made by a high level officer of Nazi forces along the Norwegian Coast.

Since the attacks were a complete surprise the German defense forces did not know the extent of the operation. There were serious communication problems between Sandnessjoen, Trondheim and Bodø and between the Army and Navy throughout the strike period. Also, the author listed numerous complaints about coding errors, lost time and channels *"constantly noisy with interruptions."*

CV-4 SORTIE #7. 10-4-43. ALT.? 6-3/8" FL.
"SAAR". UNDER ATTACK IN BODO HARBOR, NORWAY.
NEW TYPE GERMAN M/V. APPROX. 3000 GT.
SETTLING BY STERN WHEN LAST SEEN.

MALAGA under attack in Bodø Harbor by Northern Attack Group. The *MALAGA* was incorrectly identified as "*SAAR*."

CV-4 SORTIE #7. 10-4-43. ALT.? 6-3/8" FL."
"SAAR" AND M/V'S UNDER ATTACK, BODO' HARBOR, NORWAY.

Photo showing the *MALAGA*, *CAP GUIR*, and *RABAT* under attack in the Bodø Harbor. The *CAP GUIR* and *RABAT* were at anchor.

The Army and Navy shared one channel. When enemy planes attacked, the first ones to hit the airways with messages were the Army. When the Army clogged up the channel, the Navy was in no position to warn outlying posts and ships.[5]

OPERATION LEADER Strike Results[5]

- Steamship *RABAT* hit by bomb and sunk.
- Steamship *CAP QUIR* damaged by bomb under the waterline.
- Steamship *MALAGA* lightly damaged by a dud bomb.
- Steamship *IBIS* lightly damaged.
- Freight barge *MFS 231*, with 40 tons of ammunition, hit by bomb and beached.
- Troop Transport *SKRAMSTAD* hit by bomb. Burning and beached. Ship had 834 soldiers aboard. 200 killed, 15 seriously wounded, 1 Norwegian crewman killed.
- Steamship *WOLSUM* damaged by heavy strafing.
- Steamship *LA PLATA* hit by 3 bombs. Burned and beached.
- Tanker *SCHLESWIG* hit by 3 bombs, disabled.
- Steamship *KERKPLEIN* hit by 2 bombs, burned. Ship had 1,551 Russian prisoners on board. The bombing killed 14 prisoners, seriously wounds 29, and leaves 9 missing. No one on the American side knew the ship was carrying prisoners, nor was it marked as such.
- Navy *365*, a Norwegian Sleipner-class destroyer, heavily strafed.
- Steamship *VAAGEN* sunk after being hit by bomb.
- Steamship *TOPEKA* burned after being hit by 3 bombs.

Prisoners of War

Lt(jg) John Palmer's Avenger was shot down by German AA fire. One parachute was observed to open after the plane was hit. Those of us on this strike knew that Palmer's two crewmen went down with the plane. The official report was MIA.

As the unofficial historian for VT-4 after the war, I tried to locate John Palmer to obtain his ver-

sion of the strike and his capture by the Germans who were occupying Norway. Finally, in 1988, I learned that a former P-51 pilot Richard Lucas was in the same German prison camp and he knew of Palmer's location. Lucas gave me a phone number, which led to a reunion after 46 years. At this meeting with John and his wife, I presented a plaque to John with parts of his plane salvaged by the Norwegians. The salvage of Palmer's TBM was initiated by Steinbjørn Mentzoni, then a 9 year old boy who observed the crash.

A selection of John Palmer's comments on the crash and POW experiences follow: [6]

"I must have caught a shell right through the back of the plane; it went right under me and into the engine, because it caught fire. I think it must have killed Zalom and Miller. I jumped...."

"After I hit the water and got loose from my parachute, I swam to shore and waded right into this antiaircraft station. I had hailed some fishermen, hoping to get picked up, but had no luck."

"The Germans took me as a prisoner and moved me to Oslo, Norway. After a week in Oslo, the Germans transferred me to Frankfurt for a week of interrogation on bread and water, and then took me to Stalag Luft Three."

"I was the only Navy guy in this camp, and I found the other prisoners ignored me completely for about 2 weeks..., they thought I was a German plant. They showed me a German newspaper, which said the RANGER had been sunk in September.... Of course, I told them that I was off the RANGER, and they didn't believe me. They believed the newspaper."

Several other comments by John Palmer are worthy of note:

"We were flying at 1500 feet. The flight flew right over this AA battery which was not mentioned during the preflight briefings."

"I became well acquainted with John Dunn, the first American prisoner in the camp. Dunn was

LA PLATA being stafed by an F4F piloted by Lt(jg) William W. Taylor as a second F4F comes in at mask level.

TOPEKA just prior to attack by TBF 4-T-1, piloted by Cdr David W. Taylor.

a graduate from the Naval Academy, but he made a navigation error on a British Code (like a Boy Scout Code) and we interrogated every new prisoner who came into the camp."

"The Germans let the Red Cross send in clothes, books and games, and the YMCA sent us some musical instruments. We were allowed to write 2 letters and 3 post cards per month. The Germans seemed to have more respect for the Navy guys than the other POWs."

"We were liberated by the Russians and spent 2 to 3 months living off the country before an American unit took us in. I was sent back to Pensacola for a refresher and then the atomic bomb ended the war. I got out of the Navy in September 1945. Somehow, my log book was returned to me with comments by Lee Hamrick and Felix Ward."

Mr. Alf Larssturold of Bodø, Norway acquired a copy of the interrogation of Palmer after his capture. As expected, the Germans attempted to gain as much information as possible from him about the Task Force, the **RANGER**, and the aircraft component. In a concluding statement, the interrogator reports that, *"The POW... loves German music (Schumann), has trained as a singer, and has often performed at a Swedish Club in Chicago."* (Translation by Mr. Larsstuvold.) [7]

Palmer's two crewmen, Joseph Louis Zalom and Reginald Hayman Miller were believed to be killed by the AA fire that hit the plane. Reports of parachute sightings were never confirmed.

Lt(jg) Sumner Davis with Donald W. McCarley ARM2c as gunner was also shot down by German AA fire. The plane was hit during an attack on the ship **RABAT**, anchored outside Bodø Harbor. Davis ditched his damaged SBD near the small island of Prestøya by the Helligvaer islands. He and McCarley managed to inflate and climb into a small rubber raft.

The raft was spotted by Norwegians Odd Karlsen and his Father, who were fishing nearby. They took Davis and McCarley to their home. Odd

Karlsen said in an interview: [8] *"The Germans had seen the crash and had lookouts everywhere -- and also the fact that we were in small islands away from the mainland -- there was little we could do."* Germans soon located the Americans and took them as prisoners of war.

In a letter to John Carey published in the USS RANGER (CV-4) News on September 26, 1993, Sumner Davis relates his experiences as a POW: [9]

"The day after we were captured, we were flown to the Trondheim Air Field in one of these old Junkers 52. We were still in shock when photos were taken. That night we were put in separate light-less cells with nothing but saw-dust on the cement cold floor. Our 2 well-armed guards took us on a train from Trondheim to Oslo the next day."

"That was just the start of our 38 days of travel before we were released to a permanent P.O.W. camp. The bad part I hate to mention -- at the end of that time we were still in the same outfits; and never allowed to have a shower. You can imagine our condition. They also transported us on regular transportation, with the exception of the flight to Trondheim, and the 3-day travel by packed boxcar. We were in solitary in Trondheim for 10 days, While I was there, a Luftwaffe Major had me brought up to the Kolmenkollen Ski Lodge, which they took over for their headquarters. The Luftwaffe major asked me a lot of questions. When I gave him the name, rank, and serial number stuff, he just smiled. He had asked what ship I was from and what happened to the other man in my crew. Apparently he thought I was flying a TBF. He told me to look at a picture on the wall. It was a picture of a carrier taken at high altitude.... This Major was not an interrogator. He said he was sure I came from that carrier and just talked about the United States. He knew more about New York City than I did."

"The 10 days solitary in Oslo were right at the airport and I'd check the window at the top of the wall to see how many ME 109s returned from their mission. I think there was only one missing during that time."

VAAGAN being rocked by two bombs dropped by TBF 4-T-6, piloted by
Lt Homer H. Hutcheson.

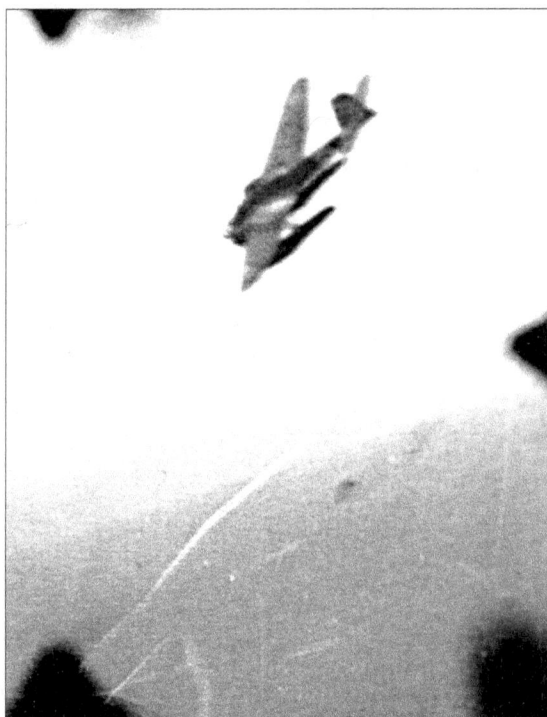

Gun camera shot of Heinkel HE-115 floatplane under attack by ***RANGER*** CAP F4Fs.
The plane was shot down. Three survivors were observed in the water but no
rescue could be attempted.

Sir Admiral Bruce Fraser congratulates the men of the *RANGER* for a successful attack on enemy shipping. Scapa Flow, Scotland. November 1, 1943.

Men decorated for OPERATION LEADER (left to right): Cdr J. A. Ruddy, Jr, Distinguished Flying Cross; Lt Cdr G. O. Klinsmann, Air Medal; Lt C. F. Weeks, Air Medal; Lt(jg) G. W. Thomas, Air Medal; Lt(jg) R. F. Ruth, Air Medal; R. F. Gray, ARM1/c, Purple Heart.

"From Oslo we went by freighter all the way to Stettin on the Baltic. We had the same 2 guards all the way. From Stettin we went by train to Berlin. From Berlin to Frankfort on Main. 20 days of bread and water, threats and verbal abuse in a huge interrogation center in Ober Russel. That's just the time the Germans were shooting down 60 to 80 B17s and B24s. They were also bringing down 15 to 30 RAF heavy bombers at night. They had their hands full with all the POWs coming in."

"During the 20 days on bread and water they send down a Captain (or Admiral) from Berlin for additional threats and interrogation. He had come in three times to talk to me but he didn't get far. He did not speak English and had to go through an interpreter."

"I was then sent to a temporary camp at the marshalling yard where I was happy to see my gunner, Mac, again. We did not have much time together because he was going to a different camp."

"That evening we were crammed into a boxcar and sent to Frankfort. You could tell Frankfort was on the Allied list of targets for air strikes. Seemed like hours went by, and sure enough, the air raid sirens started wailing. Fortunately, Frankfort marshalling yard was the decoy target and the main force turned off for the another target. However, they dropped enough bombs in the yard to shake the little RR car. I was amazed it stayed on the tracks."

*"It was about 4 days before we arrived at Barth near the Baltic again. We had another thrill in Leipzig. When the first bomb fell, the young officer that was in charge of all the guards said: '**Your comrades' calling card.**'"*

Lt(jg) Davis was finally sent to prison in Staleg Luft One. He remained a Prisoner of War for 19 1/2 months, losing 40 pounds while in prison. (The POW experiences of Davis' crewman McCarley have not been recorded.)

POWs at Stalag Luft III. Capt. Louis R. McKesson, 306BG; 1st Lt. Robert Ray Brunn, 91BG (back row, left to right). 2Lt Thomas E. Mulligan, 303BG/359BS; Lt(sg) John Dunn; Maj. Edward Wheeler; Lt(jg) John H. Palmer, VT-4 (front row, left to right). February 10, 1944. Photo courtesy of John J. Mulligan, Jr.

Chapter 3 | Origins of Torpedo Four

"He landed with his wheels sticking straight up in that cold, cold water."

Commissioned on the USS Ranger

In December 1941, shortly after Pearl Harbor, the US Navy made the decision to form a torpedo squadron from the air group aboard the *USS RANGER* (CV-4). The formal commissioning of Torpedo Four took place on January 10, 1942, while the *RANGER* lay at anchor off the sunny isle of Bermuda. Thus, VT-4 achieved the distinction of being the first torpedo squadron commissioned at sea.

The *RANGER* was the first naval vessel designed and constructed as an aircraft carrier. She was commissioned June 4, 1934. The flight deck was narrow (109.5 feet), and the 6 stacks had to be folded down during air operations. With a maximum speed of 29.5 knots, it was difficult to launch fully loaded combat planes without additional wind over the bow. Planes were usually spotted on the fantail, leaving only about half of the 769 feet of overall flight deck to be used for launch.[1]

The first pilots for the new squadron came from Scouting Squadrons VS-41 and VS-42 and the old Torpedo Squadron Three. Lt Wally Sherrill was designated as commander. The five other pilots in the original Torpedo Four Squadron were Lt Harry Bridewell, Exec; Lt (jg) Jack Warfel; Ens Homer H. Hutcheson; Ens George Cuhna; and Ens Grady Owens. Among the crew were APs Bolt, Dickson, Labyak, Stockwell, Thomas, and Ball. Laws, Rushing, Lacy, Klingfield, Sanderson, Gray, and Chema were radiomen and turret gunners.

The new torpedo squadron was assigned Douglas *"Devastators"* (TBDs) *"...that had been transferred from the training command. They were pretty decrepit."*[2]

The Devastator was designed to carry an external torpedo or a bomb load for horizontal attacks. It had power-folding wings and a semi-retractable landing gear. Although the Devastator was slow, it was easy to fly and generally popular with its crews. The AP in the second cockpit had access to dual controls. There was no doubt that the slow, lumbering TBD was a sitting duck for AA fire. The plane was destined to be replaced as soon as a more modern torpedo plane could be developed. During the battle of Midway in June of 1942, 39 of the 41 Devastators that attacked Japanese carriers were shot down.

From April 1942 to March 1943, the *RANGER* made four different runs to North Africa to ferry Curtis P-40 Warhawks to the combat zone. The Army pilots had never made a carrier takeoff, and the *RANGER* did not have a catapult at that time that could be adapted to Army aircraft.

"It scared the hell out of a lot of people... when they went off, they dropped out of sight for a while. We could listen for the engines and eventually they would come back up. Of all the flights, I don't know of a single loss (of P-40s) due to flying off the carrier."[3]

These cruises served as an opportunity for the air group to obtain valuable training. In addition, the dive bombers and torpedo planes provided necessary antisub coverage for the convoys.

After the second cruise to ferry P-40s to Africa, the *RANGER* air group became involved in *"the most ambitious Naval operation yet conducted in the European-African theater."* Simultaneous Anglo-American amphibious landings were scheduled for Morocco and Algeria in early November, 1942 as OPERATION TORCH. *RANGER* planes

The **USS SARATOGA**, CV-3 (top), **USS LEXINGTON**, CV-2, and
USS RANGER, CV-4. Pearl Harbor, Hawaii. April 8, 1938.

RANGER passes through the Panama Canal enroute to the Pacific.
January 13, 1939.

Vought SBU scout-bomber of VS-41 takes off from the *RANGER*.
March 22, 1938.

SBD Dauntless scout bomber files anti-sub patrol off *RANGER*
during OPERATION TORCH. November 2, 1942.

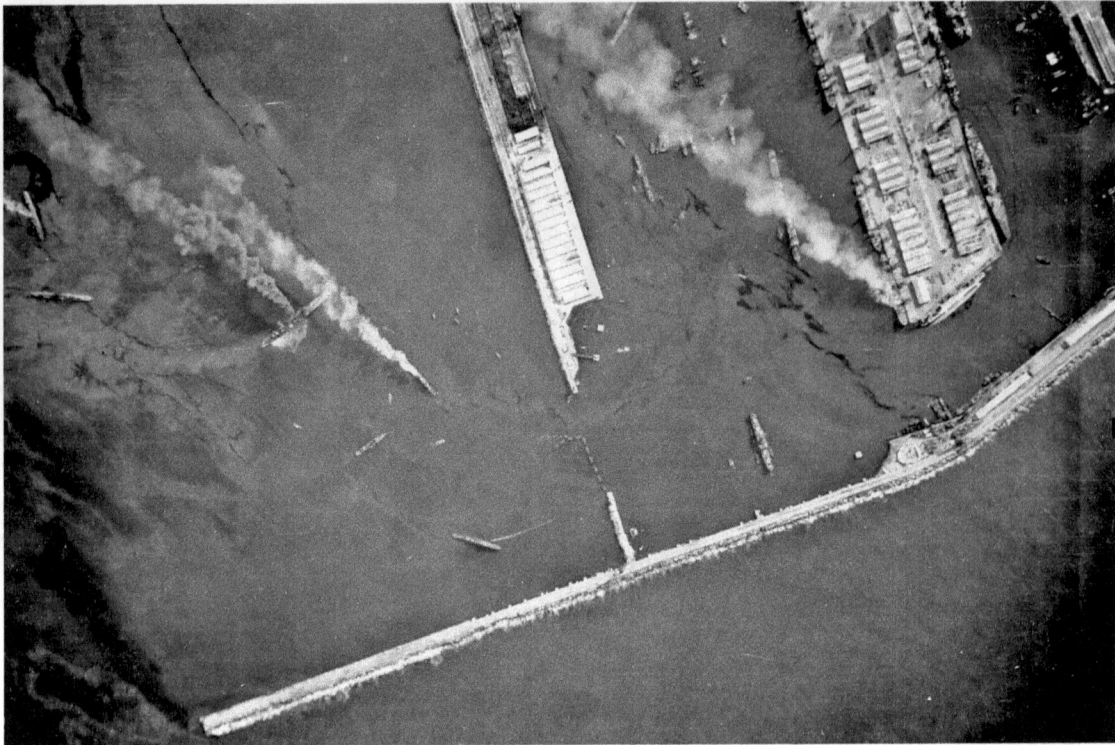

French warships under attack by planes from the *RANGER* task force.
Casablanca Harbor, Morocco, November 8, 1942.

French battleship *JEAN BART* sunk in the port of Casablanca by planes from
the *RANGER*. November 10, 1942.

joined air groups from the *USS SUWANEE* (CVE-27), the *USS SANGAMON* (CVE-26), and the *USS SANTEE* (CVE-24) to help neutralize hostile naval units and shore batteries in the Casablanca area.[1]

Nine planes from the *RANGER*, carrying 1000-pound bombs, attacked the French battleship *JEAN BART*, "and she was silenced." In the 60 assigned missions in North Africa, the *RANGER* air group demonstrated her capability as an attack force.

With the addition of a torpedo squadron, the *RANGER* air group now consisted of three squadrons: Fighting Four, flying F4F Wildcats; Bombing Four, flying SBD Dauntless dive-bombers; and Torpedo Four, with TBD Devastators. In the many practice "coordinated attacks" on our own ships, it soon became apparent that a better torpedo plane was needed to increase the effectiveness of the strike force.

Conversion to the Grumman "Avenger"

The *RANGER* returned to Quonset Point, Rhode Island, in March 1942, where the first TBF (Grumman Avenger) was assigned to the squadron. April and May were spent with a Grumman factory representative working out the bugs in the new monstrosity.

Torpedo squadrons on the *USS ENTERPRISE* (VT-6), the *USS YORKTOWN* (VT-3), and the *USS HORNET* (VT-8) received TBF-1s about the same time as did VT-4. A land-based contingent of Torpedo Eight made the first combat use of the new Avenger during the battle of Midway (June 23, 1942). In the same battle, the major portion of VT-8 was still flying TBDs from the *HORNET*. All of the carrier-based TBDs were shot down by the Japanese, and only one of the six land-based TBFs was able to limp back to the Midway airstrip.

Most VT-4 pilots were still flying the old TBDs until the end of July; then on September 8, 1942, *"the squadron went aboard and qualified in deck landings in the TBF."* [4]

The "Avenger" was the largest single-engine plane built for Navy combat duty early in WWII. The first TBFs designed by Grumman had a top speed of 271 mph and a ceiling of 22,400 feet. Defensive armaments consisted of one .50-caliber machine gun in the turret, a .30-caliber machine gun on the starboard side of the cowling fired by the pilot, and a .30-caliber machine gun in the belly set to fire aft. The large internal bomb bay had the capacity to carry one 2000-pound torpedo, two 1000-pound bombs, four 500-pound bombs, eighteen 100-pound bombs, or four depth charges. The wheels retracted outwardly, and the fully retractable tail hook was installed at the extreme rear of the fuselage.

Grumman eventually contracted the production of the Avenger to General Motors, and the TBF became known as the TBM. Also, improvements were soon made in performance and armaments, with two .50-caliber guns mounted in the wings to be fired by the pilot.

The Squadron had many shakedown problems in the first four months of operation with the TBFs. Lt Sherrill *"creamed one of the first TBFs and we sent him to the hospital."* [5] But, overall, the new planes were a vast improvement over the old TBDs.

Lt Cdr D. W. "Woot" Taylor took over as Skipper of VT-4 in December 1942. I was one of 4 new ensigns assigned to the squadron in February 1943. Bob Ruth, Felix Ward, Will Souza, and I had just completed dive-bomber training. We were surprised to be shifted to a torpedo squadron, although we were well aware of the shortage of torpedo pilots.

At least the four of us were still together -- dive bomber pilots converted to torpedo pilots by orders and not by training. Bob Ruth and I completed Elimination Base at Los Alamitos, California, at the same time. Bob was probably the smallest pilot in the Navy. He got into cadet training with the help of a pharmacist mate who obtained a waiver. Bob was an eighth of an inch too short to meet the Navy specs.

A formation of TBF torpedo bombers. Bob, Will, Felix, and I were surprised to be shifted to a torpedo squadron, although we were aware of the shortage of torpedo pilots.

"I had never seen one of those TBF monsters until we got to Quonset Point," Bob stated. Souza added, *"When Bob came up to the Avenger to sign the 'yellow sheet,' the plane captain wouldn't give it to him. **'I'm looking for the pilot,'** he said. Bob looked like a 16-year-old kid. He couldn't even get a drink at the bar without his ID."* After the war, one of our crewmen Tony DeCenso stated, *"Bob Ruth was the biggest damn pilot in the Navy!"* [6]

Will Souza went through Elimination Base at Oakland, California. He joined Bob and me in cadet training at Corpus Christi in July 1942. Souza was very conscientious, but his sense of humor added a new dimension to the flying profession. We knew of his determination to get married as soon as Lyn and the Navy could coordinate their schedules. Just for fun I drew a cartoon of Souza showing the extra 5 knots of flying speed he would need to keep from "stalling out in the groove."

Felix Ward, the other member of our inner circle, was "All-Nav." He followed the regulations to the letter and recognized the appropriate ranking system. He had applied for the "Regular Navy" while most of us were content with "Reserve" classifications. Like Bob Ruth, he was small in stature. When he was not in the cockpit, he kept a pipe in his mouth. This gave him the appearance of a calm, mature officer. Felix, too, had a beautiful girl, Peggy, from the deep south, all picked out and ready for the marriage vows at the earliest possible date.

I reported to Lt Homer H. Hutcheson, Executive Officer of VT-4 on February 23, read the manual on the TBF Avenger, received a cockpit checkout, and flew the plane for the first time two days later. On March 9, I ferried my TBF from Quonset Point, Rhode Island, to Norfolk, Virginia, and reported for duty aboard the *RANGER*.

Three days later, Bob, Will, and I were temporarily dispatched to CASU-22 (Carrier Air Service Unit 22) where we served as test pilots for reconditioned Navy planes of all types. The three of us remained with CASU-22 until April. We had a great time checking out in most of the Navy's single engine planes. We took many unnecessary chances,

including flying under two bridges in the Providence area. On one occasion we flew a three-plane formation under the Mt. Hope bridge -- one plane under each span. Later, I flew a Grumman "Duck" under a bridge where the clearance became more and more questionable as I got closer to the point of no return.

All of these wild actions were "justified," because we were being trained as torpedo pilots -- the most hazardous flying job in the Navy. Hedge-hopping was a necessary part of this training, and the civilian population around air bases "tolerated" these activities because the nation was at war. However, flying under bridges virtually stopped after a senior officer recorded the number of a plane "going under as he was driving over." The unlucky pilot was summarily charged and grounded.

CASU-22 pilots were also assigned various missions to ferry planes to other naval bases. On my second ferry hop from Quonset Point to Argentia, Newfoundland, to deliver a Grumman float plane, I was ordered back aboard the *RANGER* and reattached to VT-4. The carrier was now operating out of Argentia and providing anti-sub escort duty for convoys crossing the North Atlantic.

While the *RANGER* was in Argentia, the air group practiced simulated attacks and field carrier landings. For field carrier landing practice (FCLP), we had our regular signal officer guide us in and give us the "cut" signal for the full-stall landing on a marked area on the airstrip.

We took pride in the "tail first" touchdown. On one of my practice landings, I took the cut okay, gave the plane full-throttle to take off again, but the engine responded only by coughing and power surges. My plane was airborne at the end of the runway but in bad trouble. Because of the terrain, I had to make a quick decision -- either cut the throttle and land in the flat area beyond the runway or hope the plane would struggle over some low hills until I could position myself for another shot at the airfield. I chose to cut the throttle, switch off, and land wheels up. The plane's belly took a beating and one wing tip was slightly damaged, but the

Wilbur "Will" S. Souza.

Felix E. Ward.

landing wasn't much harder than a routine carrier landing. I was called in for an investigation and cleared of "pilot error" -- a condemnation no one wanted on their record. My TBF was *"sold to the supply officer, NAS Argentia, for the total price of $1 and a new plane was issued to Torpedo Squadron Four."* [7]

Torpedo Four was now a 9-plane squadron with 12 to 14 pilots, which allowed some opportunity for rotation of flight duty and shipboard assignments. Normally the squadron had two additional non-flying officers for intelligence and personnel. A total backup crew of 90 men, including ship's personnel, was required to put each TBM into operation. [8]

Carrier Air Group 4 attained another first when we were ordered to qualify for night flight operations. Because of the presence of German submarines, it was most important to keep the lights on the carrier at a minimum. Cdr Ruddy, who had logged many hours of flight time, stated that he would make the first test flights. He gave instructions to the deck hands to place a few lights along the flight deck and a small floodlight on the Landing Signal Office (LSO). Then he took off, came around the groove, and made a perfect landing.

"Too many lights!" he stated. *"Cut out about half, remove some of the clearance lights from the Island structure -- a sub could spot the carrier from miles away!"*

Ruddy took off again, ordered another reduction in lighting, and then said, *"Launch the other planes!"* We did just that. It was a wild scene. Pilots couldn't line up in the groove. Some got aboard with blown tires or structural damage, but most of this first flight had to be vectored to land.

On one of these night flights, Ensign G. W. Wright of VT-4 stalled out making the final approach and went in on his back. Lt Hamrick stated it this way: [9]

"He landed with his wheels sticking straight up in that cold, cold water. We all thought that was all for G. W., but the tin cans pulled him out and got him to the hospital. That was the night I took off with my wings unlocked and wondered what the loud buzzing was."

One night Otto Klinsmann, who was the Skipper of Bombing 4, lectured to all of the pilots in the Ready Room on safe techniques for night operations. He summed up by saying, *"Keep cool. Don't lose your orientation!"*

Because I was not scheduled on the night Otto gave the lecture, I went up to the bridge to watch the operation. Otto was in the takeoff spot with his SBD. He revved up full throttle, received the takeoff signal, and started down the flight deck. It was an unusually dark night with no visible horizon. About the time Otto popped his flaps, the plane started bouncing off toward the starboard before it became airborne. It disappeared over the right side of the flight deck and plunged into the drink. A deck hand ran over to the catwalk and threw in a flare to mark the point for the trailing destroyer.

We brought Lt Cdr Klinsmann and his crewman back aboard the next morning. When he was asked what happened, he simply stated, *"I lost my orientation."*

On March 15, 1944, I recorded in my journal: *"Weather foul. Night black as hell ceiling 700 feet.... Henry crashed into the Island. Plane burned but no casualties.... Planes remaining in the air were vectored to nearest land."*

Thus, the training and experimentation continued until Air Group 4 became night-qualified and ready for action.

In addition to requiring night qualifications for the Carrier Air Groups, the Navy made the decision to form more "Night Fighter" squadrons whose primary mission would be night attacks and searches. No one in VT-4 wanted anything to do with these assignments, but, sure enough, Buck Barnett was somehow selected. [10]

"I was home on a short leave. When I got back to Quonset Point, lo and behold, they had transferred me into this night squadron. I was assigned a fancy TBM with a large radar bulb way out on the wing. They sent a man with me to operate the radar, while I checked out how the blip and the plane worked. We went out and flew around the coast. The radar scope showed all the details. It was quite an experience."

"After we finished the run, I flew back to Quonset Point. You know how the runway extends into the ocean? I was hanging the plane on its prop -- like any good Navy pilot is supposed to do -- but I didn't count on that big radar out there. The wing fell off and the plane stalled in! I was in the drink!"

"We were only about 10 feet from shore, so we crawled out on the wing. My crewman pulled the rubber boat out. The fire trucks came out -- sirens full on. I had hardly got my feet wet."

*"The skipper of this night flying outfit called me in and said, **'If you don't want to stay with this night squadron, you don't have to.'** I said **'I want back in Torpedo Four!'** So that ended my night flying assignment."*

We were all glad to have Buck back in VT-4 -- not only because he was a good pilot but, after all, he was in charge of one of our poker tables. We had become familiar with his bluff, *"Call and raise, two-bits light!"*

Robert "Bob" F. Ruth.

Chapter 4 | The North Atlantic

"The U-boat attack was our worst evil."

During the spring and summer months of 1943, the **RANGER** served on escort duty for convoys going from the States to various ports in Europe. It was essential to the Allies that these convoys deliver necessary war implements, manpower, medicines, and food supplies to the European Theater.

Nearly 200 German submarines were operating in the Atlantic in the first months of 1943. Twelve merchantmen fell victim to submarine torpedoes in February, and the total tonnage sunk *"was eclipsed by March's 590,000 tons.... In one March battle, 140,000 tons was sunk in six days in history's largest convoy battle."* [1]

Winston Churchill admitted in his history of WWII that, *"The U-boat attack was our worst evil. It would have been wise for the Germans to stake all on it."* [2]

Von Bulow Decorated for Sinking Ranger

On April 25, 1943 the German radio popped off with more than its usual fervor. *"Achtung! Achtung! We are proud to announce that a German submarine has sunk the United States aircraft carrier RANGER in the North Atlantic!"*

Following this broadcast, German news releases reported that Commander Otto Von Bulow of the U-Boat U-404, personally decorated by Adolf Hitler with Oak Leaves to the Knight's Cross, had *"in addition to torpedoing four steamers, caught and sank the American aircraft carrier RANGER."*

The US Navy, concerned about the impact of the German announcement on families of **RANGER** crewmen, issued a denial of the German claim. I was aboard the **RANGER** at the time but do not believe my family knew where I was assigned. No corrections were made in the German press, and

when Torpedo 4 pilot John Palmer was taken prisoner after being shot down during OPERATION LEADER, he stated: [3]

> *"As a POW I was taken to Stalag Luft Three. I was the only Navy guy in this camp, and the other prisoners thought I was a German plant because they had seen the German news account of the sinking of the RANGER. Of course, I told them that I was off the RANGER, and they didn't believe me. They believed the newspaper."*

A major question remained with us all during the war. Were these news releases designed as propaganda or did Von Bulow really believe he sank the **RANGER**?

When the **RANGER** returned to the States -- still afloat after OPERATION LEADER -- Quentin Reynolds, noted Foreign Correspondent of CBS, interviewed Captain Gordon Rowe about the German report. In the radio broadcast dated February 15, 1944, Captain Rowe stated: [4]

> *"The story that we were sunk was a coward's trick -- spreading anxiety and fear among the innocent.... The next day we issued a denial and... on October 4 we spread panic and chaos in the Norwegian shipping lanes. Only one thing we regret. We kept looking for the Tirpitz but either she wouldn't or couldn't come out.... Meanwhile the RANGER, still very much afloat, is doing her job."*

German records on U-404 commanded by Otto Von Bulow now state that his attack on 25 April 1943 was against the British carrier **HMS BITTER** and not the **RANGER**. The U-Boat fired two FAT and two G7e torpedoes at the British carrier. All

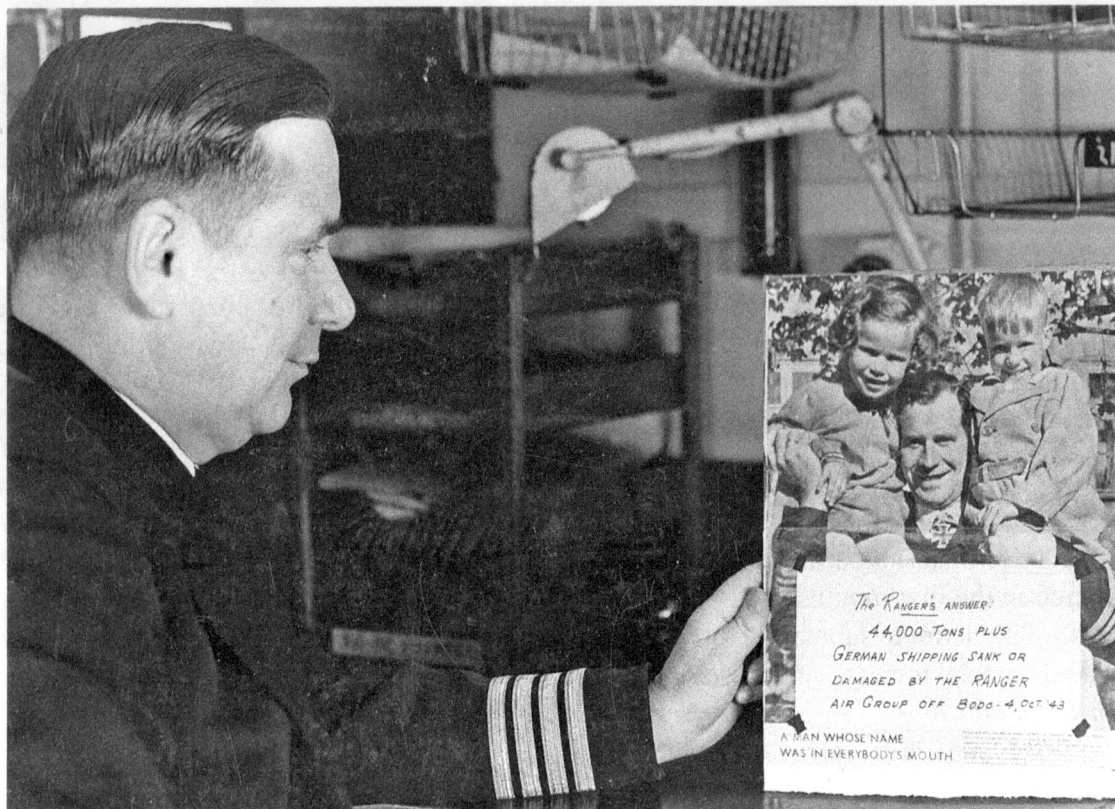

Captain Gordon Rowe, Commander of the **RANGER**, holds up a German press photo of Lt Otto Von Bulow after he was decorated by Hitler for sinking the **RANGER**.

British aircraft carrier **HMS BITTER** in Placentia Sound, Newfoundland. April 1943.

torpedoes detonated some distance away from the British warship.

Anti-submarine Patrol

The convoy run north of Norway and Sweden into the port of Murmansk, Russia, was particularly hazardous, not only because German subs were present, but also because the convoys were within reach of land-based Nazi aircraft most of the time. *"And always in the background was the menace of surviving German ships, anchored in the Norwegian fjords, which made it necessary to screen each convoy with Allied war vessels capable of slugging it out with **TIRPITZ, SCHARNHORST**, and other Nazi men-of-war."* [1]

Orders were issued by the *RANGER* Task Force Commander during night escort duty for all hands to maintain "complete blackout" as protection against German submarines, surface ships, or aircraft. One night, scuttlebutt spread throughout the ship that a lighted flashlight had been found hanging over the flight deck. That meant that a traitor was aboard who was willing to sacrifice his life to reveal the position of the carrier. This shook up those of us playing poker in the Officers' Quarters. We had already had one game interrupted when the ship rolled in a tight turn, apparently to "comb a torpedo." The turn was so sharp that the poker chips slid off the table.

We were never able to confirm the rumor about the flashlight. After the war, I checked the *RANGER* log. No such report -- but I wondered if the following entry, dated Saturday, October 2, 1943, precipitated the scuttlebutt about the light: [5]

> *"...1910 -- Promulgation of Deck Court, Staub, Edward Joseph, 250-72-73 S 1/c USN, tried by Deck Court for smoking while "smoking lamp" was out. Specifications proved by Plea and sentenced to lose $12 per month of his pay for a period of three months and to be confined for a period of 10 days."*

> *"Signed by C. L. Hodsdone"*

After I completed research on this incident, Roy Nelson, a member of the *RANGER* crew, sent the following information to the *RANGER* Newsletter: [6]

> *"...one of our tin cans sent us a message saying that we had a light showing on the starboard side of the ship just above the water line and if it was a port hole to get it closed. The word was passed for all repair parties to man their stations and we were sent out immediately to check the area that they gave us and found nothing as far as an open port hole was concerned. About this time we received a second message saying that they would do something about it if we didn't."*

> *"At that time one of the shipfitters on the hanger deck got his curiosity aroused and looked over the side in that area and he saw a flashlight hanging on a piece of white line and the line was attached to a stanchion so he cut it loose and we were all ordered to check the dogs on the hatches in that area. We found all the dogs loose on the big hatches that led down five decks to the aircraft engine storage. That was also the area where the aviation gas was stored."*

One major assignment for the *RANGER* was to escort the *QUEEN MARY*, with Prime Minister Winston Churchill aboard. Churchill was headed for the "Quadrant" conference in Quebec, Canada, August 10, 1943, to meet with President Roosevelt regarding several key decisions on the future course of the war. We had a problem escorting the *QUEEN MARY* because she was so much faster than the *RANGER*. We started early to provide anti-sub coverage as the Queen Mary approached from our rear, then we flew long flights after she passed us until other aircraft could pick up on the escort assignment.

Many hours of anti-sub patrol were flown by the torpedo planes in the cold North Atlantic during this period with periodic contacts with German submarines. Depth charges were dropped on all targets, including a few unsuspecting whales.

In his book, "Avenger at War," Barrett Tillman states: [7]

> "But with its many missions and locales, the Avenger's greatest contribution was undoubtedly in the Atlantic, where its role in defeating the U-boat wolf-packs helped to win the war in Europe. While other aircraft played prominent parts in the antisubmarine campaigns, none of them flew with such a variety of purposes -- detecting, stalking, and killing U-boats day and night -- as did the Avenger."

Several action reports from Naval Archives indicate attacks by VT-4 planes on German submarines. Charlie Barr and Labyak were flying with G. W. Bolt when, *"We caught a sub building batteries and criss-crossed same beautifully as it was going under.... However, I was in the ball turret and so full of excitement, I forgot to turn on the gun camera."* [8] A part of the action report dated February 26, 1943 follows: [9]

> "(Undated)...G. W. Bolt, pilot, sighted a U-boat and pushed over for the attack. U/B had disappeared completely about 31 seconds before release. Charges detonated about 325 - 350 feet ahead of swirl. Immediately turned to observe results and circled for about eight minutes when returned to carrier to reload and refuel. No further sighting of U/B observed...."

Interspersed between actual German sub sightings were runs on whales. Page Stephens describes one such experience. [10]

> "The only submarine contact I made really was not a submarine. I was in the landing pattern ahead of the **RANGER** when I saw something start to break water about a mile ahead of the ship. I had Andy arm depth charges, pulled up my wheels and opened the bomb bay doors. As I started to push over for a run the sub came farther out of the water and I saw it was a whale. I had Andy disarm the bombs, closed the bomb bay doors and continued in the landing pattern. The only person I know who saw my maneuver was Woot Taylor. He asked me about it and after hearing my story said, **'I'm glad you didn't drop your charges. If you had you would have been making out reports for a month!'**"

Anti-sub escort duty in the North Atlantic was shared with a number of "baby flat-tops" or CVEs. The combined efforts of these search planes and surface screening destroyers or destroyer-escorts created enough problems for the German submarine fleet that May 1943 was labeled "Black May" by the German Navy Command. During that month, *"...41 German submarines -- one third of the submarines at sea -- failed to return"* to their home ports. Admiral Donitz stated in his Memoirs, *"We had lost the Battle of the Atlantic."* [1]

The **RANGER** launched antisub patrols during all daylight hours in all kinds of weather conditions. In an undated report, R. W. Labyak, flying a TBF-1 reported: [9]

> "...sighted a large submarine with decks awash... signaled accompanying TBF on my starboard wing at 1.5 miles distance to follow and pushed over into a power glide on a reciprocal course with that of U/B... U/B which had been running on surface at 6 - 8 knots with decks awash, began crash dive, completing submergence about 30 seconds prior to bomb release point. Two 325-lb. depth bombs were released.... For 1 1/2 minutes was blinded by unusual effects from bomb drop, a number of holes being made in underside of plane. On recovery, circled for about 5 minutes at 1000 feet. It then became necessary to return to the carrier to reload."

Anti-sub patrol for the most part was unexciting. The torpedo planes were loaded with four depth charges. We normally flew a forward search consisting of a 150-200-mile outbound leg, a 50-mile cross leg, and a return vector calculated by "dead reckoning" to offset the wind direction and task force speed. It was always a relief to find the carrier at the end of the search and even more pleasant to get back aboard. The North Atlantic was usually rough, and the weather stormy with the possibility of survival in the water ranging from 15 minutes to 1 hour.

During one of the long waits in the pilot's Ready Room between antisub flights, we discussed the various ways to simplify the search process by navigation shortcuts. Woot Taylor pointed out one alternative to calculating the constantly changing return vector. *"If that's too complicated, go ahead and fly the 150 mile forward search, the 50 mile cross leg and return 'as if' there were no wind or ship's progress. Then when you complete the triangle and you find there is no carrier, calculate the elapsed time and correct for the wind vector and the ship's progress and close with a last leg."*

Will Souza thought that made a lot of sense, so he tried it. When the triangle was completed, sure enough there was no *RANGER* in sight. Because we had orders for "radio silence" he could not call for help. He plotted in the correction vector but turned the wrong direction -- 180 degrees from the correct heading. Still no carrier, so he started flying the "expanding square."

The "expanding square" concept was straightforward. Fly due north the distance of the visibility, turn 90 degrees to the east the same distance, then south twice the distance, then west twice visibility, etc. Works great on paper. But if you cut corners, you lose your position fast.

Souza had a bearing on Bear Island, but since he had missed the ship, his chances of finding Bear Island were remote. Besides there were no people on the Island and no place to land.

"I didn't know where I was or where in Hell the ship was. And, the North Atlantic was frigid -- So, I just headed south for warmer weather. The last bearing I had on

Bear Island indicated that it was 200 - 300 miles away. Damn, I was lost." [11]

At this time we had no radar or racon in the planes. However, the *RANGER*, noting that Souza's plane was overdue, picked him up on ship's radar and vectored a fighter toward the TBM. The fighter had to push the throttle to the fire wall for quite a while to catch Souza, who was "heading South" at high speed. The fighter zoomed Souza's plane and led the lost Avenger back to the carrier.

"That was a real learning experience for me," Souza stated, *"I never got lost again."*

Operations with the British Home Fleet

In September 1943, the *RANGER* task force was assigned to joint operations with the British Home Fleet. Our home port now became Scapa Flow in the Orkney Islands north of Scotland. The Orkneys were described as: [12]

"Nearly as far north as Greenland, but with the mild winters of Bournemouth; beyond the Scotland Highlands; ...its history, largely apart from that of England or of Scotland, and its population more nearly akin to that of Norway and of Normandy than to any British blend; a land which preserves an unspoilt individuality of its own and a charm which is unique...."

Unfortunately, the Americans had neither the time nor the inclination to appreciate the unique historical setting, although many of us visited some of the old castles and ruins at Kirkwall which date back to 800 A.D. The harbor, called Scapa Flow, became famous during WWI and increased in importance during the second war as the home port for a contingency of the British Home Fleet.

Each time the *RANGER* moved toward anchor in Scapa Flow, all planes from the air group were flown ashore to Hatston Air Base. We scheduled as many practice flights as possible from the narrow air strips at Hatston. At first we tried for three flights a day, but we ran into difficulty on the third flight due to the British tradition of "Tay" time.

Barrage Balloon, Scapa Flow, Scotland. Designed to block enemy planes.
Taken from the *RANGER*, September 8, 1943.

Clearing the *RANGER* flight deck of snow. Placentia Sound, Newfoundland. April, 1943.

I was on one of those late flights the first day at Hatston. We returned to the airstrip about 4:30 pm, called the tower for landing instructions, and finally received acknowledgement from a WREN. She gave us the landing runway, we landed, taxied up to the hangers, but couldn't find any ground personnel. Pilots of the Avengers dispatched their crews to chock up our own planes and assist the fighters. When we asked about the British ground crews, we were told that it was "tea time."

After a few more attempts to get a third daily flight out, we gave up and joined in on the "tea and crumpets." We also discovered that the "Limeys" shifted to warm beer early in the evening and ended up the daily routine with gin and orange. Very few of the American pilots could hold up to this British drinking challenge. However, we did enjoy the singing that inevitably resulted as the gin flowed and the evening progressed. The songs the Limeys taught us had catchy tunes with shocking lyrics. One of the milder songs contained the following stanza:

I don't want to be a soldier
I don't want to go to war
I'd rather hang around
Picadilly's underground
And live off the earnings
of a high born lady....

I have a great deal of respect for the British Navy pilots. They flew hard, they drank hard, and they took wild chances. But they seldom took a bath. We couldn't understand why many of them flew in their dress blues. At least we changed into flight gear. At tea time and in the evenings, we frequently met to exchange war stories. The Americans tolerated without comment the BO that went with our interesting discussions.

When we first flew ashore to Hatston, one of our first priorities was to get a good shower after the last afternoon flight. We rushed to the locker room and to the showers because we knew the hot water supply was limited due to wartime pressure on fuel. We wanted to beat the Limeys to the hot water. We need not have worried.

But, it wasn't only the men. The women had the same tradition -- maybe a bath once a week or every other week. That was about the same pattern we followed back on the farm on Medicine Lodge Creek in Idaho. Deodorants might have been used by some of the French in the '40s, but these new antiperspirants had not reached the general public during WWII.

Our flights out of Hatston were frequently in bad weather. Buck and I were flying wing on Ham one day trying to climb through the dense cloud layer for a simulated strike on a ship outside the Flow. We had to stay in a tight formation to keep track of each other. We depended upon Ham to watch his instruments and get us through the clouds. As we were flying in the clouds, I noticed that I began to fight my controls in order to keep on Ham's wing. Then I saw Buck pull away. I glanced inside the cockpit and noticed that the gyro horizon was almost vertical. We were also approaching the red mark in speed. About that time, I heard Buck call on the radio, *"Ham, you are in a down spiral! Pull out!"* I pulled away from Ham, fought my plane back to straight and level, and started a let-down through the clouds.

As I flew into a partially clear area, I noticed I was in the midst of barrage balloons. I was over Scapa Flow. Those numerous balloons and their hard-to-spot tie-down lines were designed to stop any low-flying aircraft from attacking ships in the Flow. I immediately climbed back up into the clouds, went out to sea, reoriented myself, and returned to base by the designated route. Buck and Ham also narrowly missed the barrage balloons as they got control of their planes. All VT-4 aircraft eventually returned to Hatston that day and in many practice flights that followed.

While the **RANGER** was anchored in the Flow, our squadron was dispatched to Edinburgh, Scotland, for a weekend of R&R. We flew through cloudy weather into a well camouflaged British air base just outside the city. I had not spotted the hidden airstrip when we broke formation to land. However, the skipper must have had some inside information, because he led us into the runway without incident. After we chocked our planes, they were immediately covered with a camouflage net.

As soon as we were relieved from duty at the hangers, I joined Makibbin for a train trip to town. While we were sitting in the station waiting for the next train, we noticed a young boy selling the *Edinburgh Times*. We decided to buy a paper, but the boy ignored us because we were foreigners. Finally, we convinced him to sell us a paper. The boy watched carefully as we started to go through the news, then he stated, *"You can't read that paper. It's in Scottish!"*

Even if we couldn't read Scottish, we had a great time with the friendly people in Edinburgh. Later on we went to London for a couple of days. Each night we were in London, the city experienced air raids from the Luftwaffe. At first, we anxiously asked the locals how to find the air raid shelters, but we soon learned that most people ignored the bombing and the AA fire and went about their business as usual. Blackout restrictions, however, were strictly enforced; so we had problems finding our way around town to the night clubs and back to the base. *"The next day we visited the bombed out regions of London and were amazed at the damage done during the first part of the war."* [13]

The **RANGER** raised anchor and left Scapa Flow with the British Home Fleet several times during October and November of 1943. A British aircraft carrier accompanied us part of the time. We had a good many laughs watching the launch and recovery process used by the British. The landing signal officer (LSO) was positioned about midway on the flight deck. We could land our entire air group and proceed into the next launch, while the British were trying to get their planes back aboard.

The British still used the old Swordfish as a torpedo plane. The Swordfish was a biplane without a variable-pitch prop. These biplanes flew so slow that they had to maintain a high throttle setting to catch up to the carrier. When there was a hard wind over the flight deck, they could land aboard without taking the slack out of the cables. They were so vulnerable to AA fire that torpedo strikes were virtually synonymous with suicide missions. Their only hope for survival was simultaneous attacks by dive-bombers or strafing by fighters to divert the attention of enemy gunners. Of course our own torpedo planes had to use the same tactics to reduce our vulnerability to AA, but at least the Avenger could get in and out much faster than the Swordfish.

The task force made a run north of the Arctic Circle to send a contingent of ships to recapture the weather station on Spitsbergen from the Germans. This weather station changed hands several times during the war. It was an important source of information to the many convoys that moved supplies in and out of Murmansk, Russia.

Air Group 4 flew anti-sub patrols and provided fighter coverage for Admiral Fraser's joint fleet during all operations in the North Atlantic. We fought rain, snow, or sleet much of the time -- and the sea was almost always rough.

One day, the snow storm was so bad that the pilots of VT-4 felt safe relaxing in the Ready Room. Then the teletype started clicking. Admiral Sir Bruce Fraser has issued orders to launch a two-plane A/S patrol. Fly a forward search and maintain sight contact with the fleet. Radio silence is essential. Hutch selected Trex and me to take the flight. We looked at the teletype for Point Option data. There was no latitude or longitude on the teletype for the ship. Hutch checked with the bridge and we were told, *"You don't need Point Option data -- maintain sight contact."* Trex and I felt naked without knowing the position of the ship, but we had no choice but to follow orders.

The flight deck was covered with snow and sleet. My plane was spotted in the takeoff position. I climbed into the cockpit and received orders to start engines as the **RANGER** turned toward the prevailing wind. While the ship was heeled over in the turn, plane handlers removed the chocks. I held the brakes but my Avenger started sliding across the flight deck. My tail slid into the catwalk, and

I held the plane on the deck only by applying full throttle. Eventually, the deck crew got a crane on the plane, and I received the cut signal.

I was then ordered to get into the Air Group Commander's plane, which was spotted nearby. I had never been in the cockpit of CAG-4's plane before. It had extra radio gear and additional items that were confusing to me. Before I could go through an adequate cockpit check-out, I was directed to taxi into takeoff position and immediately launched. Trex was sent off a few minutes later.

As soon as I became airborne, the snow storm closed in on the task force. I dropped down close to the water to maintain orientation and started dodging ships. Trex had the same problem, but he couldn't see me, and I didn't even know if he had been launched.

What a hell of a mess! In the North Atlantic in a snowstorm and we didn't even know our latitude and longitude or the ship's speed and direction. We didn't even know where or if there was any land within range, and with radio silence, we couldn't ask for help. Our only chance was to maintain sight contact, but the storm was so bad, we couldn't see the ships. Both Trex and I started circling at near water level. I almost hit several escort vessels as I tried to find the *RANGER*. Finally, I spotted the carrier as I flew over the ship at about a 90 degree angle.

After about a half hour of this wild search for the *RANGER*, the weather improved momentarily, and we were brought back aboard. After we landed, we were ordered up to the bridge. Capt Rowe said, *"Admiral Fraser sends his apologies. We should not have launched planes under these circumstances."*

In a letter of commendation to VT-4 personnel, Cdr Taylor summarized part of our activities: [14]

"During the week of 15-22 October, this squadron flew a total of 22 patrols, providing exclusive antisubmarine coverage for units of the British Home Fleet,

operating in the Greenland and Norwegian seas. Two-thirds of these flights were made between the Arctic Circle and the 76th parallel, in conditions of poor visibility and sea-level icing. In spite of the unfavorable weather, the freezing seas, the wet and icy flight deck, and the full load of depth bombs carried, these operations were completed... with such precision and dispatch as to earn a 'Well Done' from both V. A. 2 and C.T.F. 121.'"

On November 12, the *RANGER* launched the air group for a practice coordinated attack on the task force despite terrible weather. My records show that, *"Ensign Hawkins went in the drink while coming back aboard, He was picked up by a can... drowned according to reports from the destroyer -- tough luck."* [15]

During our joint operations with the British, we went through several scuttlebutt stages and a few preliminary planning sessions concerning attacks on German shipping along the Norwegian coast. One proposed strike reached the briefing stage. An approximation of this briefing, probably somewhat influenced by scuttlebutt, follows:

"We are operating under the command of the British Home Fleet. Admiral Sir Bruce Fraser has developed this grand scheme to send the RANGER air group into a secluded harbor in Norway to bomb and torpedo the German battleship TIRPITZ. The Admiral has been told that the distance from the task force to the target is too great for most of our planes. However, since the ships cannot get close to shore for fear of discovery by the Germans, the 'big plan' is to send Air Group 4 bombers and torpedo planes into the harbor to sink the battleship. Our fighters will go part way to provide cover against German planes. However, they must return to the ship early. The American dive-bombers will go in first, make their drops, and return posthaste to the RANGER. The slow, lumbering Aveng-

ers will go in last. We can anticipate no fighter cover at the strike destination. After the torpedo runs, we will rendezvous and, instead of going back to the RANGER, our torpedo planes will head for the Shetland Islands. Our planes are slow. The ships in the task force will not wait for our return, but will proceed at full speed out toward the open sea zig-zagging off course to avoid subs but, more importantly, to gain distance from shore and prevent a counter-attack by land-based German planes."

Woot Taylor, the Torpedo 4 Skipper, assured us that we, the torpedo pilots, *"could make it to the Shetlands"* by stretching our gas supply. *"Don't pump the throttle -- keep the mixture lean."* Hutch, the Exec, who was also in on the briefing with CRAG (Commander, RANGER Air Group), felt that with luck we could make it. In spite of this, Trex, Page, and a few others did some quick calculations. *"No way!"* was about all Page could say; *"No way!"* It looked like a sacrifice mission for the "Torpeckers!" Not enough gas to reach the Shetlands. Fortunately, that mission was cancelled. This aborted mission made us skeptical of the British decisions about men and machines.

OPERATION LEADER emerged as the most viable joint operation with the British because, reportedly, many potential shipping and land targets were present at the Port of Bodø, Norway. This major attack, completed on October 4, 1943, was very successful in spite of the many mistakes made by inexperienced pilots and crew.

Returning from the Norway air raid, the RANGER reentered Scapa Flow on October 8. As we moved toward the anchor position, all other ships in the Flow brought their crews to attention and Admiral Fraser *"asked for a special cheer for the Norway Raiders."* He stated, *"...the attack represents an important blow by the United States Navy Task Force now attached to the Home Fleet."* [16]

After the strike on Norway, planes from the RANGER continued missions with the British.

Several notations in my journal indicate plans for strikes on additional German targets: [15]

Nov. 9, 1943 -- *"After a two-bit poker game with the fellows... a discussion of London, commando girls, and finally the much-anticipated air raid on Norway. We are to carry torpedoes this time instead of bombs. Fighter opposition is expected and AA fire will be more severe than on October 4. Should get underway tomorrow."*

Nov. 10, 1943 -- *"Disappointment was apparent among many pilots today... because the Norway operation has been cancelled."*

Nov. 16, 1943 -- *"Flew a TBF aboard this morning while the ship remained in the Flow. No wave-offs. Lew gave me the hot dope about the big raid on Norway. Looks like I'll get to pack a torpedo against the Germans yet. Crap game tonight...."*

This last mentioned strike was scheduled for Bergen, Norway, to sink the battleship *TIRPITZ*. There is no doubt that we would have lost most of the torpedo planes if the admiral had not made a last minute change. Instead of Air Group 4, the British sent six midget subs into Bergen harbor. Three were lost in passage, and the other three were sunk after they inflicted heavy damage to the Tirpitz.

On November 21, 1943, the Commander-in-Chief of the British Home Fleet came aboard the RANGER to thank the carrier personnel for work in the European theater. This was a sure sign that the RANGER would soon leave for the States. The carrier raised anchor in Scapa Flow the next day.

The pilots and flight crews still at the Hatston Air Base did not get the word to fly the remaining planes aboard in time to stop the continuous celebration that had been going on since departure scuttlebutt had intensified. While most pilots hit the sack after a few drinks, a few held out for a much longer celebration. We had difficulty locating some personnel, when the order came to return all planes to the *RANGER*.

Climbing into my cockpit, I looked down the line and got a good indication of those pilots that had been out late the night before. Those pilots that had donned oxygen masks were the ones with the hangovers. Oxygen was supposed to sober you up in a hurry. The torpedo pilots were always more cautious and more sober than the fighters. After all, we had more responsibility -- we carried a crew. The fighters were on their own, and they tried to live up to the "Red Baron" image.

I sat on the taxi strip at Hatston, while the fighters and dive-bombers took off for the carrier. I could see we were in for some problems with those fighters who had spent most of the night on the town. One ground-looped and dragged a wing. He left his plane and came over to my TBF to hitch a ride. I took him aboard in the belly. A couple of other pilots had plane trouble and rushed to other Avengers for the ride to the ship. No one wanted to get left ashore when the *RANGER* headed home.

We had to leave about 3 planes, but succeeded in getting all extra personnel aboard the Avengers. I was the last plane in the air group to taxi out for the takeoff. Before I reached the end of the runway, a heavy-set seaman came running toward my plane. He was a member of the ship's crew -- a pharmacist's mate. He had not "got the word" that the ship had raised anchor. When he found out he rushed to the air base to catch a ride. I held the brakes while he climbed on the wing to explain his plight. My plane was already too full, but I told him to get in the belly. We did not have an extra parachute for him -- but he wasn't as heavy as a torpedo, so I gave him a lift.

When I reached the *RANGER*, most of the planes were aboard. I made a normal approach, took the cut from the signal officer and caught the third or fourth wire. I'm sure the extra passengers, and particularly the pharmacist's mate, were pleased to get aboard.

As I stepped into the Ready Room, everyone told me about the excitement topside. It seemed that one of the fighters, who had been out on the town the night before, was having trouble getting aboard. I rushed up to the bridge and chose an observation post on the aft five-inch gun mount. This pilot had taken off from Hatston long before I did but was still making passes at the carrier. He would come up the groove much too fast, usually in a skid, a wave-off from the LSO, and thumb his nose at the bridge as he flew by. He made five passes while I watched. All other planes were aboard and parked. Finally, the *RANGER* skipper passed the word to the LSO to *"get that so-and-so aboard or we will shoot him down!"* -- or words to that effect.

On a final pass at the carrier, the pilot came up the groove much too hot; the LSO was frantically giving him the "too fast, too high" signal. Then, in desperation, the LSO gave him the "cut gun" signal much earlier than normal. The pilot was slow to respond and flying in a serious skid. I could see he was not going to catch the wire with his tail hook. The plane was coming right toward me. I ducked under the armor plate as he struck the bridge below me. He wrapped the F4F around the gun mount. The cockpit remained intact, and he jumped out with the comment, *"I got aboard."* Naturally, a reprimand followed, but the Navy needed pilots so he was not grounded.

After the Wildcat crash, the *RANGER* turned out of the wind, and the task force headed for Iceland in a typical North Atlantic storm. On November 23, I recorded that we spent most of the day in the Ready Room in "Condition Eleven." Furthermore, I noted that, *"This is the roughest sea I have ever seen. This old ship bashes into the waves and shudders… even split a seam… water over the forecastle and flight deck… sure wish I was back on the farm."* [15]

Our tour of duty in the Atlantic was rapidly coming to an end. But it was hard to gauge the contribution of Air Group 4 to the total war effort at this time. We had sunk some German ships, damaged others, and shot down a few planes. Our major task, however, had been to supplement the antisub activities of the Baby Flat Tops (CVEs) and land-based patrols. During 1943, massive amounts of food and war materials with large numbers of troops had been moved in vulnerable convoys to the European theater. Our anti-sub patrols were not glamorous, but they were effective. The serious loss of German submarines prompted Admiral Donitz to record in his diary that *"The enemy holds every trump card."* [17]

The Allies were also slowly making progress toward the recapture of sections of Europe and North Africa. Landings were made in Sicily in July and Salerno in September of 1943. Mussolini was overthrown, and there were large-scale defections of Italians to the Allies. The scuttlebutt about D-Day and an English Channel crossing did not materialize while we were in the Atlantic.

The attention of Air Group 4 was always turned toward the Pacific. We were missing out on some important Naval engagements with the Japanese. And we added to our vocabulary some new names as progress was made to secure an Allied foothold in places such as Bougainville, Tarawa, Makin, Rabaul, New Britain, and the Solomon, Gilbert, and Marshall Islands.

We spent Thanksgiving Day in a fjord just north of Reykjavik, Iceland. High winds blew one plane overboard with a plane captain (James D. Westmoreland, AMM3c) in the cockpit as we pulled out of Reykjavik harbor. No rescue was possible due to heavy seas.

On the trip from Iceland to the States, the torpedo pilots took turns flying antisub patrol in the daylight and mostly played poker at night. The Atlantic crossing took 11 days.

On Friday, December 3, 1943, at 11:14 a.m., on the *RANGER* I recorded in my journal that *"... we tied up at the dock in Boston amid cheers and confusion. I rode a Navy bus to Quonset. Stopped along the way for some fruit and candy. Checked into the B.O.Q. and dropped into the 'O' club for a delicious dinner and a couple of beers."*

Sir Adm Bruce Fraser being piped aboard the *RANGER*. Scapa Flow. November 21, 1943.

Chapter 5 | Change in Command

"Bad wave-off; caught a wire and over the side, throttle full on. Radioman picked up but not Jack."

Upon reaching the States, Torpedo 4 was ordered to regroup and continue intensive training at Quonset Point, Rhode Island. Limited leave was authorized for some of the married men. I had a one-day break from flying to help turn in the old planes for the new TBF-1c. While in this process, I recorded: *"Bad plane crash today. A PV Ventura hit Hanger No. 2 in full flight, exploded and burned. Eight people killed."*

On December 5, I took one of our new ensigns, G. D. Makibbin, for an orientation hop around Providence, Point Judith, and Martha's Vineyard. We secured early and took a train for New York where we checked into the Commodore Hotel for the night. We had a two-day pass to attend Will Souza's wedding. Will had been so excited about this upcoming event that we worried about his flying. My notes on the wedding were: [1]

> *"The Raider, Radford Burley, and I rode to Staten Island for the big event, met all Lyn's relatives, and practiced the wedding procedure at the local Catholic church."*

> *"Lyn and Souz were married at 7:30 pm. Bunny was maid of honor, and I was best man. Burley Grimes and Red Raider Radford were ushers. Everything turned out beautifully. A reception was held at Bunny's house afterward, and the rum flowed freely. Had a swell time. Escorted the newlyweds back to the Commodore Hotel."*

Two days later the squadron was dropping torpedoes at Hyannis to test for altitudes and speeds of release. The Navy had developed a new torpedo warhead that was not supposed to break up or run wild when released from the air.

Torpedo 4 officially changed command on December 15, 1943. Lt Cdr D. W. "Woot" Taylor turned over the skipper responsibilities to Lt Homer H. "Hutch" Hutcheson. I recorded: *"Torpedo Four regrets the loss of the Skipper that led us in flights all over the Atlantic and in an engagement with the enemy on the Norwegian coast."* I had reference to the change in command. I did not anticipate that Woot Taylor would be transferred to a fighter squadron and get killed while checking out in an F6F.

Lt Hutcheson was soon promoted to Lieutenant Commander and he took his new assignment as Skipper seriously. He was an excellent pilot, and he expected discipline and high performance from all hands. Even on Christmas day I recorded. [1]

> *"Was supposed to have the day off but Bob woke me up at 0600 saying something about a national emergency so I rushed thru breakfast and down to the hangers. An official dispatch stated that two German aircraft carriers lay 250 miles off the coast. An attack by rocket ships was expected on New York, Washington, Boston, and Phily."*

> *"We made preparations for an attack on these ships. Tested turrets, ammunition, and loaded torpedoes."*

> *"Ate a delicious turkey dinner in shifts at noon."*

> *"Secured at 1600 with no more information on enemy mission. A drill is suspected. If the attack had come off, a good many aviators would have 'died with their blues on.'"*

Gerald (Best Man), Bernice "Bunny" Kershner (Maid of Honor), Lyn and Will Souza.
Wedding photo. Stanton Island, New York. December 6, 1943.

TBF Avenger drops a practice torpedo. 1943.

As the 1944 new year turned, the squadron was still attached to the *RANGER* but operating out of the Quonset Point. I took the standby shift at the hangars on New Year's day to replace Lt(jg) "Buck" Barnett who "just got married." While Buck and Betty were enjoying this two-day honeymoon, I "dropped a torpedo on the range near Newport." Times were tough for those of us who were still single.

Air Group 4 remained assigned to the *RANGER* until mid-April 1944. During that time we operated from the ship and from several air bases along the East Coast. The torpedo squadron practiced long-range air searches, glide bombing, and torpedo attacks. We dropped live warhead torpedoes on an island in Bar Harbor, Maine. We scheduled night flying tactics and coordinated attacks on ships in conjunction with our fighters and dive bombers.

Fighting 4 now had F6F "Hellcats" to replace the old F4Fs, but VB-4 still retained the old reliable SBDs. Our air group was rapidly becoming one of the most efficient operational units in the Navy. Many of us had now been together for more than a year. We not only flew as a team, but many of us commiserated and socialized together. We took advantage of the fact that the US propaganda machine was well oiled. All Naval aviators were treated as heroes. Our reception downtown -- even in Norfolk, which was the worst possible home-base assignment -- was great.

We tried to keep up with the news about the war, but many of the details were censored. The last two months of 1943 and the spring of 1944 brought many changes in both theaters of war. China was now a major factor in the formula -- not because of its contribution to Naval warfare but, more importantly, because this huge nation could shape the direction of the peace and the geopolitical future of Asia. On November 22-26 Chiang Kai-Shek[2] *"participated directly in Allied war planning for the first time with Churchill in the Cairo conference."* Chinese troops were to become increasingly involved against the Japanese, and China agreed to support B-29 bases at key locations in their country

for attacks on Japanese held territory.

At the Tehran conference on Nov 28-Dec 1, 1943, Stalin agreed to enter the fight against Japan. American and British troops had landed at Anzio Beach on January 22, 1945, and the European War was shifting in favor of the Allies.

Several quotations from my journal indicate the nature of Torpedo 4 operations during our last few months on the *RANGER*: [1]

Feb. 1, 1944 -- *"Bad weather. The flat-top went into Narragansett Bay and anchored. We were launched at anchor due to high winds."*

Feb. 5 -- *"VNF-77 qualified aboard in F6Fs today. No trouble. The Hellcat is a wonderful plane."*

Feb. 8 -- *"Spotted Felix, Buck, Bob, and their wives in the Garden restaurant celebrating Felix's wedding. Joined the party."*

Feb. 21 -- *"Lt(jg) Edwards was killed last night during carrier landing... just married. Memorial service today."*

Feb. 24 -- *"Night qualifications... Mak got a prop taxiing."*

Feb. 28 -- *"Two dive-bombers collided due to poor visibility. Hovey chewed Phillips' tail off and he and his radioman bailed out. They were picked up okay."*

Mar 5 -- *"Don (Henry) landed an Avenger on a Dauntless in the gear -- tore both planes up. No one hurt seriously."*

Mar 15 -- *"Weather foul. Night black as hell -- ceiling 700 feet... Henry crashed into the island. Plane burned but no casualties... Planes remaining in the air were vectored to nearest land."*

Mar 25 -- *"Got a 'butch' haircut today. The squadron comment on it was, 'Now,*

Gerald. Boston, Massachusetts. March 3, 1944.

Gerald beside his Avenger. Quonset Point, Rhode Island. May, 1944.

they won't even let you in the snake pit.'"

Mar 28 -- *"Ens Allander got vertigo in a cloud and was last seen spiraling down in his plane. The Avengers and Dauntlesses spent the remainder of the day searching for survivors or wreckage. No luck."*

Apr 3 -- *"Night takeoff... It was Jack Fulnecky's turn tonight. He has been on this tub 14 months now and never had any trouble. I was in the air when it happened. Bad wave-off; caught a wire and over the side, throttle full on. Radioman picked up but not Jack. I can name 19 pilots (with crews) lost since I got on the RANGER. No wonder the air group is p.o.'d."*

Apr 4 -- *"Standing by in the Ready Room, Condition Eleven, with Candyman (Lt(jg) William H. Canty), as strike group in case of sub contact. They are firing the 5-inchers top-side at a towed sleeve as the only interruption in the monotony of waiting.... Later, VF-7 practiced carrier landings. Leo Norman was almost added to the list when he caught an F6F slipstream and almost went in on his back. Crap game in the bunk room tonight."*

Apr 16 -- *"Spent the day packing and moving off the RANGER. Air Group 4 has been detached from the RANGER to Fort Devens, Massachusetts, to be enlarged to a 90-plane outfit. Lunch aboard today was probably my last meal on that flat-top. I'm leaving with some vivid memories, centering around hazardous day and night carrier landings, rough seas, foul weather, crap games, bull sessions, good friends, Argentia, Scapa Flow, Iceland, London, Edinburgh, and the Norwegian coast. The ability of personnel to start and spread scuttlebutt will not be forgotten, either. Rumors never ceased concerning yard periods, next operations, transfers, and so on. She's a great old ship, the RANGER, cussed and loved by many people, honored*

and spat on, but always the same when she's the only landing spot in an enormous ocean -- a welcome sight to the naval aviator coming up the groove."

Apr 18 -- *"Received the Air Medal aboard the RANGER officially today. Captain Rowe made the presentation and read the citation. Bob Ruth, Cy Weeks, and Lt Cdr Klinsmann also received Air Medals. Cdr Ruddy received the DFC."*

Several other Air Group 4 pilots received decorations as a result of the Atlantic operations. As was the Navy custom, the pilots received the recognition, while the crewmen were seldom cited for their sacrifices. This was an unfortunate military inequality. To carry out the awesome responsibilities in the turret and the belly of the TBM -- not knowing if the pilot was functioning -- required a depth of skill and confidence beyond imagination. Captain W. B. Chace in *Avenger at War* called these assignments *"the cheap seats."* He stated: [3]

"The tunnel did not provide much comfort. It was a noisy enclosed capsule with very limited visibility. After days of intensive combat, it became encrusted with and smelled of engine oil and transmission fluids. There was no physical access to the cockpit, therefore it could produce a discouraging claustrophobia for the uninitiated."

Our experience over Norway clearly demonstrated the challenge facing our crew members in combat situations. When my crewman C. P. Jackson accidentally pulled his parachute rip cord in the plane, I became much more aware of the crew's problems. From that time on, I spent more time with my own crew in the pre-combat briefings and escape procedures. Captain Chace, a former belly gunner, described the responsibilities in the belly of the Avenger very well. [3]

"The crew compartment, manned by two, consisted of the tunnel and an armored turret with a .50-cal above. The tunnel, en-

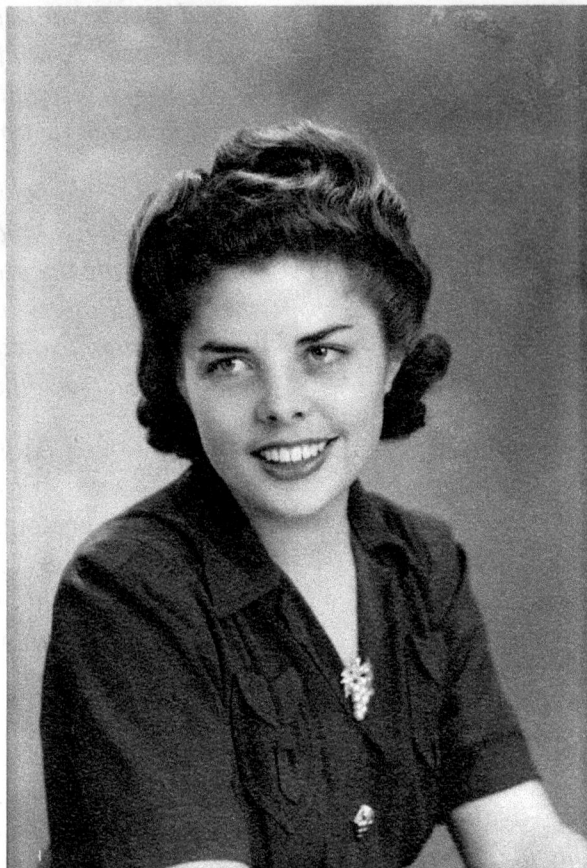

"In one of Jean's letters she enclosed a photo which I was proud to show to some of my squadron buddies."

Gerald home at Medicine Lodge Ranch, Idaho, on an 8-day leave. April 24, 1944.

compassing about half the total airframe, was equipped with a bench seat (room for two), radio, radar, navigating board, and armament gear on a convenient forward bulkhead. Aft there was a .30-cal 'stinger' gun. Within this area, an experienced crewman could create a crude but effective airborne CIC (Combat Information Centre) to support his pilot and advance the mission. Whatever this mission might be, antisub patrol, glide bombing, night low-level attack, or interdiction of enemy airfields, the ability and response of this great aircraft was a challenge and a joy."

A Too-Brief Visit Home

On April 20th I was authorized an 8-day leave. This was my first chance to visit my parents since I was assigned to Torpedo 4. To lengthen the time at home, I flew by commercial airlines arriving at Missoula, Montana on the evening of the 21st. After a couple of days in Montana I drove down to Idaho and home.

While in Idaho I learned that Jean Ellis, the daughter of a Clark County rancher, was teaching school in Pocatello, Idaho. We had met several times at county dances before the war. Her family had a ranch about 20 miles from ours.

I took a chance and called her up for a possible dinner date. To my surprise, Jean accepted and she brought her sister, Lois, along for a pleasant evening meal and visit. This meeting resulted in periodic correspondence while I was in the Pacific. In one of Jean's letters she enclosed a photo which I was proud to show to some of my squadron buddies. Most everyone had a photo of their wives or sweethearts in their locker on the ship.

Detachment From the RANGER

On April 29th, I returned to the Air Group 4, which was then detached from the *RANGER* and assigned to Fort Devens Airfield.

From May 7 to June 3, 1944, I was dispatched with Ted Newell, Mak Makibbin, and several other pilots from Air Group 4 to VD-2, a special photography unit at Harrisburg, Pennsylvania. This additional training meant new responsibilities for us during future strikes.

On May 20, I recorded in my journal, *"Red letter day."* My brother, Byron, who was attached to the *USS KASAAN BAY* came down from Washington to Harrisburg for a brief visit. I showed him around the base and the next day took him up for a hop in my TBM. I had a great time showing him the mountains and valleys of Pennsylvania at treetop level. However, Byron did not fully appreciate the ride from the belly of my Avenger.

During my brother's visit, I introduced him to Mary -- a good-looking girl I had met in Harrisburg. That was the end of my relationship with Mary. Byron fell in love with her, kept in contact during the war, and married her on August 3, 1945.

Back to the squadron on June 4, I recorded that we flew over Hyannis Field in parade formation; the tower called up and said *"Victor 39 -- a beautiful formation!"*

We flew our planes back to Quonset Point on June 29, 1944, where we checked them into the base command. Then most of the personnel of Torpedo 4 were loaded on a train for an unforgettable coast-to-coast ride to San Diego. The trip terminated at Brown Field. After a short but pleasant stay there with brief interludes at Dago and Tijuana, the squadron boarded the *USS BARNES* for transportation to Hawaii. The *BARNES* departed San Diego on July 13 and docked at Pearl Harbor on July 21, 1944.

While we were en route to Hawaii, Saipan in the Marianas was invaded by the Marines. The battle of the Philippine Sea was raging. Our submarines had already sunk the Japanese carriers *Shokaku* and *Taiho*. US planes added the carrier *Hiyo* to the list. Two US battleships, two carriers, and a heavy cruiser were damaged. We lost 130 aircraft, while the Japanese lost 476. This damaging blow caused the Japanese to pull back to Okinawa.

Flight Reconnaissance Training. Harrisburg, Pennsylvania. May, 1944.
Front: Lt(jg) G. D. "Mak" Makibbin and Gerald. Others unidentified.

Two Navy brothers meet in Harrisburg, Pennsylvania. Byron from the
USS KASAAN BAY and Gerald from the *RANGER*. May 20, 1944.

Chapter 6 | Tragedy Strikes Night Operations

"Three VT-4 planes collided during night operations and the squadron lost nine men, including one of the most capable skippers in the Navy."

Headquarters for squadron operations for the next several weeks was the airbase at Hilo, Hawaii. Here the squadron carried on intensive operational training with a new note of seriousness, for now the real test was just around the corner. All personnel worked hard and played hard to take advantage of their much-needed break from carrier duty.

Lt Cdr Homer H. "Hutch" Hutcheson was a good pilot and a hard-driving Skipper. He wanted to make every minute of our land-based stay at Hilo productive. We usually made two training flights a day and numerous night flights, often in bad weather. Sometimes we flew a tight formation at night with all lights out, relying only on exhaust flames to stay in touch with wingmen.

Hutch drove us so hard that there was a building resentment from the pilots. We all thought we took too many chances with the weather. We had a few vertigo incidents, which were shocking to both pilots and crew. The "needle-ball-airspeed" seat-of-the-pants trained pilots of VT-4 probably were more subject to the hazards of vertigo than the modern instrument-trained flyers of today.

On one occasion, a night flight was scheduled from the Hilo airstrip in very bad weather. It was so dark that there was no visible horizon for orientation. I took off with the proper spacing behind another plane. We were flying with a minimum of external lights. As I became airborne, I glanced briefly at my cockpit instruments to check on critical readings, then looked ahead to try to join up with the other plane. I thought I spotted his taillight as he was making a join-up turn. But this plane in front kept going slower and slower. I glanced into the cockpit frequently to check my airspeed and couldn't understand why the lead plane was so

slow. I was about to join up on this light when my radio altimeter turned red. I immediately advanced the throttle, just barely missing a house on the side of the volcano. The light I had been trying to join up on was not one of our planes in the air but a light from a house on the ground. I hope I didn't break any windows as I flew full-throttle over the rooftop. This kind of vertigo experience was not unusual for pilots caught between instruments and formation responsibility. We had to split our attention, but the major charge was to hold our position in the flight division.

Lt(jg) William H. "Bill" Canty joined Torpedo 4 at the same time as Lt(jg) C. N. W. "Scott" Vogt, as we moved from the Atlantic to the Pacific theater of war. Both pilots were transferred to us from Torpedo 8 -- recently reformed after the disastrous loss of all planes (with Ensign Gay as the sole survivor) during the Battle of Midway. Even though Scott and Canty had trained only briefly with squadron Torpedo 8, that association with the now famous squadron, where all members made the supreme sacrifice, carried an aura of glamour. We respected these transfer pilots and did not know at the time that both would suffer the same fate as that of their original squadron buddies.

I felt very close to Bill Canty. I don't know who first tacked on the label "Candyman," but it was a natural. He was a redhead from the Midwest with a pleasant smile and a good sense of humor. Unmarried, he was a logical teammate for several of the junior pilots. Consequently, we went on liberty together, usually restricted to short trips to downtown Hilo, Hawaii. A couple of times we had an afternoon off to play golf at the Hilo Country Club on the slope of Mauna Loa.

Bill "Candyman" Canty and Gerald. Hilo, Hawaii. August, 1944.

Our Skipper Lt Cdr Hutcheson stealing second base during a squadron baseball game. Others unidentified. Hilo, Hawaii. August, 1944.

Some of us were in downtown Honolulu on a night after the Fifth Marines returned from combat in the Pacific. We were shocked to observe the animosity of the Marines toward anyone who resembled the Japanese. After a few drinks, some innocent Hawaiians also felt the wrath of these Marines on R&R. Shore patrols were kept busy breaking up the fights. Curfew and blackouts were blessings for both natives and military personnel.

The skipper of Torpedo 4 had designated me as "Material Officer" for the squadron, so one day I was ordered to fly from Hilo to Barber's Point, Honolulu, for some squadron supplies. Candyman was to accompany me in another Avenger. We made the flight to Barber's Point without incident but had some trouble with our contacts on the base where we were to pick up the supplies (mostly flight gear and spare parts). Consequently, we were later than expected for our departure back to the Hilo airstrip.

The weather had closed in on the Big Island when we reached it. We could see the top of the volcano, but there was a solid cloud layer covering the field. Our planes were not equipped with sophisticated radar, and there were no ground control techniques to guide the planes onto the runway.

We circled Mauna Loa a couple of times. Candyman was flying on my left wing. I called the tower and received word that the visibility was limited but we should be able to get in. I radioed Canty that we would go out to sea a short distance, then come in from the north at near-ground level. The main problem was to stay clear of the volcano which covered much of the island. Our orders were to return that day, so neither of us considered a possible flight back to Pearl Harbor.

We finally made it back to the airstrip after an anxious letdown through the soup. That was only one event in a long series that made our training hazardous while we were awaiting assignment to go aboard the ***BUNKER HILL***.

On September 21, 1944, during night operations out of Hilo Air Station, three VT-4 planes ran together in a severe rain squall, and the squadron lost one of the most capable skippers in the Navy, Lt Cdr Hutcheson. Lt(jg) Canty, Ens M. S. Stocker, and all crew members were also lost and never found in the sea search that followed.

Lt(jg) Page Stephens stated the circumstances as follows: [1]

"I was with Hutch the night they ran together. I was not scheduled but Trex and Makibbin had dates with some girls in Hilo so I was persuaded to take it. We were doing one of those exercises where a flare plane split from the group and dropped flares on one side of the target while the rest of the flight stretched out in a line and made a torpedo attack from the opposite side. I drew the task of the flare plane so when we were airborne I joined up on Hutch's section. Canty was his wingman on the starboard; the other two were Binder on his port, and Stocker directly below 'in the well.'"

"There were some clouds that night and as 'Hutch' approached one, he gave his usual directive, 'Close up.' We did, and once in the cloud I could see Binder's wing lights and beyond that, Hutch's. The cloud became thicker and Hutch's lights faded out."

"There I was, in the middle of the cloud flying wing on Jolly Ed Binder who was without doubt the worst instrument pilot in the squadron. Instinct told me to check my artificial horizon and when I did, I realized we were banking into an ever-increasing steeper turn. My reaction with instant. I pushed over, dropped about 200 feet, and pulled out heading away from the formation. By that time I was under the cloud and could see no other planes. A few seconds later I saw quite an explosion down on the water. Later I realized this must have been the three planes hitting the water."

"All I could do then was to try to contact other planes and tell them to go back

The three pilots lost in the mid-air collision, September 21, 1944. Ens Merrill S. Stocker, Lt Cdr Homer H. Hutcheson, and Lt(jg) William H. Canty.

The cartoon of Hutcheson that I had drawn and taped to our barrack's wall prior to the accident. Note the knife marks.

to the field. I am not sure who else was on that flight but I believe Bob Ruth was. The next morning when it was light we searched the area but found nothing more than an oil slick."

That night when word reached the barracks of the crash, many of the pilots and crew got drunk -- very drunk! Scott Vogt took on a "crying jag." The loss of Bill Canty, his Torpedo 8 buddy, was too much for him.

Before the crash I had drawn a cartoon of Hutch and had it tacked to the barracks wall. The cartoon depicted our skipper, sitting on top of a pile of Navy regulations, issuing one of his frequent memos to officer personnel. The cartoon was drawn in jest. Nevertheless, after the 3-plane collision, some of the surviving pilots became very critical of Hutch's rigorous training schedule and the numerous flights in bad weather. After a few drinks they spotted my cartoon on the wall and started cursing and throwing their knives at it. I rescued it after it received two direct hits.

We lost some good pilots and crew members in this accident. It was impossible to place the blame on any one individual. The real culprit was the weather. However, some resentment and responsibility continued to be placed on Hutch. Later, when we got back into combat, most of us were thankful that Hutch had put us through some important and rigorous training -- perhaps saving some lives later. Who knows?

There is no doubt that we lost one of the best Torpedo skippers in the Navy in Lt Cdr Homer Hamby Hutcheson. While he demanded high performance, he had a special concern for each of his pilots. His wife June stated[2] *"Before the Squadron left the States... he had invited all his new Ensigns to his home for Sunday dinner. That's why I remember so many of you."*

We continued the search for possible survivors for three days after the crash -- without success. Memorial services were held the next Sunday in St. Joseph's Church, Hilo, Hawaii, for Torpedo 4 pilots and crew. A portion of the service in Our Lady of Victory Chapel follows:

IN MEMORIUM

In your charity we ask you to pray for the happy repose of the souls of nine of our Shipmates, who during this past week gave their lives for God and Country.

To:

Homer Hamby Hutcheson, Lt Cdr, USN
William H. Canty, Lt(jg), USNR
Merrill Silver Stocker, Ens, USNR
Henry N. Karsemeyer, ACRM(AA), USNR
Edward James Dooner, ACOM(AA), USN
Thomas Charles Bradley, AOM2c(T), USN
William Laverne Finkenbinder, ARM3c, USNR
Harry Lester Johnston, AOM3c, USNR
Raymond N. Glew, ARM3c, USNR

We say: God reward you and Well Done!

Lt Paul J. Davis, Jr.

Lt Lee L. "Ham" Hamrick.

Lt Page P. Stephens.

Lt Burt R. "Trex" Trexler.

Lt Davis was named Commander of Torpedo 4 after the tragic loss of Lt Cdr Hutcheson.
Lt Hamrick moved into the Executive Officer position.
Lt Stephens and Lt Trexler became senior division leaders.

"... minimal advice on evasive action against AA fire."

USS LONG ISLAND to Saipan -- A New Command

Lt Paul J. Davis, Jr., fresh out of instructor training, assumed the difficult position as Skipper of Torpedo 4 on September 21, 1944. None of us had the confidence in P. J. that we had flying under "Woot" Taylor or Hutch. I believe P. J. knew this because he seemed confused in the leadership position. He had not asked for the command but happened to have the lowest serial number.

After I returned from one flight out of Hilo under P. J.'s leadership, I confronted him with the comment, *"That was the most dangerous flight I have ever been on, including combat!"* P. J. shrugged, but he could have chastised me for insubordination. On the flight P. J., in the lead with 18 planes flying on him, had changed the throttle setting many times, made sharp turns into the formation, and dodged in and out of severe cumulus clouds, which periodically obscured about half the planes. This erratic leadership made it difficult to avoid a midair collision. Nevertheless, Torpedo 4 now had a new skipper, and he was the senior man in the squadron. A lousy time to be heading into combat with the Japanese!

With only a short training period under new command, the squadron was loaded aboard the *USS LONG ISLAND* and ferried to Saipan in the Marianas. We departed Pearl Harbor on October 22 and arrived in Saipan November 2, 1944. At this time Saipan was largely secured, but Tinian remained in Japanese hands. Our air group, while on shore, was subjected to periodic sniper fire and one bombing raid by Japanese planes. The sniper fire, even though it was in the distance, gave us a chill as we stood in the chow lines with the Marines still involved in mop-up operations.

I was lying on a canvas cot in a tent on Saipan when Japanese bombers came over the island. As our shore-based antiaircraft fire started, I rolled onto the ground and under the canvas cot -- great protection against the strafing and bomb blasts!

The damage to the facilities on Saipan was minimal. Evidently, Japanese air raids on the island were common. Saipan was first invaded by the 2nd and 4th Marine divisions on June 15, 1944, and supposedly secured on July 9. US Marine and Army casualties during the occupation of Saipan were over 14,000, with 3126 killed in action. The Japanese garrison of 27,000 was almost completely destroyed. [1]

Four months after the island fell, American troops were still involved in mop-up operations. All of the Torpedo 4 personnel survived the air raid and the remaining duty on the island while awaiting an assignment to our aircraft carrier. We were pleased to see the *USS BUNKER HILL* pull into Saipan Harbor on November 4, 1944.

Transfer to the USS BUNKER HILL

Air Group 4's first tour of duty in the Pacific started with our assignment to the *BUNKER HILL*. This was our first experience on an Essex-class carrier. Launched on December 7, 1942, the *BUNKER HILL* had been in the Pacific theater since November 1943 and had already established a reputation as a hard-fighting ship.

I was thrilled to be on the *BUNKER HILL* -- a great ship carrying a name important to American history. This assignment was the terminal point of months of operational training. It represented the ultimate challenge to a Naval aviator -- carrier duty in the Pacific -- an opportunity to have an impact

Launching of the **USS BUNKER HILL**. Fore River, Mass. December 7, 1942.

BUNKER HILL burning after being hit by Kamikaze. May 11, 1945.

on the Pacific War.

The **BUNKER HILL** (CV-17) had a flight deck that was 103 feet longer (overall length 872 feet) and nearly 40 feet wider than the **RANGER**. These larger dimensions and a top speed of 33 knots increased the margin of safety for launch and recovery. With a complement of 100 planes and 3500 men, we were now attached to one of the best carriers in the fleet -- a carrier that went on to earn the Presidential Unit Citation. Unfortunately, the **BUNKER HILL** later took two Kamikazes during the invasion of Okinawa, resulting in 346 dead, 43 missing, and 264 wounded.[2]

On November 5, 1944, the **BUNKER HILL** log states that she was "underway for the Philippines" and a very brief shake-down cruise. Our carrier moved with Task Force 38.4 under Admiral Davidson to the combat zone. We would be operating side-by-side with the carriers **ENTERPRISE**, **SAN JACINTO**, and **MONTEREY**. Ulithi Lagoon would now serve as the base of operations.

The shake-down cruise of three days provided the first opportunity for Air Group 4 to perform together on an Essex-class carrier. Cdr George O. Klinsmann, formerly Skipper of VB-4, was designated as Air Group Commander. As he stated in a later report to his task force superiors: [3]

"...The group reported aboard with very little carrier experience since being reformed in May 1944; the entire air group never having been on board together. It was fortunate that about 40% of the pilots were carrier experienced. It was most opportune that the ship's schedule was such that the Coordinating Officer could and did make it possible for the group to have three days of operations prior to going into action. This short time was invaluable and from then on, only minor trouble was experienced."

"The group also reported aboard without an experienced signal officer... an experienced signal officer who knows the ability of each pilot in carrier operations will

greatly relieve the additional mental hazard this condition creates, as well as expedite carrier operations...."

Cdr Klinsmann could also have said that Torpedo 4 went into combat with a Skipper fresh out of instructor's training. In addition, *"a typhoon was encountered on November 7, and throughout the action, flights were more or less hampered by high winds and heavy seas."*

During the four-day training period ship's records show that Air Group 4 lost two planes operationally and six ended up in the barrier. We were very lucky that no lives were lost.

In spite of these problems, we had some darned good section leaders, and we knew each other's flight habits. Furthermore, landing on the flight deck of the **BUNKER HILL** was a dream compared to trying to get aboard the old **RANGER**.

Tactics and ID Briefings

During our three-day shake-down cruise on the **BUNKER HILL**, the pilots of VT-4 received the most in-depth briefing we had experienced since OPERATION LEADER. When we were not studying maps of the Philippines or discussing "coordinated attacks," we were required to attend ID movies showing all of the Japanese aircraft we might encounter.

The major deficiency in our briefings concerned how to avoid anti-aircraft fire. We were provided only minimal advice on evasive action against Ack Ack. We knew we had little choice on the inbound run as we pressed home a torpedo attack or committed to a glide-bombing drop. However, we did have some options on target approach and we certainly should have received more advice on the escape, rendezvous, and return flights. It seemed that everyone had to "learn the hard way" -- by combat experience. Cozy Cole put it this way: [4]

"I think it was the expediency of the moment -- the war and all. The Navy was putting warm bodies in the planes without adequate experience. Some of us would not

*have made it through preliminary train-
ing in today's Navy. We had damn near no
briefing. P. J. didn't have any background
to help us. But why didn't they have some
veterans of a couple of combat cruises talk
to us?"*

The concept of a coordinated attack, designed
to permit maximum effectiveness of the dive
bombers and torpedo planes, theoretically provided some diversion from enemy gunners. The whole
idea was for the fighters to go in first, strafe the
target to reduce Ack Ack, then the dive-bombers
and torpedo planes would attack amid the height of
the confusion. However, there was never enough
confusion to stop the 20s and 40s from concentrating on the Avengers locked in on a torpedo drop.
**"Fly straight and level, maintain your altitude,
no skids, no turns -- that's the only way the torpedo will hold its course toward the ship."**

During simulated attacks when I was not scheduled for a flight, I watched the planes of Air Group
4 make their runs on the carrier. I positioned myself behind a 20-mm mount and followed the gunner's moves as he concentrated on an approaching
torpedo plane. The pilot of the Avenger held steady
for the drop, then started what he considered "good

evasive tactics." He rolled his wings from side to
side as he turned, but the plane was cumbersome.
What the pilot conceived as sharp turns were ac-
tually very easy to follow by the ship's gunner
with a slight side-to-side motion. However, any
up and down movement of the plane created more
problems for the gunner. After watching a few of
these simulated attacks from the ship, I changed
my mind about how to evade AA -- radical up-and-
down moves instead of rolling turns. These moves
were hard on the crew, but they may have saved
our lives in actual attacks.

After watching practice torpedo attacks from a
position behind the ship's guns, I could easily visu-
alize the heavy VT losses at Midway: [5]

- Out of 41 torpedo planes from 3 carriers, only
  6 returned.
- All planes in Torpedo 8 were shot down.
- Torpedo 3 lost 10 out of 12 planes.
- Torpedo 6 lost 10 out of 14 planes.

The precedent established by VT-3, VT-6, VT-
8, and other squadrons in the Pacific theater did
not bode well for Torpedo 4. But we had a job to
do, and to my knowledge, no one questioned the
upcoming assignments.

Burned planes on the flight deck of the ***BUNKER HILL*** after Kamikaze strike. May 11, 1945.

Chapter 8 | Introduction to the Philippines

"Carrier planes sank two destroyers, two DEs, and four attack transports."

Ormoc Bay -- Strike Able -- 11 November 1944

The recapture of Leyte in the Philippines, by Army and Marine troops under General MacArthur, began on October 20, 1944. The Japanese had decided to hold the Island by sending 25,000 reinforcements into Ormoc Bay to support some 16,000 troops that were already on the island.[1] Our task, as a part of the Third Fleet, was to prevent additional Japanese support for the island.

Since this was the first strike for Air Group 4 against the Japanese, there was a high level of excitement during the briefing in the Ready Room on the morning of November 11, 1944. We were informed that there would be two strikes during the day. Both strikes would be designed as coordinated attacks involving Hellcats, Helldivers, and Avengers. During the previous short shakedown on the **BUNKER HILL** we had practiced for this type of attack against shipping, but no one knew how well we could carry it out under combat conditions.

Strike Able was launched from the **BUNKER HILL** shortly after daybreak. It consisted of 20 F6Fs, 8 TBMs, and 11 SB2Cs. The target was the Japanese Convoy entering Ormoc Bay with troops and supplies. Lt Cdr K. G. Hammond, VF-4, was assigned the lead for both fighter cover and attack coordination. Although enemy Zekes and Oscars were observed in the area, our formation was not attacked. Part of the official report follows: [2]

"The target area was approached from the north at 12,000 feet. There was a strike group from Air Group EIGHTY (Ticonderoga) 10 miles ahead and another attack group from Air Group TWENTY (Enterprise) on the port beam."

"The enemy shipping, consisting of 4 APs, 5 DDs, and 1 DE, was sighted on an easterly course in the strait between Leyte Island and Ponson Island entering Ormoc Bay from the west. During the approach the 4 APs were observed burning and smoking. The air group coordinator directed the group to attack the leading AP, but before attack could be executed, APs #1 and 3 exploded, and Aps #2 and 4 were burning fiercely. The group was then ordered to attack DD #10 with bombs and to strafe the other DDs and DE which was putting up AA fire." (AP, AO, and AK are designations for Japanese auxiliary ships. DDs are destroyers, and DEs are destroyer escorts.)

Fighting 4 made the first bombing and strafing runs with fair success. Damaging near-misses were reported by those Hellcats carrying bombs and *"The strafing attack was effective in silencing most of the AA fire...."* Fighters also reported that, *"A small fire was seen to start near the torpedo tubes on one of the DDs."* The DE was also burning.

This was the first strike for Bombing 4 using the new SB2C Helldivers. Each SB2C was loaded with a 1000-pounder and two 100-pounders. The Helldivers dived almost vertically from 10,000 feet as the last fighters were in the attack. Most of the dive-bombers pulled out at about 1000 feet and proceeded at low level to the rendezvous location. Hits were confirmed by Lt McReynolds and Lt(jg) Jackson. Several near-misses also produced damage. Lt Cdr Johnson, who led VB-4, reported after the strike that, *"It was felt that two 500-pound GPs (general purpose bombs) would have been more effective than the 1000-pound SAPs (semiarmor piercing bombs) against this type target."*

Avenger taking off. Unidentified carrier. Pacific.

Ships burning following Ormoc Bay Strike Able by AG-4. November 11, 1944.

Those of us in the Torpedo squadron had the opportunity to see a part of the attack by planes from the *TICONDEROGA* and *ENTERPRISE*. We also saw some of the results from attacks by our own fighters and dive-bombers. There was still some antiaircraft fire coming mostly from the Japanese destroyers and DEs as we pushed over.

Our 8 TBMs were loaded with four 500-pound SAPs. Our orders were to follow the dive bombers but to come in from different directions to confuse the Japanese gunners. The VT-4 tactical organization was as follows: [24]

Strike Able - November 11, 1944

P. J. Davis, Jr. (pilot)
   R. F. Gray and N. J. Schmolke (crew)

C. N. W. "Scott" Vogt
   Leo E. Halvorson and R. E. Kelly

G. M. "Buck" Barnett
   Joseph C. Cohen and C. Christopher

W. F. "Willie" Walker
   S. A. Hastings and G. F. Zeimer

Page P. Stephens
   A. Beard and Andy "Marge" Mocsary

Vernon A. Landre
   A. "Tony" DeCenso and Charlie C. Statler

Gerald W. "Jerry" Thomas
   J. E. Holloman and Don H. Gress

R. M. "Hoppy" Hopfinger
   F. W. Wilson and A. W. Yarman

We made the approach to Ormoc Bay from the south side of Ponson Island. The Japanese ships, especially the DDs and the DE, took evasive action as we dived down for the attack. Even though the fighters and the dive bombers had made their run, the antiaircraft fire seemed to increase. At least there were plenty of tracers floating toward our plane. Because this was my first encounter against the Japanese, I was excited; but I was so busy with the check-off list and attack maneuvers that there was no time for fear.

The first division, led by P. J. Davis, pushed

over from 9000 feet at a glide angle of 40-50 degrees. P. J. and Scott Vogt went in on one of the AKs. Davis' bombs failed to release, and Vogt scored a near-miss.

Buck Barnett led the second section in on the destroyer. Buck *"released two bombs that struck near the port beam of the DD, but no damage was observed."* His other two did not release. Willie Walker, flying on Buck's wing *"dropped his bombs on the DD, the last bomb hitting squarely amidships."*

Page Stephens led our division in the dive about the time P. J. pushed over. Page and Vernon Landre dived toward one of the other destroyers in a formation run. *"One of the bombs hit the DD on bridge. It was impossible to determine whose bomb it was. Stephens brought one bomb back."*

Hoppy started out on my wing as I pushed over to attack one of the AKs, then he turned toward one of the Japanese destroyers. *"Hopfinger released his bombs on the DD, one bomb exploding on the fantail."* In the meantime, I held my nose on the AK as it took evasive action. Unfortunately, I *"... dropped three bombs along the starboard side of the AK with no damage claimed."*

During the attacks, Halvorson, Cohen, Beard, and Mocsary fired on the ships with the belly guns as their planes pulled out of the dive.

In spite of the "hung-up" bombs, the strike was an overall success. We learned from the experience. The official report also states: [2]

> *"It is assumed that enemy personnel casualties were extremely high for it is believed the shipping attacked was en route to Ormoc to land reinforcements. Several pilots and crewmen reported seeing large numbers of enemy personnel in the water."*

Ormoc Bay -- Strike Baker -- 11 November 1944

In the second strike of the day, assigned targets were again the four damaged destroyers and one destroyer escort in Ormoc Bay. Cdr Otto Klinsmann (CAG-4) led this attack. He assigned 4 Hellcats as high cover, 4 as intermediate cover, and he and his wingman stayed in close to the bombers. The approach was made southwest-ward across Leyte Island over Ormoc town to the bay. All the ships, except one, were burning at the time the flight arrived.

Enemy Zeros, Oscars, and Zekes were encountered during the strike. As a consequence, Klinsmann ordered his fighters to maintain cover instead of strafing as a part of the attack. Seven Oscars that attacked the formation were engaged by Lt Boykin's fighter division. One Oscar was hit but not observed to crash. Lt(jg) Peabody received damage to the port wing and fuselage. [2]

"Our fighters were able to turn into the enemy attack and scissor with them. At times the enemy VF showed good tactics by bracketing our VF with two planes on either side and leaving the remaining three Oscars as high cover for them. However, they did not press their attacks closely, and neither the Oscars nor our own fighters were in position to fire except in head-on runs."

Lt Keers's division of fighters was engaged by four Japanese Oscars at 11,000 feet over Ormoc Bay. Lt(jg) T. J. Graham *"got in a good burst on one of the Oscars... forcing it to retire from combat."*

Three divisions of dive-bombers were also on Strike Baker. *"Lt Weeks scored a direct hit on the bow (of the DD) forward of the superstructure with near-misses by Lt(jg) Baker and Ens Kinder. The DD was left in a sinking condition."*

Eight torpedo planes were scheduled for this flight under the leadership of Lt Hamrick. However, when Souza and Cole manned their planes on the flight deck, they found that they were not loaded. Consequently, only six VT were in on the attack as follows: [2]

Strike Baker - November 11, 1944

Lee L. "Ham" Hamrick (pilot)
  W. M. Hardin and R. A. Trembley (crew)

Don A. Henry
  E. A. Shirley and A. G. Schiesz

Felix E. Ward, Jr.
  Don M. Applegate and C. J. Warrington

J. E. Hewitt
  C. W. Lathrop and L. P. Shuman

E. A. "Ted" Newell
  W. J. Lace and D. E. Venderville

W. J. Hopkins, Jr.
  Stan W. Coller and R. E. Simendinger, Jr.

No direct hits were recorded in the glide-bombing attacks by VT-4 due to evasive action by the Japanese ships. Schiesz and Warrington fired on the targets from the turrets while Shirley and Applegate followed up with the tunnel guns as the planes went over the ships.

On the return flight, over Leyte Island, the dive-bombers noted seven Zekes engaged by Army P-38s. One of these Zekes made a run on the formation and slightly damaged Lt(jg) Fallgatter's Helldiver. Our bombers confirmed that at least one Zeke was shot down by a P-38.

All planes from our air group returned to the **BUNKER HILL**. Our first day of action in the Pacific left us with a healthy respect for the gunners on the Japanese warships and a fleeting view of fighter interception. The poker game that night was frequently interrupted with war stories.

BUNKER HILL records show, *"On the 11th carrier planes found the ships and sank one large destroyer, one (medium) destroyer, two DEs, and four attack transports."* [3]

Chapter 9 | Cavite and Manila Harbor

"As aircraft retired both DDs were seen to explode."

Cavite, Luzon -- 13 November 1944

After the strikes on Ormoc Bay, **BUNKER HILL** records show that November 12 was used for refueling. Routine combat air patrols and anti-sub flights were launched.

Although we did not hear the news until later, November 12 held additional significance for us since this could be considered the day for the final destruction of the German Navy. The battleship **TIRPITZ** was finally sunk by the Royal Air Force, taking about 1200 crewmen to their deaths.[1] We couldn't help wondering if the job could not have been done one year earlier by Torpedo 4 when our flight was cancelled by the British Home Fleet.

On November 13, 1944, we were again scheduled to go back to the Philippines. Strikes were made throughout the day on Luzon, Manila Bay, and Cavite by various combinations of fighters, dive-bombers, and torpedo bombers. Statler reported in his diary that *"at least 40 or more enemy ships were sunk by our task force (TF 38.3)."* [2]

We sent one four-plane F6F division under Lt H. T. Houston to fly a combat air patrol (CAP) over the "lifeguard submarine," which was in the Subic Bay area to pick up airmen shot down by the Japanese. The sub was never spotted, and attempts to contact it by radio failed. However, this CAP did engage enemy aircraft. Lt(jg) Gilbert shot down a Japanese Lily (Kawasaki Bomber) in flames at the entrance to Subic Bay. No one was seen to bail out. Later the group spotted another Lily, which Lt Houston attacked. This plane was also shot down in flames with no apparent survivors.[3]

Lt Cdr K. G. Hammond led 16 planes in an early morning fighter sweep over Clark Field on Luzon. Five Tojos (Nakajima Fighters) intercepted the Hellcats. Lt G. M. Harris, Jr. and Lt P. H. Gordon shot down two of these and Lt(jg) Hal Avants damaged another. The sweep group destroyed at least seven aircraft at Clark Field and damaged others.

The first coordinated strike group was launched in the morning of November 13. Cdr Klinsmann and 7 other Hellcats again led the group. Nineteen Helldivers under Lt C. F. Weeks and 14 Avengers under P. J. Davis were scheduled, but Bob Ruth's TBM wouldn't start, so he was left behind. Klinsmann reported that: [3]

"Standard formations were flown by all squadrons, and before reaching land, VF began its escort weave."

The "fighter weave" was developed at an early stage in the Pacific war. The technique was effective in confusing enemy fighters if they had not encountered it before. The major purpose of the weave was to provide continuous cover of the tail of your fellow pilots. In case of an attack, there was always a fighter pointed toward the intruder. It was effective if properly executed. The torpedo planes had a turret gunner to serve this purpose.

Shortly after reaching the area, planes were assigned targets at Cavite. Most of the fighters attacked several of the AKs in the harbor.

Lt Byrd's and Lt Hancock's fighter divisions were assigned to strafe ahead of the VT but lost the VT as they let down through the clouds. By this time the Japanese AA gunners were well in position and ready for the attack. White puffs of smoke burst in most of the cloud openings.[3]

"Lt (jg) A. F. Summer's plane was hit in the engine... forcing him to make a wa-

BKHL-378-13 NOV 44 (-9)1530 K-20 6% ALT VAE CAVITE BAY Conf

Japanese warships burning in Cavite Bay following VT-4 strike. November 13, 1944.

A second view of the Cavite Bay strike. November 13, 1944.

ter landing in Manila Bay about four miles east of Corregidor.... He and his radioman, George Bogel, were successful in inflating their life raft." (CAG-4 reported the location of the raft to rescue facilities. Final outcome unknown to this author.)

The 13 Avengers for this strike were loaded with 2000-pound torpedoes. The tactical organization was as follows: [3]

Strike Able - November 13, 1944

P. J. Davis, Jr. (pilot)
 R. F. Gray and N. J. Schmolke (crew)

C. N. W. "Scott" Vogt
 Leo E. Halvorson and R. E. Kelly

D. C. Pletts
 J. E. Ganley and R. C. Mann

G. M. "Buck" Barnett
 Joseph C. Cohen and C. Christopher

W. F. "Willie" Walker
 S. A. Hastings and G. F. Zeimer

J. F. Zook
 L. E. Thomas and P. J. Baughman

B. R. "Trex" Trexler
 C. W. Barr and J. W. Aldrich

G. M. Bell
 A. J. Tankard and R. R. Pittman

L. C. Gray
 J. F. "Forrest" Ballard and C. L. McConnell

Ed S. Binder
 W. D. Jenkins and A. B. Tranflaglia

H. J. Deimel
 C. L. Ely, Jr., and L. S. Leach

G. D. "Mak" Makibbin
 J. C. Gerke and R. Campbell

W. H. Cannady, Jr.
 J. J. Supanich and E. A. McGuire

Because the TBMs were carrying torpedoes, they had to come in low in a different approach. Davis led the group along the south shore of Manila Bay. All VT attacked the same target, a float-

ing drydock. The dropping altitude was 400-500 feet at about 230 knots. At least 4 torpedoes were observed definitely to hit the drydock. Credit was given to Davis and Vogt for two of the hits. *"It was not possible to establish credit for the other two known hits. The attack completely destroyed the 'bay side' of the drydock."* [3]

During the attack, Kelly and Zeimer strafed from their turrets, and Halvorson, Hastings, Tankard, and Ely used their tunnel thirties.

As Buck Barnett was recovering from his run, he flew over the top of one of the islands. *"Shrapnel from AA fire came through the side of the plane and hit my belly gunner, Cohen, behind the ear. He was bleeding like a stuck pig. We both thought he was dying, but we got him back aboard and into sick bay. His wound turned out to be minor, and he was scheduled out the next day."* [4]

Cavite, Luzon -- Strike Baker -- 13 November 1944

Before the second coordinated attack of the day, the ***BUNKER HILL*** launched another fighter sweep over central Luzon. Lt L. M. Boykin led this group of 10 F6Fs to Tarlac and Clark Fields to strafe and damage as many Japanese planes as possible.

The fighter runs on Tarlac led to the conclusion that most of the planes on the ground there were non-operational or dummies. The group then went on toward Clark Field. En route, Lt Hendricks and wingman engaged a Tojo, smoked the plane, and observed the pilot bailing out.[3]

Lt Boykin's division attacked 4 Tojos just below the clouds east of Clark Field. Boykin's shells caused one plane to burn, but no one verified the crash. Peabody shot down one of the remaining planes. In another encounter, Garrigan and Blackwell both obtained kills. The group returned to base at 1621 hours.

The second major strike of the day in the Cavite area involved 4 fighters, 18 dive bombers, and 14 torpedo planes. I'm not sure as to the reasoning for the lack of fighter cover. At any rate, we did not run into any enemy aircraft.

Cdr Klinsmann led the group to the assigned targets -- two Japanese destroyers alongside the docks at Cavite. The 4 fighters went down first -- no direct hits but some damage. Lt(jg) Martin pulled out so fast he lost most of his horizontal stabilizer, so he returned directly to the ship. Avant's plane was hit with AA fire, and he too lost about half of his stabilizer and elevator.

The SB2C Helldivers, led by Lt Cdr Johnson, made their customary breakoffs, rollovers, and near-vertical dives. Bevis laid his 1000 pounder on the bow of one destroyer. Guttery hit the second DD with a 250-pound bomb, and several other bombers had near misses which caused damage. Tutwiler hit a Fox Tare Charlie. Kinder scored a direct hit on an AK or AO.

All except 3 of the 14 Avengers were loaded with 4 500-pound SAP bombs. Ruth, Hopfinger, and I carried 500-pound GPs (General Purpose bombs). The tactical organization for Torpedo 4 was: [3]

Strike Baker - November 13, 1944

Lee L. "Ham" Hamrick (pilot)
  W. M. Hardin and R. A. Trembley (crew)

Don A. Henry
  E. A. Shirley and A. G. Schiesz

Felix E. Ward, Jr.
  Don M. Applegate and C. J. Warrington

J. E. Hewitt
  C. W. Lathrop and L. P. Shuman

E. A. "Ted" Newell
  W. J. Lace and D. E. Venderville

W. J. Hopkins, Jr.
  Stan W. Coller and R. E. Simendinger, Jr.

Will S. Souza
  D. L. Huston and T. R. Sims

L. A. "Cozy" Cole
  N. H. Knox and N. L. Shiverdecker

Page P. Stephens
  A. Beard and Andy "Marge" Mocsary

Strike Baker - November 13, 1944 (continued)

Vernon A. Landre
  A. "Tony" DeCenso and Charlie C. Statler

Gerald W. "Jerry" Thomas
  J. E. Holloman and Don H. Gress

Robert F. "Bob" Ruth
  J. F. "Forrest" Ballard and C. L. McConnell

B. O. O'Brien
  R. H. Stradley and R. D. Biddle

R. M. "Hoppy" Hopfinger
  F. W. Wilson and A. W. Yarman

We flew into the harbor area at 10,000 feet. Anti-aircraft fire was very heavy -- some coming from the ships below and some coming from emplacements on Cavite and on the Luzon shore southwest of Cavite.

Hamrick's 4-plane section attacked a medium AK. All drops were near-misses except Hamrick's, which set the ship afire.

Four of us attacked the two Terutsuki-class destroyers docked at Cavite. These two Japanese DDs put up more AA fire than any we had experienced so far. I held the nose on the target as long as I could, probably dropping below 2000 feet.[3]

"Lt(jg) Thomas scored with all four of his bombs. Lt Stephens put two bombs on one of the DDs and two on the adjoining dock. Lt(jg) Ruth also scored two hits on the DDs and his other two bombs demolished a nearby building. Lt Newell hit the DDs with two SAPs.... As aircraft retired, both DDs were seen to explode."

Six VT attacked a medium AK or AO. Landre made a direct hit amidships and Souza scored a near-miss on the port bow. *"The ship was burning badly as aircraft departed."*

Three crewmen, Schiesz, Coller, and Simendinger strafed the targets but were not able to evaluate the extent of the damage.

Ens "Cozy" Cole was flying on Souza's wing as they pushed over into the glide bombing attack. He stated: [5]

"This was my first strike with VT-4. I saw so dad-gum many ships down there and so much AA fire! I picked out a ship and dove toward it. Just as I released my bombs, I got hit by anti-aircraft fire. It was more like a solid 'pop' than an explosion as it went through my port wing. Shiverdecker grabbed his intercom and shouted, 'Are you all right?' I was too busy checking to see if my controls would work to answer immediately, but I was pleased that the crew was OK."

"The projectile, probably more than a 20-mm, had just missed my gas tank. It knocked out my aileron control, but I could skid around with the rudders. I was a little skittish about getting too close to Souza and was dragging behind in the formation. Souza gave me hell for not closing up."

"When we reached the ship, I orbited until they had everyone else aboard. They didn't want me to mess up the deck. But we got aboard OK."

Shiverdecker stated, *"That hole in our wing was large enough for one ground-crewman to climb through."* [6] The records show that Cole's TBM required a wing change but was repairable on board.

Felix Ward's Avenger was also hit by Japanese gunners. His turret gunner, Norm Applegate, described the experience: [7]

"It was a terrifying moment. I was riding in the turret facing toward the tail. I felt this big thump on my back. I thought, 'Oh my God! to hit behind me it must have got Mr. Ward.' Was I glad when he pulled out of the dive. We made it back with a big hole in the starboard wing."

The rendezvous was all fouled up. Our Skipper, P. J., was not where he told us he would be. There was too much AA fire in the area to hang around long, so I joined up with Page and we headed home on our own.

In the meantime, two other VT-4 planes were in trouble. During the dive on the two Japanese destroyers docked at Cavite, AA fire hit the planes flown by Bob Ruth and by Ens O'Brien. Bob Ruth stated: [8]

*"My plane was hit by a projectile which came up through the bottom of the plane between me and the engine. The cordite odor was very strong, but the plane did not catch fire. No controls were damaged, but we sweated out the 200-mile return flight. My wingman, O'Brien, whose plane also took a hit, requested permission for an emergency landing on the first carrier he could find, the **LANGLEY**. O'Brien crashed into the barrier and fouled up the flight deck, so I was sent to another carrier, the **YORKTOWN**."*

Forrest Ballard, flying as gunner for Bob Ruth, stated that their Avenger had been hit and they were streaming gas. *"I was worried about a fire, but we made it to the **YORKTOWN**. They fixed our plane and we flew back to the carrier the next day."* [9]

In view of the intense AA fire over Manila, we were lucky to get by with only 4 damaged planes. Hopkins pulled a very foolish stunt in the raid. He decided to convert his TBM to a fighter and go back down for a strafing run. His crewman, Stan Coller, said, *"We dove on this Japanese freighter. Hoppy strafed with the forward guns, I opened up with my 30, and Simendinger fired from the turret. When we pulled back into the formation and heard about the other planes damaged or shot down, we considered ourselves very very lucky. No more strafing runs for us!"* [10]

November 13 had been a busy day for Air Group 4. We could point to significant damage to

Avenger pulls away after dropping a 500-lb bomb. Cavite Coast. November 13, 1944.

Japanese ships burning in Manila Harbor. November 14, 1944.

the Japanese. But sadly the enemy had taken a toll, particularly, of our dive-bombers: [3]

Lt(jg) Arthur G. King's SB2C was hit as he pulled out of the dive. There was a large flash under the fuselage and the plane immediately dived into the bay. His gunner was Richard A. Smart, ARM3c. Listed MIA.

Ens James I. Hawkins' plane was last seen just prior to the pushover. Someone saw a large flash toward the north end of the bay. His gunner was G. P. Curtice, ARM3c. Listed MIA.

Lt(jg) C. J. Fallgatter's plane ran out of gas as he was making a landing approach. He was knocked unconscious but his crewman, E. F. Flanigan, ARM2c, extricated him as the plane sank. They were picked up by one of our destroyers.

South Harbor, Manila -- 14 November 1944

Word spread as reveille was sounded about 0400 that we were going back to Manila Harbor. That meant another day of exposure to heavy anti-aircraft fire. We were in the Ready Room for briefings at 0600 and launched at 0732. The Torpedo 4 tactical organization was as follows: [3]

Strike Able - November 14, 1944

P. J. Davis, Jr. (pilot) (returned before attack)
  R. F. Gray and N. J. Schmolke (crew)

C. N. W. "Scott" Vogt
  Leo E. Halvorson and R. E. Kelly

G. M. "Buck" Barnett
  Joseph C. Cohen and C. Christopher

W. F. "Willie" Walker
  S. A. Hastings and G. F. Zeimer

Page P. Stephens
  A. Beard and Andy "Marge" Mocsary

Vernon A. Landre
  A. "Tony" DeCenso and Charlie C. Statler

Gerald W. "Jerry" Thomas
  J. E. Holloman and Don H. Gress

R. M. "Hoppy" Hopfinger
  F. W. Wilson and A. W. Yarman

Strike Able - November 14, 1944 (continued)

B. R. "Trex" Trexler
  C. W. Barr and J. W. Aldrich

G. M. Bell
  A. J. Tankard and R. R. Pittman

G. D. "Mak" Makibbin
  J. C. Gerke and R. Campbell

L. C. Gray
  J. E. Ganley and R. C. Mann

Twelve TBMs were launched without incident, but Lt Davis returned to base shortly after takeoff because of engine trouble. He jettisoned his bombs before landing aboard. Lt Trexler assumed VT lead for the 200-mile flight to Manila.

We were accompanied on this strike by 8 Hellcats and 10 Helldivers. Otto Klinsmann served as CAG-4 in his F6F, and Lt Weeks led the dive-bombers. All 8 F6Fs were loaded with bombs, so they had a multipurpose responsibility.

Cdr Klinsmann and his fighters went in first. Their reports show bomb hits on an AK by C. L. Martin, flying on Otto's wing, and W. C. Guyles. From the second fighter division, Lt Hendricks hit a different Japanese AK.

The dive-bombers started their attack from 11,000 feet, diving out of the sun to reduce their vulnerability. Lt(jg) Dondero was credited with a probable hit on an AK, and McCanley, flying with VB-20, also hit an AK.

VT pushed over from 9500 feet under heavy AA fire. Seven VT attacked a large AO or AK, two attacked the boats in the seaplane basin, one attacked the Natori-Class CL, and one attacked a large AK. Debriefing reports show the following results: [3]

"Five bombs bracketed the AO, three credited to Ensign Landre and one each to Lt Trexler and Lt(jg) Thomas. Debris was seen to fly with the bomb explosions and the ship was observed to be afire as VT departed. Ensign Landre, Ensign Bell, and

VT-4 strike on Manila Harbor. November 14, 1944.

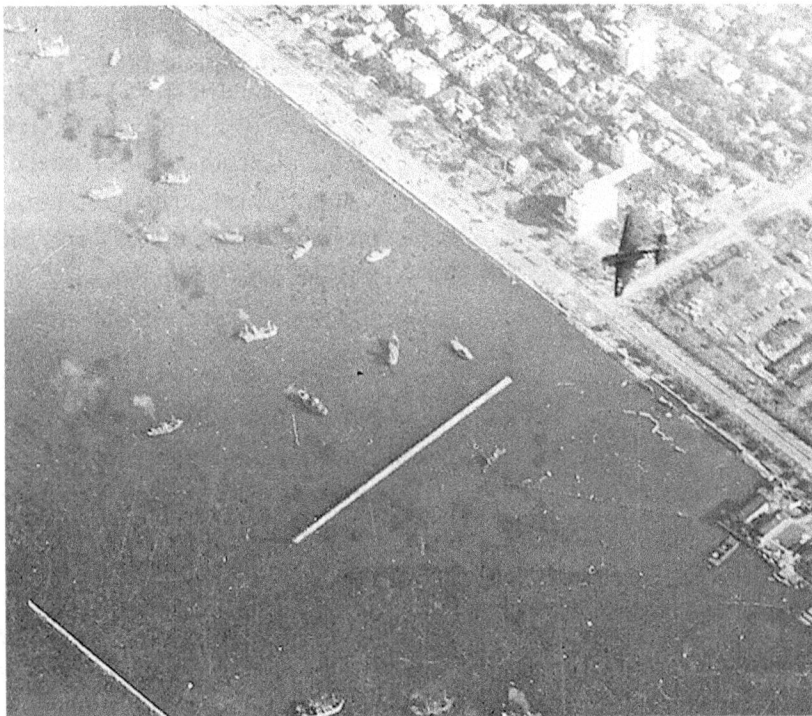

Detail of the above image showing a VT-4 Avenger going in for a strike.
Manila Harbor. November 14, 1944.

Trexler each retained one bomb, which they were unable to jettison on the return trip to base. Lt(jg) Barnett and his wingman, Ensign Walker, dropped on the boats in the seaplane basin. Barnett's bombs were not observed."

"Two of Walker's bombs struck boats and two fell on land installations. Much debris was seen to fly with the bomb explosions. It is believed that at least two boats, possible PT boats, were destroyed."

"Lt(jg) Makibbin attacked a large AK. One of his bombs was a near miss on the starboard quarter which started a fire." [11]

Lt(jg) Scott Vogt picked out the most challenging target in the Bay. He chose a Natori-Class Light cruiser. The record shows that Scott *"scored a hit just forward of the bridge and a near miss on the port bow."* Leo Halvorson, one of Scott's crewmen stated it this way: [12]

*"Coming out of there the Ack Ack was pretty heavy, but I saw our bombs hit -- not one but two direct hits! I called Scott and asked if we were going to attack that cruiser and I asked how he wanted the bombs set. He said '**at 700 feet.**' So I set them. But as we got closer I thought '**What the Hell! You're a better bomber than that.**' So, I reached in and reset for 400 feet. We ended up with two direct hits."*

*"But as we were pulling out, I felt a boom over the roar of the plane. I went back to operating my peewee 30-caliber. Then I got this sting in my leg, and the gun jammed. Pretty soon I could feel blood in my shoe. I called Scott and said '**Let's get the hell out of here!**' He never answered and I called back. He said, '**We sure fooled the Japs that time.**' I said, '**How's that?**' and he answered, '**I used the gas in the***

*right wing going to the target, and just before we went in to bomb, I switched to the left wing. Boy did we fool those Japs!'** We had a 2-3 foot hole in the right wing!"*

After the attack, join-up was effected over the center of Manila Bay. This was certainly not the best place to rendezvous! We should have firewalled it back to a safer area to regroup. Two of our Torpedo 4 planes were hit by AA fire, and one rear gunner was wounded.

As the Air group proceeded back to the **BUNKER HILL**, we counted our losses.[3]

Ens William N. Ostlund, Fighting 4, was not seen after the dive. It is believed that his plane was hit by AA and he crashed. He was listed as MIA.

Ens Kenneth W. Watkins, VF-4, was hit by AA fire and crashed in flames.

Lt(jg) Don Dondero's plane was hit by AA fire, and two persons were observed to bail out hitting the water between South Manila Harbor and Cavite. McReynolds saw one person in a life raft, and one in a life jacket. Their chances of being picked up by 'friendlies' were minimal.

Don Dondero was a close friend of the Torpedo pilots -- usually accompanying them on liberty or participating in the VT-4 poker games. Don had a rough time after he was shot down, but he was able to return to the States after the war and open a photography shop in Reno, Nevada.[13]

Summary records from the **BUNKER HILL** show the following results from this second day over Manila Harbor: [14]

"A destroyer was sunk, a medium AK heavily damaged, and five medium AKs, a large AK, a large AK or AO, a Natori-Class CL, a large destroyer, and a large AP damaged. An antiaircraft battery on the southeast side of the harbor was also hit."

Japanese ships under attack. Manila Harbor. November 14, 1944.

Airport, Manila Harbor. November 14, 1944.

Chapter 10 | BUNKER HILL: Recap and Critique

"We must accept losses of personnel in these attacks."

Flight operations in the Manila area were concluded on November 14, 1944. The **BUNKER HILL** then departed for Ulithi, with a refueling stop en route on November 16 in a "safe area." The ship finally dropped anchor in Ulithi Lagoon on the 17th.

The return trip was utilized for the necessary reports to the higher levels of command. Air Group 4 had flown 277 Target Sorties, 38 Search Sorties, 102 Combat Air Patrol Sorties, and 46 anti-sub patrols. We had dropped 91.8 tons of bombs and fired 13 aerial torpedoes against the Japanese.[1]

During this 12-day period, Air Group 4 had lost 7 pilots and 4 crewmen in combat. Torpedo Four had lost only one plane, but combat (combined with operations) had cost us 4 F6Fs and 7 SB2Cs. VF-4 fighters were credited with shooting down seven Japanese planes, plus two more "probables" and two "damaged."

We had made a good record for the **BUNKER HILL** in terms of the loss of Japanese ships, damage to shore installations, and the destruction of more than 15 enemy planes on the ground. Nevertheless, there was plenty of room for improvement.

Report by Commander, Air Group 4

Under the date of November 20, Cdr Klinsmann presented a summary report on Air Group Four's operations in the Leyte-Luzon combat zone over the period November 5-17, 1944.[2]

Included in this report are the following observations (emphasis added):

"An analysis of the forwarded reports reveals that too many targets were attacked scattering light damage to many ships rather than concentrating on the destruction of particular targets. When a large number of targets of equal importance are present, pilots naturally tend to attack readily available targets in the vicinity of their division leader's attack. Further indoctrination in divisions attacking as a team will bring about a selection of fewer targets and a greater number of sinkings."

"The continued increase in the accuracy and intensity of Japanese anti-aircraft fire must continue to receive the serious consideration of all concerned. It is believed that shipping in well-protected harbors will receive greater damage during continued strikes if the anti-aircraft positions are first attacked, and that during strikes, VF equipped with rockets, make diversionary attacks on these installations. **We must accept losses of personnel in these attacks;** *however, it is firmly believed that we could greatly reduce the number and increase the percentage of hits. At MANILA HARBOR heavy and medium antiaircraft fire encountered was of the barrage type making it necessary to pass through it to reach a target. A diversionary attack by VF in coordination with the strike group would divert the volume of fire during the attack."*

"Radio discipline must be improved, especially when a large number of planes are in a target area. Unnecessary transmissions often prevent target assignments from getting through resulting in attacks not being properly coordinated and delivered against less profitable targets."

"It is believed that every effort should be made to give spare air groups more carrier work during their training, either on the mainland or in the forward areas."

"The group also reported aboard without an experienced signal officer."

Signed: G. O. Klinsmann, Cdr, CAG-4

All of these observations by Otto Klinsmann were valid -- targets too scattered, increasing losses from AA fire, poor radio discipline, the need for more training, and the value of a good LSO (Landing Signal Officer).

The problem of radio communication deserves special mention. During the confusion of the strikes, the airways were so cluttered with frantic calls that we couldn't tell whose message was getting through. It was particularly important to receive acknowledgement for "May Day" or rescue calls. At this time we were all using channel "Charlie." The final *BUNKER HILL* action report recommended that two other VHF channels be utilized for part of the transmissions.[1] This change was not made until much later. In the meantime all pilots were again reminded of the importance of strict radio discipline -- no frivolous or unnecessary calls!

As we completed our tour of duty on the *BUNKER HILL*, we were again asked to send a "form letter" home. Evidently, some service men were not communicating very well with their parents or relatives. Personally, I think this form letter was designed by someone who had little concept of its possible adverse impact.

"Dear (fill in name of parent or guardian)"

"Hold on to this letter; it will tell you a lot of things you may need to know while I'm away. The Navy wants you to have this information."

"First, there's my service number: _____. Always use it when writing the Navy Department...."

"If you are unable to pay any federal income tax I may owe when it is due, go to any office of Collector of Internal Revenue and fill out their form explaining the reason you can't pay, and requesting that payment be deferred until six months after my naval service ends."

"If I am wounded, you may be notified, although of course I will probably be writing you myself. If I am disabled, and entitled to disability benefits after my discharge, these will be arranged through the US Veterans Administration, Washington 25, D.C."

"If I am reported missing, missing in action, or captured by the enemy, my pay and allowances will go right on. My insurance and war bond allotments will continue, and so will any allotment for the support of a dependent, if designated as such."

"If I should die while on active duty, you are entitled to six months' pay in a lump sum. Claim blanks for this will be sent to you. If you do not receive them, write the Bureau of Naval Personnel, Navy Department, Washington 25, D.C. Settlement will also be made of any pay remaining due me, and savings on deposit with the Paymaster."

"If the landlord should want to evict you get legal advice."

"Signature _____"
"Rank _____"
"File No. _____"

Air Group Four transferred off the *BUNKER HILL* at Ulithi on November 17, 1944. She went home for repairs and was back on duty in the Pacific for the February strikes on Japan. On May 11, 1945 the ship was put out of action by a Kamikaze attack.

Chapter 11 | Phylogeny of a Torpedo Pilot

"Thomas... I guess you know you gave me a lousy ride!"

The first combat tour in the Pacific on the **BUNKER HILL** gave those of us in Torpedo 4 a conception of our ultimate mission. We could now understand why everyone did not choose to be carrier-based torpedo pilots. Why and how we got to this point can be illustrated by my own experience.

My second ride in an airplane took place after I joined the Navy as an aviation cadet. The flight instructor took me up to about 5000 feet in a "Yellow Peril," rolled the plane on its back, and dove straight for the ground. It took some time for my stomach to catch up. *"That, Cadet Thomas," my instructor stated, "is what a dive-bombing run is like! Do you think you can take it?"* I gasped an affirmative through the speaker tube that connected our cockpits, but I wasn't so sure.

Certainly, this was much more exciting than my first ride when my brother, Daniel, and I paid $2.50 each at a Los Angeles airport in 1937 for a short but thrilling flight in a Piper Cub. After that I spent several hard-earned quarters on a tied-down propeller-driven Lynk trainer at a San Diego amusement park. Then too there were those books back home about the "Rover Boys" and their flying machines. The desire to fly was in my blood.

I was working for the US Forest Service on a Timber Stand Improvement project near Yellowstone National Park when the Japanese bombed Pearl Harbor. I learned about the declaration of war two days later when I went to Island Park for groceries. I was camped with a small forest crew about 35 miles from Island Park. We were living in tent houses and working in about two feet of snow -- mostly girdling "bug" trees with a hand ax or piling brush after a timber cut.

The work was hard, and the crew came into camp every night wet, cold and tired. My notes taken a few days before Pearl Harbor state.[1]

"Another miserable day of ax swinging. The picture of the day shows the four major articles of our household. The alarm clock which wakes us up so regularly (at 5 a.m.). The coffee pot on which our very existence depends and contains more rings than we have miseries. The complicated philosophical remarks found in Shakespeare's works keep our tongues and minds active throughout the miserable day. The remaining article in the picture, as you may have guessed, is a roll of tissue paper. It deserves mention because it is a very important item in our backwoods life. With the end of this roll near, our one remaining luxury passes on. The defense program has brought about this major tragedy -- it is with the deepest regret that we again return to catalogs because, my friends, tissue has gone up to six cents a roll."

Under these circumstances it is not hard to understand why I responded to President Roosevelt's declaration of war by attempting to join up. I told the Forest Ranger that I was going to enlist in the Army Air Corps. He said to go ahead since the snow was getting too deep to work anyway. I loaded my gear in the old Model-A and drove back to the ranch at Medicine Lodge. I left the Ford and most of my belongings on the ranch, and a few days later I hitchhiked to Pasadena, California.

The attack on Pearl Harbor changed everyone's attitude about the war. I found one of the letters I

Like "Old Faithful," the Model-A that I relied on for my Forest Service work overheated
on me regularly. Nicholia Canyon, Idaho. 1940.

had written to Mother while I was a student at the University of Idaho. This letter indicates that I, too, was caught in the wave of isolationism that was sweeping the country. The date was November 11, 1939.

"Dear Mother,"

"Today is Armistice Day. Just 21 years ago today the World War ended, and a treaty was signed by all the major countries of the world, a treaty which supposedly would end all world conflict for many years to come. Yet we find Europe now engaged in another war. We can only hope that the United States does not foolishly become involved."

"Here, at the University, the major opinion seems to be that we will not be drawn into the conflict. As long as we can keep the propaganda machine in check, I am certain that we can remain a sane country. History has proven that war can accomplish nothing. I sincerely hope that the people will realize this and not be influenced by those who profit by war...."

"Love,"
"Gerald"

Most of us did not know about Hitler's solution to the "Jewish problem" or his dedication to conquer the world. We only wanted to continue a peaceful existence and to recover from the Depression. Pearl Harbor and new revelations about the Fuhrer changed us all.

I was now eager to get into the Service to fight the Japanese and the Germans and defend my country. The trip to California added to my excitement about enlistment. When I visited my cousin, Delbert Rice, I found that he had not only decided to enlist in the Army, but he, like many other young men "rushing off to war," wanted to get married before they left the States. On January 1, 1942, I recorded in my journal:[1]

"At 1:30 this morning Delbert and Irene were married in the Abbot home (in Las Vegas, Nevada) with Loeva Jean as bridesmaid and me as best man. After the very interesting ceremony we climbed into Delbert's car and drove out on the desert... camped under a bridge. Del and Irene spent their wedding night in my sleeping bag (it was larger), I slept in Delbert's and Loeva Jean slept in the car.... We were back in Pasadena by 3:30 pm for a big wedding feast at Aunt Flora's."

Delbert tried to talk me into joining the Army but I wanted to fly. Before I got to the Air Force recruitment office I learned that the Navy also had an air arm. So I decided to join the Navy and try to get into flight training.

I soon found out that it wasn't that easy to get into the Naval pilot training program. I met the first criterion, a college degree, but I ran into trouble with the Navy doctor. After a rigorous physical and psychological exam I was told that the Navy would not consider me unless I had my tonsils out and a tooth filled at my own expense. The doctor also had reservations about the shape of my nose.

The civilian dentist that I consulted couldn't find any cavities, so I dropped that issue. The more serious problem concerned my tonsils. I did not know I had tonsil trouble, but I had to respond to the Navy request. The doctor that took my tonsils out gave me a local anesthetic. My constant gagging during the operation made it tough on me as well as on the doctor.

I stayed with Chet and Helen Woods in Pasadena during a brief recuperation period. Then, with a great deal of apprehension, I returned to the Navy recruitment center.

On February 5, 1942, my journal shows that I *"completed the enlistment procedure for aviation cadets, US Navy, at Los Angeles, California."* I was sworn into the Navy by Wayne Morris, a movie star, who was in the Navy Reserves at that time. He was between phone calls to some girl in Hollywood. Morris later became a member of "McCampbell's Heroes" in Air Group 15 with five Japanese planes to his credit.

After the brief swearing-in ceremony, I was told to go back home and await call to active duty. I returned to Pasadena expecting the follow-up call on a day-to-day basis. It finally came two months later. On April 9, I began active training as an aviation cadet at the Naval Reserve Air Base, Long Beach, California.

Flight training in the early years of WWII started with assignments to one of the several "Elimination Bases" in the States. The concept of an E-Base was to prescreen prior to official aviation cadet training. "Elimination" was the key word, and the instructors set about this task with a vengeance. No one should get through this stage unless they showed good promise for the eventual attainment of the coveted Wings of Gold.

During approximately three months of E-Base training we were given the rank of Seaman Second Class. This was a classification which gave the Navy several options if we washed out -- including return to civilian life. Perhaps these options were the excuse used by the Navy to refuse government insurance coverage. If we completed E-Base training without being washed out, we became regular Aviation Cadets. At that time we were required to purchase a $10,000 life insurance policy -- a modest consolation for the families of the trainees killed during the elimination process.

The competition was intense. Everyone feared the "down checks" which would lead to a washout. I don't have the statistics on the failure rate at the Elimination Base or in later cadet training, but we were told that less than half of us would get through.

The letters that I wrote home during flight training were saved by my mother. These letters, which I quote in part, recapture some of the excitement and stress of the times. They were written in more detail because of my teenage brother's interest in flying.[2]

April 18, 1942, Long Beach, Calif --
"Glad to hear from you but I don't need the money. We are getting a total of $110 per month. When we start flying in about two weeks we get an additional $18 per month flight pay. So, I'm happy about the whole thing."

"At night we can do anything we want providing we get our studies. Consequently, we do nothing at night because we have to study harder than in college. Anyone who flunks a test is restricted to the base until 8 pm every night without supper until he passes the test or they kick him out of the service. About half my class is on restriction for radio and physics I have to raise my score in radio (Morse Code) to 15 words per minute."

"...So far this training has been the most interesting and exciting of any period in my life...."

April 18, 1942 was even more exciting for Lt Col James Doolittle. On that day, Doolittle and 15 other B-25 Mitchell bombers were launched from the aircraft carrier **HORNET** 800 miles out, with orders to bomb the Japanese homeland. Seventy-one of the 80 men involved in the Doolittle raid eventually got back to the States.[3]

The attack by Doolittle was a great morale booster for all Americans. It was also a special topic of conjecture for potential Navy pilots, because we knew that B-25s were not designed for carrier operations. The next week I wrote home to say that I had:

May 1 -- *"...started in the 'Lynk trainer.' As you may know, this is a fastened-down job that has the controls and instruments of a real plane. I put it in too steep a climb without enough throttle and stalled it... then went into a tail spin. I'm glad I was* *in the Lynk and not a P-38."*

"...The ground school doesn't seem nearly as hard now as it did at first. However, four fellows washed out last week... gosh, I sure would feel bad if I didn't make the grade...."

May 2, 1941 -- *"...my rudder and stick coordination can stand some improvement.... I didn't get the throttle open enough and unconsciously pushed on the right rudder pedal. The fields below start revolving (as I go into another spin). The instructor's voice reaches me thru the ear phones. 'Open the throttle wide, push your stick clear forward, and kick the left rudder!' he shouts... 'and keep your eyes open!'"*

"That's the first time I've thought to watch for enemy planes and on glancing around I see a German Messerschmitt directly overhead. I point it out to the instructor and it disappears. A squadron of five Stukas is under my right wing and a Focke-Wulf pursuit is on my tail."

"'You're a dead pilot, I hear thru the phones,' then, 'keep your head on a swivel after this. That is the most important thing in wartime flying.'"

"During all this time I've never left the ground over 6 ft. because the plane is fastened down, the scenery is painted, and the enemy airships are flashed on and off with light switches. But it's fun and it is a prelude to what is to follow in my future training."

Corregidor surrendered on May 6, and the Japanese captured 16,000 Philippinos and Americans.[3] Burma had essentially fallen to the Japanese forces. These events in the Pacific and the continuing exploits of the German sub fleet increased the pressure on the Navy to hasten the flight training program.

May 7 -- *"Today I passed the final check in the Lynk Trainer. Monday we start flying real planes. Another fellow washed out today because he couldn't land the plane good enough to suit the Navy. We are being tightened down considerably regarding military regulations."*

I finished these final checks in the Lynk Trainer as the battle of the Coral Sea raged in the Pacific. *"From May 4-8, 1942, the Japanese suffered their first setback of the war."* [3] Navy pilots from the *LEXINGTON* and *YORKTOWN* sank the Japanese light carrier *Shoho*, the destroyer *Kikuzaki*, and three auxiliaries. US Navy losses were the carrier *LEXINGTON*, the destroyer *SIMS*, and the oiler *NEOSHO*. The *YORKTOWN* was damaged but repairable.

May 13 -- *"I received my first actual instruction in the air yesterday. Landing is the hardest because you can't judge just where the ground is. Everything looks so soft from above that it seems you could land anywhere."*

Jun 3 -- *"I'm writing this letter to let you know that I soloed today.... Here is the procedure. I go up with a different instructor and he puts me through the paces, including tailspins and emergency landings. I gave him what I considered a poor showing but he says it's OK so I get an up-check from him also. Then he crawls out of the front cockpit and tells me she is all mine. I taxi out for the takeoff very conscious of the fact that the front cockpit is empty. A little air work and a couple of landings then my first solo flight is over. The first step to become a US Navy flier is completed."*

The day I soloed Japanese carrier-based aircraft bombed Dutch Harbor and Fort Mears in Alaska, part of Tokyo's diversion plan to draw the US fleet from Midway. Fortunately, we had already broken the Japanese code and learned of some of their plans.

The Naval Air Station, Corpus Christi, Texas was commissioned March 12, 1941.
The first flight training started May 5, 1941.

Naval Air Station, Corpus Christi, Texas. July 20, 1942.

Midway turned out to be one of the most important Naval engagements of World War II. Four Japanese carriers were sunk -- ***Kaga***, ***Soryu***, ***Akagi***, and ***Hiryu*** in addition to the heavy cruiser ***Mikuma***. The US lost the ***YORKTOWN*** and the destroyer ***HAMMANN***.

Those of us in Naval Flight Training were alerted to the significance of carrier-based aircraft during the Midway encounter. We lost 147 planes, and the Japanese lost 332. Only 6 of our 41 torpedo planes survived the battle.

Jun 10 -- *"I have been flying regularly since I first soloed. So far my instructor has been satisfied with my flying. I hope I don't disappoint him."*

Jun 21, Los Alamitos -- *"All the cadets are moving into the barracks at the new base east of Long Beach. From now on we will be confined to Base except Saturday night to Sunday. We have been very busy with flying and ground school. Some of the navigation problems are very difficult Another fellow washed out of my class yesterday. It is so easy to do things wrong. I can think of nothing that would hurt me worse than not making the grade as a flyer."*

Jul 2 -- *"The B-check is the most important flight in this preliminary training. I passed it OK.... We call these planes 'Yellow Perils' because they are painted yellow, but they are technically known as N3Ns. We are practicing 'Circle Shots' -- landing in circle 100 feet in diameter. I tried five times and finally hit one on the nose.... Also emergency landings. The instructor cuts the engine without notice and you look for a place to land.... I was also required to do some precision spins. I was told to recover after the instructor put the plane in the tightest and fastest spin I was ever in. We were fairly close to the ground when I pulled the plane out of the spin."*

"On top of all this we had what is known as small field procedure, steep spiral, slips and enough other stuff to baffle me thoroughly. I had made many mistakes and deserved a down-check. However, the instructor was a swell guy, and after telling me how to remedy my errors, he gave me an up-check. He said he liked my attitude. Every time I made a mistake, he looked around and saw me laughing. After I climbed out of the cockpit he saw me grinning and said, 'Thomas, you are a funny guy . . . I guess you know you gave me a lousy ride.' I grinned and said I made a good many mistakes. After about 15 minutes of discussion, he gave me a thumbs up and wished me good luck at Corpus Christi."

"Tomorrow is my birthday. As you know, I will be 23 years old. At this rate I should be a fairly wide experienced man at 30. I get homesick about once a week but they keep me so busy I get over it. Love, Gerald."

This was my last letter from the E-Base at Los Alamitos, California. I felt lucky to have passed the various check points, and I felt sorry for those who got washed out.

The excitement of the move to Corpus Christi was somewhat dampened by the news from both war fronts. Japan's empire had reached its maximum, ranging from the Aleutians to the Dutch East Indies -- from Manchuria to New Guinea and the Solomons. Hitler's forces had taken over parts of North Africa and his Luftwaffe planes were regularly bombing the British Isles. We felt the urgency to speed up the flight training programs.

An Aviation Cadet at Corpus Christi, Texas

Jul 8, 1942, Naval Station, Corpus Christi -- *"The big trip from Long Beach to Corpus Christi is over. It sure was a swell vacation from the military routine of*

Naval Air Training Center

United States Naval Air Station
Corpus Christi, Texas

Know all men by these presents that

Ensign Gerald Whitlett Thomas, A-V(N), USNR

has completed the prescribed course of training and having met successfully the requirements of the course has been designated a

Naval Aviator

In Witness Whereof, this certificate has been signed on this 27th day of November 1942 and the Seal of the Naval Air Station hereunto affixed

Navy Wings Graduation Photo.
November 27, 1942.

GERALD W. THOMAS RECEIVES WINGS

Gerald W. Thomas, son of Mr. and Mrs. D. W. Thomas of Small, Idaho, has been awarded the coveted "Navy Wings of Gold" and commissioned an ensign in the U. S. Naval Reserve at the Naval Air Training Center, Corpus Christi, Texas.

Ensign Thomas received his wings with the designation of a Naval Aviator from Admiral A. E. Montgomery, USN, Commandant of the training center, at class graduating ceremonies today.

Thomas volunteered for flight training last February and received preliminary instruction at the Los Almaitos, Calif., reserve aviation base. Upon completion there he was transferred to Corpus Christi for intermediate training at the world's largest naval air station.

In addition to flight instruction Thomas completed a thorough ground school course, including navigation, gunnery and bombing theory, communications and allied aeronautical subjects at the "University of the Air."

Thomas attended Pasadena Junior College and the University of Idaho where he was a member of the Forestry Club prior to his enlistment.

Clark County Enterprise-Banner,
December 4, 1942.

the past three months. I've always wanted to see this Southwest Country but I certainly never expected to do so at Uncle Sam's Expense. We had a Pullman all to ourselves and were allowed $1.00 meals in the diner so we couldn't very well kick about traveling conditions."

"The train was held over five hours in San Antonio. Fortunately, a rich woman from the USO met us at the train and escorted us in her private cars out to a very ritzy country club. We went swimming and had the run of the place. About suppertime we were hauled downtown to a high-classed hotel and enjoyed a $1.25 meal. The entire class was sorry when we left the town."

"The Naval Air Station here is really a big place. I've seen nearly every type of aircraft in the Navy... including the mammoth PBY boats. I perspired more than I did on top of that haystack back home. I reckon I will get used to the heat if they will let me get my hands on one of those beautiful planes that fly around here."

July 13, Cabaniss Field -- *"Today was my first day in the air here in Texas. Let me tell you it's really different from Long Beach flying. Here we have from 150 to 200 planes taking off and landing at the same time. They swarm around this field like bees."*

"On just this one outlying field we have nine practice fields and each field has a different flight pattern to be learned. Which way to turn, how high to fly, etc. are just a few of the things you have to know for each field."

Jul 19 -- *"This letter will be somewhat short since it is about time for taps. Today is Sunday but instructors pile on so much work we never see any relaxation. I have been working all day on navigation problems. Yesterday I passed the final check*

in N3N planes. The next training stage is aerobatics. Boy, it will be fun doing loops, snap rolls, split S's, etc. About half of my class from Long Beach got at least one down check since they arrived here. I didn't miss it far myself. P.S. Texas is the hottest state in the Union I believe."

Jul 23 -- I recorded in my journal that *"almost wound up in an inverted spin as I fell out of an Immelmann. Also one cadet couldn't get one wheel down so he was forced to fly out to the bay where he made a crash landing by the rescue boat 'MARY ANN'"*

Aug 2 -- *"I fly every day 3-4 and one-half hours either in the morning or afternoon. Last week I passed the two toughest checks in this stage of flying, the C and D Checks. They had me worried for a while but I slipped through. If my luck continues I will get my wings in about four months. One of the fellows just informed me that he had a perfect record until he wrote and told his folks, then the next day he got his first down check. Hope that doesn't happen to me."*

"The C Check was the toughest ride. It consisted of aerobatics (Immelmanns, split S's, loops, snap rolls, inverted spins, wingovers, slips to circles, small field procedure and flying Pylons)."

"On the D Check smooth flying was the main thing. I wasn't sure I had passed it when the instructor took over and landed at one of our outlying fields. He climbed out of the front cockpit and told me to change places with him. I knew then that I had received one of those 'up in the front cockpit' OKs."

"Saturday I began my E Stage -- formation flying, which is an art in itself. We sure fly close together. 'Peeling Off' is sure fun."

"This week I will also begin night flying. After Thursday I'll take an E Check and if I pass I will be moved to Cuddihy Field for training in Vultee monoplanes. This primary training is supposed to last five weeks."

Aug 13, Cuddihy Field -- *"On Monday I began training in Vultee SNV planes. They carry a 635-horsepower motor which is double the power of the N2S. My luck is still holding out so I was given the honor of soloing these babies this afternoon. From these planes I go to OS2Us, commonly called 'Kingfishers.' These planes are used in actual combat in the fleet. They have pontoons on Cruisers and are catapulted into the air. Their primary purpose is observation and scouting as they are not equipped with many guns."*

"I do not know whether I told you or not, but I now have the privilege of choosing between an Ensign Commission in the Navy or a Second Lieutenant Commission in the Marine Corps. I don't know which is better. The main difference would be that if I went into the Marines I would probably be land-based instead of on a carrier. I have always had a fascination for the Marines... but, they are no better as flyers because the training is the same."

The pros and cons of each branch of service were discussed vigorously in the barracks. None of my close friends seemed to have any inclination for the Marines. This influence plus the fascination for carrier duty ultimately shaped my decision to stay with the Navy. Also reports coming from the Pacific and European theaters indicated more excitement with a Navy career.[3]

- PM Tojo called on Australia to surrender.
- Guadalcanal was invaded by the 1st Marine Division on August 7.
- Allied Naval vessels suffered one of their most severe losses in the battle of Savo Island on August 9.

- German subs were laying mines in US Atlantic harbors.
- Stalingrad was under siege by the Germans.

Sep 4, Corpus Christi -- *"I am now up to my neck in instrument flying. Many students meet their downfall when they crawl 'Under the Hood.' It is surprising what unusual feelings you get when you cannot see anything but a panel of instruments. For example, you cannot feel a turn. Then when you stop turning you think you are turning in the opposite direction. You are tempted to disbelieve the instruments. (This is 'vertigo.') However, in every case the instruments are right."*

"Another obstacle in this stage of flying. I am now learning to 'fly the beam'. This is not very simple because radio beams are not always constant."

"Tell Walter that he is not the only one getting gun practice. Movie stars pay plenty to shoot the skeet that we get free. This afternoon we start on the machine gun and pistol."

"I received some discouraging news from the Navy Department. In the form of a memorandum which stated the customary 15-days leave granted graduating cadets would be withheld until these newly commissioned officers completed 2 to 3 months of very vigorous training in actual dive-bombing, scouting, and fight. Liberty will be at a minimum and all officers are advised not to get married."

The pressure to rush cadets through the training process was still building. The September 9 air attack with incendiary bombs on continental US by a submarine-based Japanese plane stirred up public concern, even though the only damage was a small fire in a forest near Brookings, Oregon. The carrier **WASP** was torpedoed and sunk, and the battleship **NORTH CAROLINA** damaged on September 15.

Sep 11 -- *"Since you are wondering about my insurance, here is the dope. Immediately on my arrival here in Corpus, the Government took out for me a $10,000 policy.[4] They make the payments until I get my commission then I have to make them. You need not worry about the validity of the policy. The Chaplain handles all of the insurance so it is on the square."*

"My paycheck is now $75 a month. We are required to put 10 percent of our pay in defense stamps.... Social life here is far from ideal. The town is overcrowded with workers and service men. We get into town about every 2 weeks and about all there is to do is eat and stand in line for a show."

Sep 24 -- *"Don't trade my sorrel mare off. I want to keep her. I should have a pretty good start in the horse business by the time I get out of the Navy."*

"I bought my uniforms downtown last weekend. This is the price list. They are expensive."

- *1 cap set complete -- $18*
- *Green cap cover -- $2.50*
- *Overseas cap -- $3.00*
- *1 set Blues -- $62.50*
- *2 sets Khakis -- $39.00*
- *1 set buttons -- $1.00*
- *Gold Wings for Blues -- $4.85*
- *Line Officer star and stripe -- $7.50*
- *1 set greens -- $65.00*
- *Extra green pants -- $19.50*
- *Wings for green suit -- $4.85*
- *Conversion of Cadet blues -- $11.50*

"Total: $240.05. The Government gives us a uniform allowance of $150 upon graduation so I will have to pay $90-100 out of my own pocket."

Oct 2 -- *"Just completed training in instruments. My orders now direct me to Kingsville, Texas for advanced training*

in dive-bombers. The training in dive-bombing is the best in the world. We will get workouts in aerial gunnery, navigation hops, bombing runs and aerobatics. Will probably be carrier-based. I chose this field because it is a tough field to get thru and because it is at all times exciting."

Oct 12 -- *"Busy flying. Finished up with the Curtis SNCs Saturday. Got a check and soloed the SNJ today. This is the plane I have been looking forward to flying. Sure is a honey. Cruises about 160 mph and has a top diving speed of 250. Fixed machine gun forward and a flexible machine gun in rear cockpit. The Army calls these planes AT-6."*

"Last week I flew formation mostly. It is really a sight to see 18 planes flying around you. Every once in a while the leader swishes his tail and all planes fall into a column. The leader sights a farmhouse and peals off into a dive. Each of the other planes peal off in order. We dive about 4,000 feet and zoom farms all over this country. Sure is fun to watch chickens, dogs and cows scatter. I don't imagine the farmers like being dived on but they always wave as we zoom by. The other day all 18 planes dove on a car running along the highway. The driver ran into the ditch, got out and ran across the pasture. He figured the Japs had attacked for sure."

While I was having a great time zooming farms and chasing coyotes on the King Ranch, Navy pilots in the Pacific were in the middle of another critical engagement. Admiral Halsey took command of the US Naval Forces in the Pacific on October 23. Three days later, in the Battle of Santa Cruz, the carrier **HORNET** and the destroyer **PORTER** were sunk by the Japanese at a cost of 100 of their planes. Intense fighting continued on Guadalcanal. (3)

Oct 30 -- *"My flight is ready for gunnery now. This should be the most fun of train-*

US Navy SNJ (AT-6) trainer made by North American Aviation.
Corpus Christi, Texas. July 1, 1942.

PBY towing a "sock" for gunnery practice.

*ing so far. We get fixed and flexible gun-
nery. Flexible gunnery is firing from the
rear cockpit with a swivel machine gun."*

Nov 4 -- *"We go out over the ocean for
all gunnery hops so that no one will be
shot by mistake. We use .30-caliber machine guns for practice."*

*"You would have enjoyed night flying with
me last week. We flew in 9-plane formations. It was very dark and there was a
solid layer of clouds about 5000 ft. high.
We had to fly very close together in order
to have the wing lights of one plane light
up the fuselage of the next one. If you slid
out of formation in the least you couldn't
see anything but a small red light on the
other planes. Well, we flew up thru the
clouds anyway. To our surprise, there was
almost a full moon out. We skimmed over
the top of this cloud layer about 140 miles
an hour. Sure was pretty up there."*

Nov 8 -- *"Just finished flying for 4 hours.
The first two hours was an altitude hop.
Took an SNJ as high as it would go. **I
got to 23,050 feet.** Had to use an oxygen
mask. Also had a heavy pair of sheepskin
pants and wool-lined boots. My thermom-
eter registered over 20 degrees centigrade
below zero. I boosted my plane higher
than any of the other fellows. The record
for an SNJ is 25,500. Most of the fellows
stalled out at about 20,000 feet and one or
two of them went into tailspins."*

Nov 12, 1942, Kingsville, Texas -- *"Regarding graduation, here is the dope. I
have nine more hops left."*

*"Graduation exercises here are simple -- a
matter of about 30 minutes. Upon completion of flight training I receive a $100
check for clothing allowance. Also flight
gear, heavy coat, helmet, suitcase, and
other minor articles. With my wings comes
a pay allowance amounting to $200-250*

*per month. This is a lot of money per
month but it is reduced by the donations,
insurance rates, etc, which I have to pay
upon being commissioned."*

*"I will then be an Ensign in this Navy
which means I must assume greater responsibilities. In many ways I regret losing
the carefree life of an Aviation Cadet."*

*"By the way, I was complimented today by
several officers. It seems that my gunnery
record is abnormally high for a student
pilot. We fire with a machine gun forward
at a canvas sock towed by another plane.
We make nine runs from various angles
and the hits are counted at the end of each
hop. (Each plane has a different color on
the bullet.) Well, anyway, I have 114 hits in
5 runs. The next closest student has 25 hits
and several have only 4 or 5. I was called
into the gunnery office and questioned
about this record. They asked how I aimed,
how much I lead the target, what was my
experience, etc.... So I am to be given special tracer ammunition from now on as an
experiment. This gunnery is more fun than
hunting rabbits."*

The experiment with special tracer ammunition
did not go well. My guns jammed on every pass.
But I was again approached by the Command to
consider a transfer to fighters. I continued to state
that I would stay with dive bombers.

Another major engagement took place in the
Pacific off Guadalcanal at this time. Americans
claimed a victory in this battle which raged from
November 12-15, 1942. The Japanese sank the US
cruisers ***ATLANTA*** and ***JUNEAU***, plus seven destroyers. Japanese losses were the battleships ***Hiei***
and ***Kirishima***, three destroyers, and eleven transports.[3]

On November 15, 1942, the five Sullivan
brothers from Waterloo, Iowa, were lost when the
JUNEAU sank. This widely publicized loss of five
members of the same family prompted the Navy to

My Navy Wings graduation class. I'm the third person from the right, back row.
Corpus Christi, Texas. November 27, 1942.

Insignia for Torpedo Squadron 4
(VT-4) designed by Walt Disney.

Our nickname was the
"Torpeckers."

formulate a new policy that would prevent similar tragedies in the future. Under this new directive no two members of the same family would be assigned to the same ship or unit in the Navy. In April, 1943, a new destroyer was named in honor of the Sullivan boys. Seven of us from Torpedo 4 owe our lives to the crew of the *USS SULLIVANS* for rescuing us from rubber boats as Task Force 38 was leaving the South China Sea on January 16, 1945.

Nov 23, NAS Corpus Christi -- *"I completed my flying in Squadron 15 last Thursday, checked out, and moved back here to the main station at Corpus Christi (awaiting orders to Operational Training). I have not flown for about 5 days and already I miss the roar of airplane motors. Flying sure gets in a persons blood."* (My logbook shows that I had 139.1 flight hours in the pilot's seat when I finished cadet training.)

Nov 27 -- My new orders stated: *"Completed active duty undergoing training, accepted appointment as Ensign, A-V (N), USNR, executed oath of office, reported for active duty, and detached this date. In compliance with reference C you will proceed and report to the Commanding Officer, Naval Air Station, Miami, Florida, for pre-operational training."*

Operational Training in Dive-Bombers

Dec 5, 1942, NAS, Miami -- *"Graduation exercises at Corpus Christi were comparatively simple. We received our diplomas from Admiral Montgomery, saluted and were dismissed as officers. Two other fellows and myself packed out clothes and got tickets to Miami via Independence, Kansas. The Government gave us $150 plus $30 back Cadet pay. We paid $80 down on our uniforms and used the remainder for expenses on our trip, which was very enjoyable. This journey con-*

sumed the entire 6 days, which we were allowed for travel time."

"Since my arrival in Miami I have been occupied with the necessary routine steps of checking in and getting acquainted with my new life as a Naval Aviator and officer."

"Should be ready to start flying in the next few days. Operation training lasts from 4 to 8 weeks. We fly long hours and are treated nearly the same as Aviation Cadets, liberty being limited to one day of 8."

"I'm still with about the same bunch of fellows that were at Corpus. Of course they all have wings and officer's strips now, which makes them seem somewhat older. Otherwise we are the same carefree lot. A few of the boys took advantage of the new ruling which allows marriage after being commissioned. As for myself, I have no such intentions at the present."

With the issuance of the orders to Opa-Locka, Florida, several options were closed out. First, my application for "lighter-than-air" -- an assignment to blimps -- was rejected by the Navy. This turned out to be an unexciting deadend for a few pilots. Second, I chose a Navy commission instead of the Marines -- primarily because I wanted to be carrier-based. Third, I lucked out and escaped an assignment to Corpus Christi, Texas (NAS) as a flight instructor. Last, I turned down the opportunity to be a "fighter" pilot.

My selection of dive-bombers over fighters probably was influenced more by the fact that I didn't want to leave my buddies than any other factor. Bob Ruth, Will Souza, Felix Ward, and I wanted to stay together. None of us knew at the time that after we finished dive-bomber training the Navy would arbitrarily assign us to a torpedo squadron. Worst of all, an assignment to VT-4 meant duty in the cold North Atlantic while all the exciting action was taking place in the Pacific.

Carrying a torpedo or going in for a glide-bombing attack did not have the glamour of a dog fight. The fighters had the opportunity to engage in plane-to-plane combat -- a challenge of skills; we had to fly low and slow into the face of AA fire. Furthermore, a fighter could get credit for "kills" -- could perhaps become an "ace;" no "torpeckers" were ever classified as aces.

The only famous torpedo pilots that I know of were Ensign Gay and Lt(jg) George Bush. Gay received notoriety since he was the sole survivor of Torpedo 8. George Bush became President of the United States -- not because of his assignment to torpedo planes but for other reasons.

A flight of TBF torpedo bombers. We looked forward to flying this wonderful plane, the US Navy's largest carrier-based plane at the time. Undated photograph.

Chapter 12 | Shakedown on the ESSEX

"Upon departure of VT, #1 burning, #2 damaged, #3 dead in the water, #4 capsized and sinking."

Transfer at Ulithi Lagoon

On November 17, 1944, the **BUNKER HILL** returned to Ulithi for refueling and R&R for all personnel. Word spread like wildfire that the carrier was headed back to Pearl Harbor. This scuttlebutt turned out to be true.

The departure of the **BUNKER HILL** raised the question about the fate of Air Group 4. We had already served in both theaters of war. Two cruises in combat zones were considered adequate for rotation back to the States. However, our assignment on the **BUNKER HILL** had been brief and our combat losses minimal. Consequently, we were not surprised to receive orders to report aboard the **USS ESSEX**.

The **ESSEX** was the first of a new and powerful class of aircraft carriers to join the US fleet. It was built at Newport News, Virginia, and launched April 28, 1941. She passed through the Panama Canal and reported for duty to the Commander, US Pacific Fleet, on May 16, 1943.[1] The **BUNKER HILL**, was of the "Essex Class," so we knew what to expect in terms of quarters and air operations. These carriers carried a complement of approximately 3,000 men.

The Logbook of the **ESSEX** states, "Nov. 18-21, 1944. Anchored in Berth 27, Ulithi Islands... replenishing." Air Group 4 reported aboard as a part of that "replenishing." On November 21, 1944, I wrote to Mother and Dad:

*"...I write every chance I get to send mail out, but that is rather infrequent. I hope you don't worry about me.... The censors have agreed to let me say we were in the Hawaiian Islands. Also that we are no longer on the **BUNKER HILL**. Cannot*

give the name of the present carrier."

The **ESSEX** had already been labeled the "fightingest ship" in the Navy and her Air Group 15 had an outstanding combat record and had sustained heavy combat losses.

It was obvious that the **ESSEX's** crew did not believe that the new air group could come up to the standards of their old group -- so we had to overcome some resentment. Our fighters were really under pressure:[2]

"Replacing Air Group Fifteen on the carrier was more of a job than it appeared at a casual glance, for Air Group Fifteen had set an all-time record at planes destroyed in the air -- 310. The seven planes to our credit by this time did not look very impressive. Consequently, there was an air of scorn about."

Cozy Cole, one of our VT-4 pilots, said he would have to take some credit for the poor reception we received when we went aboard the **ESSEX**.[3]

*"When we were transferred to the **ESSEX** at Ulithi, they sent me and a couple of fighters to Falalop Island to pick up some replacement planes. That night we sat on the beach, watched the moon rise, and did away with the whole bottle. The fleet sortied at sunrise the next morning. We were ordered to fly aboard as soon as the ship could get into maneuvering position. The two fighters got aboard very quickly. I think I got more wave-offs that one morning than all the rest of the time I was in the Pacific. It was a rather poor introduction to ship's company for Torpedo Four."*

The *USS ESSEX* enters Portsmouth, Virginia for commissioning. December 31, 1942.

Ulithi, Caroline Islands. Much of the Fifth and Seventh Fleet of the US Navy
at anchorage. February, 1945.

The attitudes of ship's personnel about Air Group 4 changed substantially after several combat missions and the advent of the Kamikaze.

As the **ESSEX** left Ulithi on November 27, our air group was placed under the same pressure as we had experienced on the **BUNKER HILL** -- inadequate time for a proper shakedown. We had to work out flight schedules while the ship was en route back to the Philippines. During the shakedown and for several strikes thereafter, our Avengers carried two different identification markings. This led to some confusion by later historians, particularly those who researched the records of Air Group 15 ("McCampbell's Heroes").

Japanese Subs Penetrate Ulithi

While the **ESSEX** was anchored in Ulithi and Air Group 4 was getting bunk assignments, two Japanese minisubs got through the submarine nets. One torpedoed the US tanker **MISSISSINEWA** anchored near the **ESSEX**. The tanker exploded and burned in the show of a lifetime.

It was very early in the morning (0550 hours), but I was on the flight deck preparing to take pictures of the squadron with the K-20 camera we had used on our last strike. At the time of the explosion I swung around and snapped several pictures of the action. I was excited since I was probably the only person in a position to record the first stages of the torpedo attack on film. When I rushed the camera to the darkroom to have the film developed, we discovered that there was no film in the camera. The K-20 would show a film advance even though it was empty. Pictures of the **MISSISSINEWA** burning were taken a few minutes later from a nearby ship.

Scuttlebutt was that both Japanese subs were sunk and two dead crew members were picked up, which proved true.

Strike on Santa Cruz

On November 25, 1944, the ship's records state, *"Operating in TG 38.3 about 100 miles E of Luzon launching strikes against shipping and land targets in the Manila area."*

Early in the morning the **ESSEX** launched the usual Combat Air Patrol and a morning fighter sweep against Clark Field on Luzon. Lt Boykin led the VF sweep in the attack on Clark Field.[2]

"As they rendezvoused after the attack, they were set on by a group of 18 Tonys, four of which were shot down. Boykin, Marn, Nicholson, and Carruthers were credited with the kills."

The main strike group made preparations for an 0730 takeoff under the command of Otto Klinsmann. There were 18 TBMs and 21 2B2Cs and only 6 fighters scheduled for the strike. I recorded in my journal: [4]

"Two Helldivers went in the drink while VT-4 was turning up on the fantail (the VB-4 skipper, Lt Cdr Johnson, and Lt(jg) Deputy. Johnny and his gunner got out of the plane, but Dep was never picked up.)"

One of these Helldivers went in the water as it cleared the flight deck due to power failure and it is believed that the other closed his flaps too soon after the takeoff and spun in.[5]

The torpedo planes, loaded with four 500-pound semi-armor-piercing bombs, under the command of Lt Davis, *"proceeded to target employing a formation of four, four-plane divisions in stepped-down diamond."* The tactical organization of VT-4 was as follows: [6]

Strike Able - November 25, 1944

P. J. Davis, Jr. (pilot)
  R. F. Gray and N. J. Schmolke (crew)

C. N. W. "Scott" Vogt
  Leo E. Halvorson and R. E. Kelly

G. M. "Buck" Barnett
  Joseph C. Cohen and C. Christopher

W. F. "Willie" Walker
  S. A. Hastings and G. F. Zeimer

USS Mississinewa burning after being hit by a Kaiten Kamikaze torpedo in Ulithi Harbor.
The oiler carried over 400,000 gallons of aviation fuel. 63 sailors were killed in the explosion.
November 20, 1944.

Kaiten suicide torpedo recovered in Ulithi Harbor following Kamikaze attack on November 20, 1944. The front part of the Kaiten is destroyed.

Plane handlers readying Fighting Four F6F Hellcat for takeoff prior to strike on Santa Cruz. *USS ESSEX*. November 25, 1944.

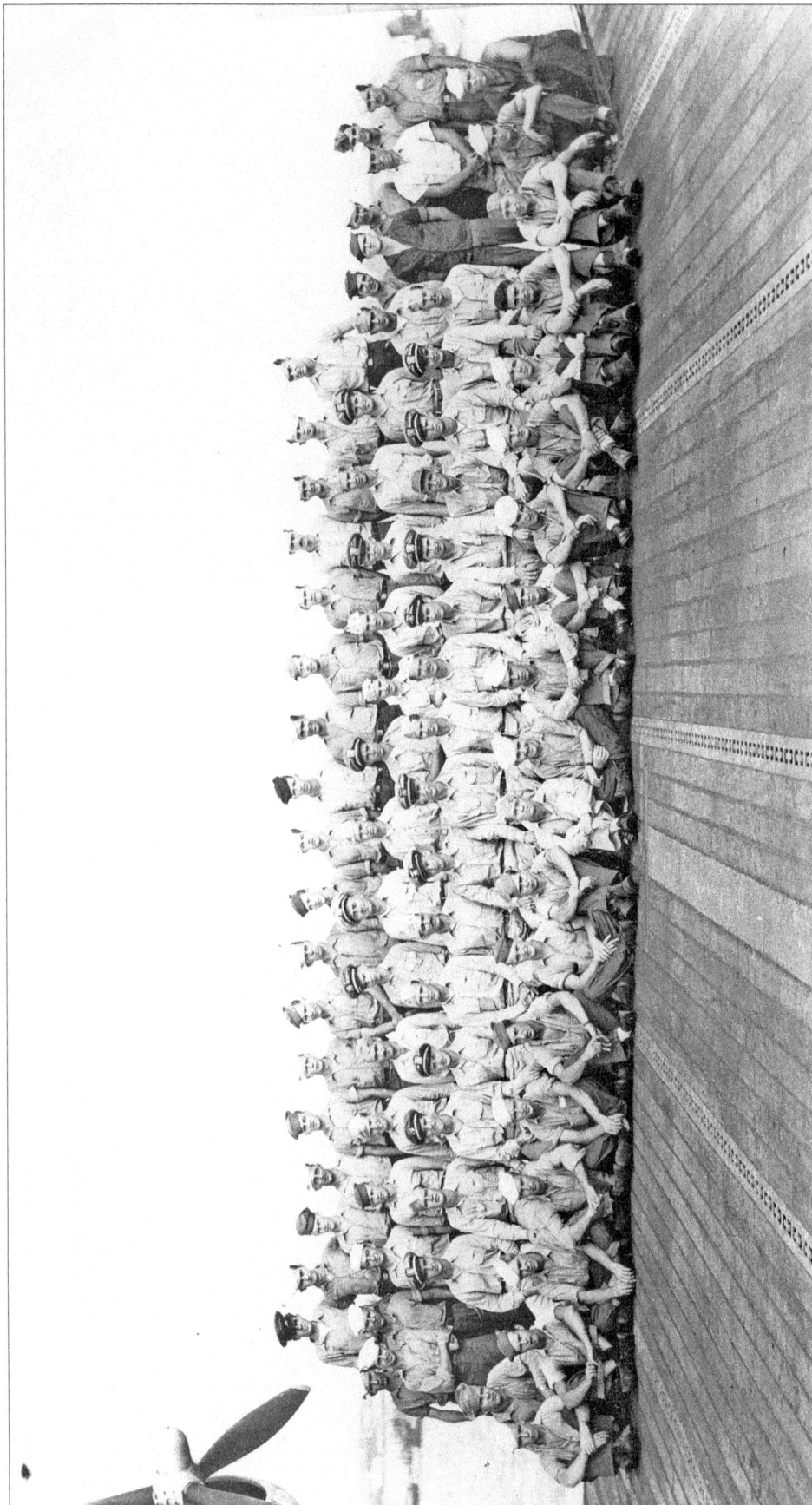

Torpedo 4 aboard the *USS ESSEX*. Ulithi Lagoon. December 1, 1944.

Front row: J. E. Ganley, J. W. Frost, A. J. Tankard, R. R. Pittman, C. L. Ely, J. W. Aldrich, J. F. Ballard, S. A. Hastings, T. R. Sims, H. L. Blalock, G. J. Rauch, R. A. Trembley, E. A. Shirley, D. L. King, R. E. Simendinger, N. J. Schmolke, D. H. Gress, W. T. Lundry, W. S. Lace, H. R. Green. **Second row**: G. D. Makibbin, L. A. Cole, R. B. Cline, G. M. Barnett, B. R. Trexler, E. S. Binder, Scott Vogt, P. J. Davis, L. L. Hamrick, J. W. Harriss, G. W. Thomas, L. C. Gray, R. M. Hopfinger, J. E. Hewitt, L. G. Gardemal, P. P. Stephens. **Third row**: A. Beard, D. E. Venderville, L. S. Leach, J. J. Pinkney, L. E. Halverson, E. A. Newell, V. A. Landre, W. H. Cannady, D. A. Henry, J. D. Clemenson, H. J. Deimel, R. F. Ruth, W. F. Walker, F. E. Ward, W. J. Hopkins, G. M. Bell, W. S. Souza, C. Christopher, W. D. Jenkins, A. P. Robistow, C. J. Galeano, J. S. Serafin, N. L. Shiverdecker. **Back row**: M. A. Clark, F. W. Wilson, S. W. Coller, A. DeCenso, J. C. Gerke, C. J. Warrington, G. F. Zeimer, R. E. Kelly, J. E. Holloman, D. L. Huston, N. H. Knox, A. Mocsary, C. L. McConnell, D. M. Applegate, R. C. Campbell, C. C. Statler, L. P. Shuman, A. G. Schiesz

Strike Able - November 25, 1944 (continued)

Page P. Stephens
  A. Beard and Andy "Marge" Mocsary

Vernon A. Landre
  A. "Tony" DeCenso and Charlie C. Statler

Gerald W. "Jerry" Thomas
  J. E. Holloman and Don H. Gress

R. M. "Hoppy" Hopfinger
  F. W. Wilson and A. W. Yarman

B. R. "Trex" Trexler
  C. W. Barr and J. W. Aldrich

G. M. Bell
  A. J. Tankard and R. R. Pittman

Robert F. "Bob" Ruth (did not take off)
  J. F. "Forrest" Ballard and C. L. McConnell

L. C. Gray
  J. E. Ganley and R. C. Mann

Ed S. Binder
  W. D. Jenkins and A. B. Tranflaglia

H. J. Deimel
  C. L. Ely, Jr., and L. S. Leach

G. D. "Mak" Makibbin
  R. B. Montague and R. Campbell

W. H. Cannady, Jr.
  J. J. Supanich and E. A. McGuire

J. F. Zook
  L. E. Thomas and P. J. Baughman

D. C. Pletts (did not take off)
  A. P. Switaneck, Jr. and L. E. Wood

The target coordinator sighted a Japanese convoy just south of Santa Cruz and ordered Air Group 4 to attack these ships. The fighters went in first, diving on a destroyer escort and firing rockets. Lt Lew Lepp's belly tank came off as he began the run, so he pulled out and was ordered to return to base. Lt Harris's rockets hit an LSM, setting it afire. The ship exploded and lost headway.

The 16 Helldivers from VB-4 rolled over from 10,000 feet and dived on the DE and 3 LSMs. Lt(jg) Hanson's bomb hit the stern of one LSM and Ens F. W. Wilson hit another.

The first division of Avengers, led by our skipper, P. J. Davis, attacked one LSM.[5]

"...pushing over from 8000 feet, employing a glide angle of 40-45 degrees, with an average speed of approximately 300 knots of glide, releasing at 2500 feet, and pulling out at about 1800 feet. One hit forward by Lt Davis and a near miss forward by Lt(jg) Vogt were reported. Damage was not immediately observed, but ship was dead in water as aircraft retired."

Buck Barnett was leading the second section of P. J.'s division with Willie Walker on his wing. As Buck was pulling out of the run, his plane was hit by antiaircraft fire. Joseph Cohen, ARM3c, who was manning the belly gun, was wounded by shrapnel. The plane's controls were not damaged and Buck was able to fly the plane back to the carrier.

I was in the second division with Page Stephens in the lead. We pushed over on the destroyer escort. It was taking evasive action as the Japanese gunners concentrated on the diving Avengers. We pulled out of the run at about 1000 feet. Surprisingly, none of us was hit.

"Ens Hopfinger scored a direct hit on the bow of the ship. Damage was not immediately observed, but DE appeared to be burning as VT departed."[6]

"Trex" Trexler took the third division into a glide bombing attack on one of the LSMs. *"Though several bombs hit close to target, no damage was observed or claimed."*[6]

"The fourth division, led by Lt(jg) Binder, split its attack with two planes attacking the auxiliary transport and two planes attacking the LSM. Planes pushed over from 6000 feet and made individual rather than section runs. Dive angles employed varied from 35-50 degrees. Lt(jg) Binder straddled the bow of an LSM with two bombs.

Debris was seen to fly from ship with the bomb explosions. Lt(jg) Makibbin scored a hit directly amidships on this same ship, which caused an explosion on board. The LSM capsized almost immediately after the attack. The two other VTs of this division, attacking another LSM, caused no apparent damage."

"Upon departure of VT, the convoy appeared to be in the following condition: #1 burning; #2 damaged but under way; #3 dead in water; #4 capsized and sinking. En route to base, pilots heard planes from sub- sequent attack group report all four ships sunk."

After the strike we rendezvoused about 5 miles east of the target at 5000 feet. When Landre, Hopfinger, and I joined up on Page Stephens, we again noticed Page's erratic flying pattern. We had finally become accustomed to this strange behavior. Page always had to use the "P" tube after an exciting strike. To operate the relief tube in a Grumman Avenger was always a challenge. There was no way you could fly straight and level while engaged in this activity.

Avengers taking off from the **USS ESSEX**. November, 1944.

Chapter 13 | ESSEX Takes a Kamikaze

"A suicide bomber flew thru heavy flak into the ship."

Strike Able had just returned to the ***ESSEX*** following a strike on Luzon when several Japanese planes began attacking the task force. A suicide bomber flew through heavy flak into the ship, hitting the forward part of the flight deck. A quote from my journal follows: [1]

> **Nov 25, 1944, afternoon** -- *"Second attack group prepared to take off. Several Jap planes began attacking task force. Suicide bomber hit us on forward part of flight deck. Killed 14 men and injured many others. I was in wardroom and only got shook up. Fire put out and flight deck temporarily repaired. Second attack group took off. VT carried torpedoes (third division) and hit two ships off San Bernardino Point. Scored four torpedo hits out of nine. VB lost Lt(jg) Binder, another photo pilot, leaving six out of the nine of us that went to Harrisburg to photo school."*

Three other aircraft carriers were hit by Kamikazes on the same day -- the ***USS INTREPID***, ***HANCOCK***, and ***CABOT***. Some historians say that, if the Japanese had known the extent of damage to the American fleet by these suicide planes, they might have followed up with a different strategy during this critical period in the Pacific war. The Navy was so concerned about these attacks that they issued orders to all personnel returning to the States even as late as the summer of 1945 (when Torpedo 4 was transferred stateside) to refrain from any mention of the word "Kamikaze."

The origin of the word Kamikaze goes back to 1570, when a Mongol Emperor, attempting to conquer Japan with a fleet of ships, was met with a typhoon which dispersed his invasion fleet. The Japanese were convinced that the typhoon had been called up by the gods, and they named it Kamikaze, or "Divine Wind." [2]

Periodic reports of Japanese "devil divers" or suicide planes, relentlessly flying through flak to reach their targets (with bombs attached) started showing up as early as September 1944. Historian John Toland, in his book, The Rising Sun, states: [2]

> *"But it was not until Vice Admiral Takijiro Onishi arrived in Luzon -- just before the American landing at Leyte -- to take command of Fifth Base Air Force and learned he had fewer than a hundred operable planes that the Kamikaze Special Attack Corps was officially organized."*

> *"'**In my opinion,**' he told his commanders, '**there is only one way of channeling our meager strength into maximum efficiency, and that is to organize suicide attack units composed of Zero fighters equipped with 250-kilogram bombs, with each plane to crash-dive into an enemy carrier.'**"*

> *"Onishi's proposal was explained to the pilots. '**Their eyes shone feverishly in the dimly lit room,**' reported one commander named Tamai. '**Each must have been thinking of this as a chance to avenge comrades who had fallen recently in the fierce Marianas fighting, and at Palau and Yap. Theirs was an enthusiasm that flames naturally in the hearts of youthful men.'**"*

> *"Onishi's Kamikaze group was created specifically to support Kurita's raid on Leyte Gulf, and the first attack had come earlier that morning. Six suicide planes*

Kamikaze flown by Yoshinori Yamaguchi dives through intense gun fire toward the **ESSEX**.
The plane was identified as a "Judy" (Yokosuba D4Y3 dive bomber), tail number 17.
The pilot was aiming at the flight deck, but the ship's defensive fire deflected him forward
and to the left. The streaks are tracer fire. November 25, 1944.

and four escorts took off from Mindanao at 6:30 a.m. and went north. While Taffy 3 was fighting off Kurita, the Special Attack planes came upon Taffy 1. One Zero crashed into **SANTEE** *and another into* **SUWANEE**, *but both of these jeep carriers were soon back in action. Nevertheless, all those who had seen the Japanese boring in with such fatalism were still shaken by the experience. It was a preview of things to come."*

The Kamikaze hit the *ESSEX* after I returned from the first strike on Santa Cruz. I took off my flight gear in the Ready Room and went to the ship's wardroom with the other returning pilots for a late noon meal. I was eating my dessert and listening to the periodic anti-aircraft fire laid on by our ship. It was easy to separate by sound the 5-inchers from the 40-mms and 20-mms. The firing intensified just before the high explosion as the Japanese Zero hit.

The impact of the Kamikaze was so severe that I could see the paint bounce off the bulkheads in the wardroom before smoke filled the room. My immediate thought was, *"We have been hit by a torpedo or a bomb!"* I looked around the room and noticed that nearly everyone else had ducked under the wardroom tables. I thought, *"That seems kind of silly since the explosion is over."* Then I thought about delayed-action fuses. *"They are expecting a second explosion!"* So I got under a table too.

The ship's crew secured the hatches almost immediately after the Kamikaze hit. Those of us in the wardroom were confined to the area until orders were given to open the hatches and to make the room available for emergency aid to the wounded.

There were varying reactions from the pilots and crews in the loaded planes on the flight deck as the suicide plane pressed home his dive toward the ship. Some of the turret gunners charged their guns and started firing, others were without power as the pilots switched off the engines and scrambled out of their planes.

"All I could think of as the Jap bore in was 'I'm sitting on top of this 2,000-pound torpedo. Let's get the hell out of here!' So I cut the gun, climbed out of the cockpit, and ran forward on the flight deck. I slid under an F6F. When the smoke cleared, I raised my head and bumped against a 1,000-pound bomb loaded on the Hellcat. If that bomb had shaken loose I would have been a goner -- even if the bomb didn't explode." [3]

This comment from Souza reflected the excitement and confusion topside on the *ESSEX*.

Andy Marge was in the crew's Ready Room. *"When that plane hit, a flash came into that Ready Room. I slammed that hatch and ran out the other way and hit the deck."* [4]

Don Gress was standing on the catwalk. He stated: [5]

"I saw all the 20-mm and 40-mm guns shooting at it... it seemed like it was coming in very slow... It was smoking but no one could shoot it down. I jumped back into the Ready Room as it hit. After the explosion, I ventured back on the flight deck -- and I wish I hadn't -- all those people killed -- most burned to death!"

Another crewman reported *"I rushed over to help get a man out of a 20-mm gun mount. I tried to pull him out of the fire but part of his arm came off... I got sick."* [6]

J. F. Ballard had a similar experience. *"I ducked into the Ready Room, grabbed my survival kit, and ran onto the flight deck. I seen these fellers with short sleeves, the flesh hanging. I grabbed a big tube of Ungentine and tried to rub it on one guy's arms. The skin came off in my hands."* [7]

My division leader, Page Stephens, had completed his meal and gone to his quarters. *"I was getting ready to crawl into the sack where any up-and-coming naval aviator should be. I remember Trexler saying,* **'Well, they can blow that thing**

Stills from film of Kamikaze hitting the **ESSEX**. November 25, 1944.

Detail of Yoshinori Yamaguchi's Kamikaze showing the "17" tail marking.

ESSEX crew responds to the fire caused by the Kamikaze strike.

The fire is brought rapidly under control.

The Kamikaze struck along the port side gun mounts. The 16 men killed were manning these guns. 44 men were wounded. If the Kamikaze had hit the flight deck with its munitions-loaded planes, the damage would have been much worse.

Funeral service for the men killed in the Kamikaze attack on the *ESSEX*.
November 25, 1944.

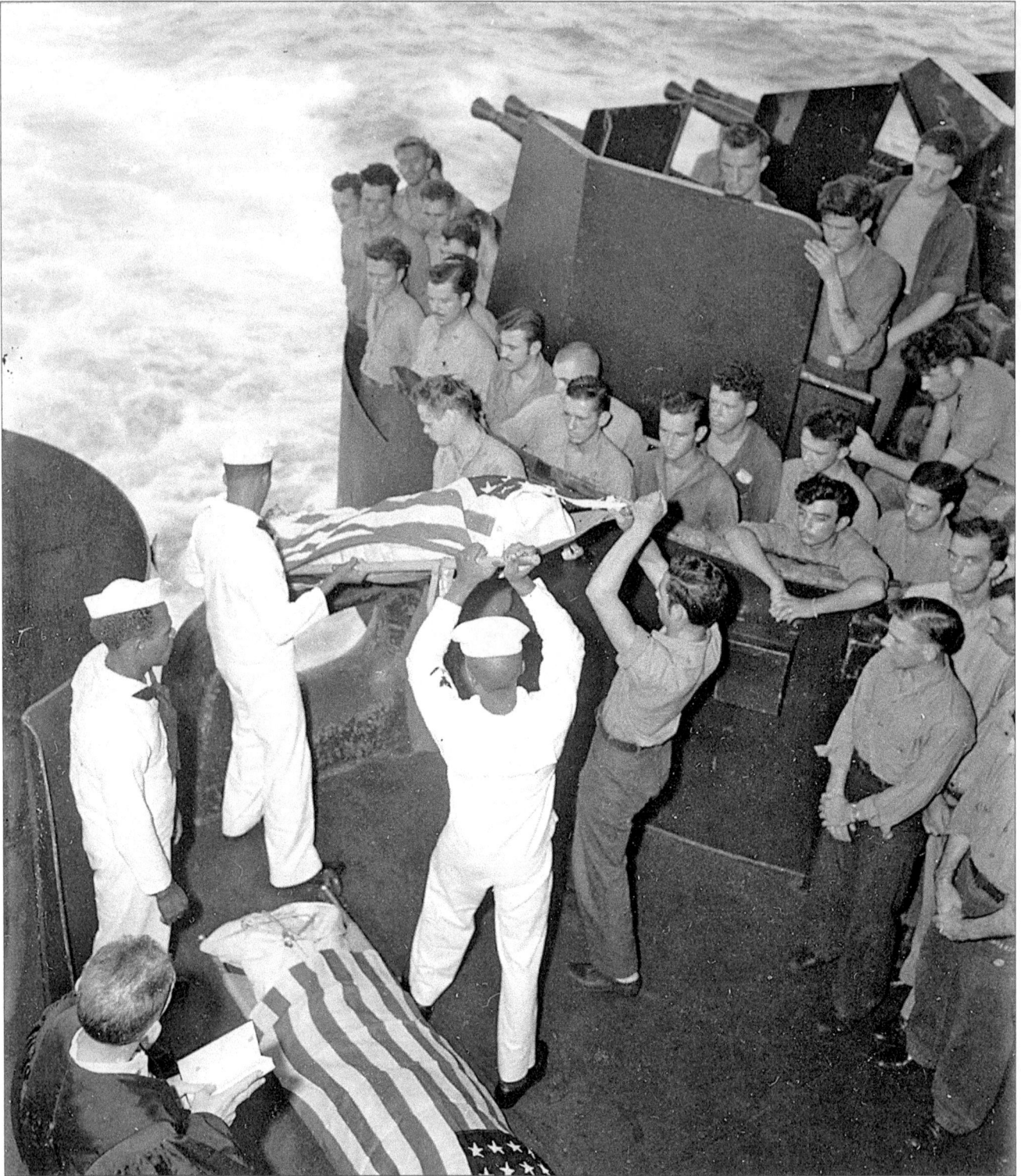

Burial at sea for the men killed in the Kamikaze attack on the **ESSEX**.
Combat made it impossible to return the bodies for land burial.
November 25, 1944.

*(General Quarters) all afternoon, they're not go-
ing to get me out of here.'* Then there was that terrific concussion because it hit not too far over our
room so Trex said, *'I've just changed my mind!'*
We headed for the wardroom and everyone was under the tables."[8]

The record shows that 16 men were killed and
44 were wounded. *"Skillful fire-fighting and superb damage control localized the damage."*[9] The
ship's log merely states:

> *"1256 - **ESSEX** hit on port edge of the
> flight deck at frames 69 - 70 by a Japanese
> suicide torpedo aircraft (Judy)."*

> *"1326 - Flight operations were re-
> sumed."*

Fear of those suicide attacks spread throughout
the fleet. In fact, some of the ship's crew had become so nervous and trigger-happy that our pilots
worried about being shot down by our own gunners as we approached the task force on our return
from a mission.

On one occasion, after we were hit by the Kamikaze, I saw some of our ship's gunners actu-
ally fire at late-returning planes. As a precaution
against this, the admiral started deploying a destroyer about 50 miles from the task force, with
the requirement that our planes returning from a
strike made an identification circle around the de-
ployed destroyer before approaching our own carriers. This change in flight policy was instituted as
a result of the following confidential recommendation from Lt Col Millington after he took over as
commander of Air Group 4:[10]

> *"As a result of friendly aircraft being
> fired on during the enemy airborne attack
> against the fleet on 21 January, this group
> feels the need of a general plan which could
> be effective for all returning strikes to fol-
> low when the fleet is under attack. As a sug-*

> *gestion, the following plan is submitted:"*

> *"All returning sweep and strike leaders,
> on reporting their ETA and upon receiving
> word to stand clear of the disposition due
> to enemy attack, should take station with
> their flights at the nearest TOM CAT or
> PICKET, circling to the right and remain-
> ing below 2,000 feet. The leaders should
> then report to that TOM CAT or PICKET
> the CAP calls of their flights and the state
> of their ammunition and fuel. Thus, the DD
> concerned becomes the controlling base
> for all flights stationed there and can ad-
> vise the Force Fighter Director. All flights
> remain there until the all-clear signal, or
> in the event traffic becomes congested they
> can be vectored by the controlling DD and
> the fighters can be utilized as CAP if condi-
> tions so dictate. Such a general plan might
> relieve excess radio transmissions between
> all flights and their bases under such emer-
> gency, since they would stand by for orders
> from the DD, relayed from Force Fighter
> Director. Moreover, those planes particu-
> larly low on gas would be vectored by the
> DD direct to the carrier indicated by the
> Force Fighter Control as being available
> for emergency landings."*

This new directive was fairly effective but it
did not stop all of the problems with gunners who
confused our own low-flying planes with potential
Kamikazes. The risk of improper identification
continued as the Kamikazes increased. By the end
of the Pacific war records show that:[11]

■ 7,465 Kamikazes flew to their deaths

The Allied fleet paid dearly with:

■ 3,048 sailors killed
■ 6,025 sailors wounded
■ 120 ships sunk

The damage to the **ESSEX** flight deck by the Kamikaze was minimal.

The flight deck was repaired and air operations resumed in about an hour.

Chapter 14 | San Fernando Harbor

"Lt Newell and Lt(jg) Souza each scored direct hits on the port beam both torpedoes exploding."

The Kamikaze attack was only one of a series of events that involved Air Group 4 on November 25, 1944. Declassified records show that our **ESSEX** Combat Air Patrol already in the air sighted a flight of six Zekes (Mitsubishi A6M Zeros) flying at 9,000 feet on an easterly heading.[1]

> *"Lt Hendricks made a high side run on one Zeke as the Zeke turned toward him. Lt Hendricks continued toward the enemy making a head-on run. Just before getting in range, the Zeke made a steep climbing turn to the left. Lt Hendricks and his wingman Lt(jg) Hovey turned with him and fired short bursts. The Zeke began to trail smoke and the pilot bailed out."*

> *"Lt Burnett, after making a high side run on another Zeke, saw the enemy trail smoke, lose altitude fast, and go out of sight."*

> *"In the meantime, Ensign Zdancewicz made a high side on a Zeke, which burst into flames and crashed into the water."*

> *"The remaining enemy had apparently seen enough for they scattered among the clouds and disappeared from the screen."*

Since most of our fighters were launched from the **ESSEX** before the Kamikaze hit, they were vectored to bogeys sighted by the Task Force. How many of these were potential suicide bombers no one knew, but the word from the ship was *"Get those SOBs before they hit any more ships!"*

The Combat Air Patrol under Lt L. M. Boykin was vectored out on a bogey which proved to be a Japanese Frances (Yokosuka P1Y Navy Bomber). Lt(jg) Peabody and Ens Keenholts were able to bracket the enemy. It burst into flames and crashed near the beach on Ildefonso Peninsula, Luzon.[1]

A two-plane "Jack Patrol," with Lt Blackwell and Ens Olson, sighted a Zeke at 700 feet being pursued at a distance by 4 F6Fs.[1]

> *"Lt Blackwell initiated a beam run on the Zeke which turned into the attack. Both aircraft fired but neither was effective. As Lt Blackwell passed over the Zeke he anticipated that the enemy would turn back to his westerly heading and away from the division of F6Fs engaged in the pursuit. Accordingly, Lt Blackwell turned west and his foresight was rewarded in that this maneuver placed him on the Zeke's tail. As the Zeke dived for the deck, Lt Blackwell gave it several good bursts of effective fire. Debris began to fly from the Zeke and at an altitude of about fifty feet it started a roll to the right and crashed into the sea."*

Back on the ship, after the flight deck was repaired, the remainder of Strike Baker was launched. Cdr Klinsmann was designated strike leader and target coordinator to lead strike groups from the **ESSEX** as well as Air Group 80, each composed of 8 VF, 18 VB, and 9 VT.

Concussion from the explosion of the Japanese suicide bomber had damaged the elevator and rudder of four of the SB2Cs, so only 14 dive bombers were launched from our ship. Air Group 4 rendezvoused and departed for the target area at 1330 hours.

Otto assigned Air Group 80 to a camouflaged cruiser in the southern part of Santa Cruz Bay. *"Our flight arrived just in time to witness two torpedo hits on this cruiser causing her to capsize and*

Yokosuka P1Y Navy Bomber, code named "Frances." The twin-engine
plane could carry either bombs or torpedoes and had a crew of 3.
Undated photograph.

A VT-4 Avenger drops a torpedo on a Japanese ship in San Fernando Bay.
The target is rapidly heading for the relative safety of the shore.
November 25, 1944.

sink with her bottom awash." [2]

Will Souza added *"That **Ticonderoga** air group made a beautiful coordinated strike on that Japanese cruiser... and they sank the darned thing! Then we had to look for other targets."* [3]

The **ESSEX** strike group was ordered by Cdr Klinsmann to proceed northward to San Fernando Bay where several Japanese ships were spotted. Anti-aircraft fire was very intense from several gun emplacements on San Fernando Point. Fighting 4 strafed these positions as the dive-bombers and torpedo bombers pushed over into their runs.

The Helldivers had climbed to 11,500 feet before they started their attack. Lt Weeks, leading VB-4, reported that the Japanese withheld their AA fire until the divers started, in order to avoid disclosure of the gun positions. Then they really laid down a barrage.

One Helldiver was shot down. This plane was piloted by Ensign Billy Nye Kinder.

It was believed that the pilot was hit by AA fire since the plane went directly into the bay. ARM3/c Donald R. Follweiler also went down with the plane. Three other SB2Cs were hit by Aak Ack but made it back to the **ESSEX**.

The dive-bombers of VB-4 had dealt a hard blow to the enemy ships. One medium AK *"was probably destroyed as a result of a hit on the stern with a 1000-pound bomb by Longley and 2 hits with 250-pound bombs... by Tutwiler and Zaremba.... The small AK was smoking from the attacks by McCauley and Peters."* [2]

The 9 Avengers from Torpedo 4 were loaded with torpedoes. Our Exec, Lee Hamrick, was leading the group.

After circling off San Fernando Point, five VT broke off to attack a Fox Tare Charlie beached between San Fernando Point and Darigayos Point. The remaining 4 planes turned southeastward to attack a Fox Tare Charlie which appeared to be beached between San Fernando Point and Bauang

Town. The Fox Tare Charlie to the north appeared to be previously damaged and abandoned; the Fox Tare Charlie to the south was in good condition. [4]

The Torpedo 4 tactical organization consisted of: [4]

Strike Baker - November 25, 1944

Lee L. "Ham" Hamrick (pilot)
   W. M. Hardin and R. A. Trembley (crew)

Don A. Henry
   E. A. Shirley and A. G. Schiesz

Felix E. Ward, Jr.
   Don M. Applegate and C. J. Warrington

J. E. Hewitt
   C. W. Lathrop and L. P. Shuman

B. O. O'Brien
   R. H. Stradley and R. D. Biddle

E. A. "Ted" Newell
   W. J. Lace and D. E. Venderville

W. J. Hopkins, Jr.
   R. B. Montague and R. E. Simendinger, Jr.

Will S. Souza
   A. W. Butler, Jr. and T. R. Sims

L. A. "Cozy" Cole
   N. H. Knox and N. L. Shiverdecker

Hamrick's 4-plane division made a torpedo run on the beached Fox Tare Charlie, dropping from 1500 yards at about 215 knots.

"Lt Hamrick and Lt(jg) Ward each scored hits on the starboard quarter of the ship, the explosions blowing the stern off the ship. Two torpedoes missed the target on either side; one was seen to explode on the beach while the explosion of the other was not observed. A fifth torpedo made an erratic circular run." [4]

The 4 torpedo planes led by Ted Newell attacked a Fox Tare Charlie which had not been damaged by previous runs. The planes went in low (275 feet), kept the air speed below 210 knots, and dropped from 1400 yards.

"Lt Newell and Lt(jg) Souza each scored hits on the port beam, both torpedoes exploding. A third was seen to explode on the beach. The performance of the other torpedo was not observed."

"Both ships were rendered useless as a result of the torpedo hits." [4]

As the last strike group and fighter sweep returned to base on November 25, the *ESSEX* could claim one of the most exciting days of the Pacific war. Our fighters had shot down at least 15 Japanese planes, we had sunk or destroyed several enemy ships, the *ESSEX* gun crews had fired at several bogeys, and, most important, we had survived our first Kamikaze.

A Torpedo 4 Avenger drops a torpedo on an unseen target. San Fernando Bay. November 25, 1944.

Chapter 15 | Meanwhile, Back on the Ranch

"...rounding up the horses and... planting spuds again today."

"Food will win the war!" That's what they told my Dad when they excused him from military service during World War I. *"We need you back on the ranch to raise horses and produce food for our boys in the trenches."*

That motto was reiterated during WWII as our agricultural and industrial back-up system became more and more critical to the sustainability of the war machine. Again, during the Korean and Vietnam conflicts, adjustments were made to "maintain our food production potential." As late as the Cuban Missile Crisis, one of President Kennedy's first orders was to tie up all CCC grain stocks until our future relationships with the USSR could be clarified.[1]

Major wars have always had a significant impact on agricultural history. Even though a country at peace may be in a period of apparent surplus production, the outbreak of war produces food problems of immediate international concern. After WWI, one economist with the US Department of Agriculture stated: [2]

"Then came the World War."

"Suddenly the productive industries felt the impact of a force wholly new to that generation, a force so powerful that it could and did dominate the economy of this country and of much of the world. Almost overnight, as history is reckoned, production had to fit itself to an altered pattern of trade and consumption.... Under the stimulus of price and patriotism -- finally of outright inflation -- the farm business labored and expanded and provided the sinews.... Every form of educational propaganda that could be devised was employed to stimulate

wheat acreage... and the US produced."

The experiences of WWII were similar. One of the greatest food shortages occurred in the province of Honan, China, in 1943. An excellent description of this famine and the conflicts between Chiang Kai-Shek and the Communist leaders, which led to mass starvation, is contained in Theodore White's book ***In Search of History***. White reported that: [3]

"Five million people starved to death in the province of Honan.... In a famine where there are no marks on the people who die: nature itself is the enemy.... Following famine and widespread corruption, came anarchy... a condition where no order prevails.... Compassion, kinship, customs and morals were swept away.... Food was the only idea, hunger the only command."

During the siege of Stalingrad and Leningrad, virtually no food supplies could get through to the cities. Thousands died of starvation. Similar situations were occurring all over Europe. Russia's serious food shortages were only partially offset by the numerous convoys that moved into Murmansk -- convoys that were protected by the anti-sub patrols of VT-4 and many other squadrons of Avengers that operated from aircraft carriers in the north Atlantic.

As the war progressed in the Pacific theater, Japan became increasingly vulnerable to food shortages. Our Naval blockades, which preceded the occupation of each Japanese-held island, brought a virtual halt to supplemental food supplies. Even though the vast Japanese Empire encompassed some highly productive farm areas, there was no way, without Naval support, to move rice and other essentials to the homeland.

My family's ration books and some of the stamps necessary to buy food items during the war.

As a final blow to the hungry Japanese, OP-ERATION STARVATION was put in place in the summer of 1945. The impact was devastating to the far-flung Japanese Empire. Food shortages became so acute that the government called on the civilian population to collect 2.5 million bushels of acorns to be converted into eating material. The average Japanese had to survive on a daily intake of 1680 calories, or about 78 percent of the minimum required for health and physical performance. Agricultural experts were projecting over 7 million deaths by starvation if Japan stayed at war through 1946.[4]

On May 24, 1945, shortly after the defeat of the German armies, War Food Administrator Jones sent a letter to all members of Congress in which he stated:

> *"The United States has produced 50 percent more food annually in this war than in World War I. With 10 percent fewer workers on farms, twice as much food has gone annually to the armed services and for overseas shipments as was used for these noncivilian outlets each year of the last war."* [5]

Food had helped win the war. And it would certainly shape the peace that followed. But some of those left "back on the farm" did not fully appreciate their role in the war effort. In our family, Byron and I had joined the Navy, Daniel was married and working in Alaska as a carpenter for the Army, John and Bill were too young to work. So that meant my teenage brother Walter was left to help Dad and Mother with the farm and ranch chores. Walter, therefore, became one of my primary sources of back-home information and, without his knowledge, a sort of counselor.

Walter's letters became a focal point for many of my discussions with squadron buddies. In one of the earlier letters I received from Walter, he wrote that he and his cousin Bill had spent the day rounding up horses and, after considerable trouble, corralled a part of the herd: *"When daddy seen them*

he said that we had rounded up every horse except the right ones." Dad often said, *"that Walter, he can't ever do anything right!"*

This and other statements that Dad made about Walter's work on the ranch led to the squadron label of my favorite brother as "Worthless Walter." We all looked forward to the next mail call outlining Walter's troubles back on the ranch.

I saved most of Walter's letters and reread them many times while awaiting the next strike. These letters revealed something of the struggle and sacrifices made by our civilian population. Those of us in the service may have been subject to more risks, but we also held the glory assignments.

> **Sep 2, 1943, Small, Idaho** -- *"Mother bought a place in Montana, around $5000... school starts up there the 7th. I wanted to start but daddy said I had to stay home and help thresh, pick spuds, fix fence and a million other things... a feller never gets to do anything he wants to anyway so I shouldn't have ever figured on it.... I'm going to get in the Navy when I get old enough so I can help get this war over with.... Love, Walter"*

So Walter stayed in Idaho to help on the ranch. The workload increased even more when the folks rented Lidy Hot Springs. Lidy's was the traditional summer resort for Clark County, Idaho. It had natural hot water for the large outdoor swimming pool, a bar, and dance hall. In addition, Dad and Walter moved most of our cattle from Medicine Lodge to Lidy's.

The move meant that Walter had to ride 10 miles to school from Lidy's to Medicine Lodge on old "Dime." As he stated in one letter, School District N 24 had just received a typewriter and he "kinda liked" learning to type.

> *"This typewriter cost the school $19.00.... so I could learn on it last winter please dont mind the mistakes im out of practitous and spilling too."*

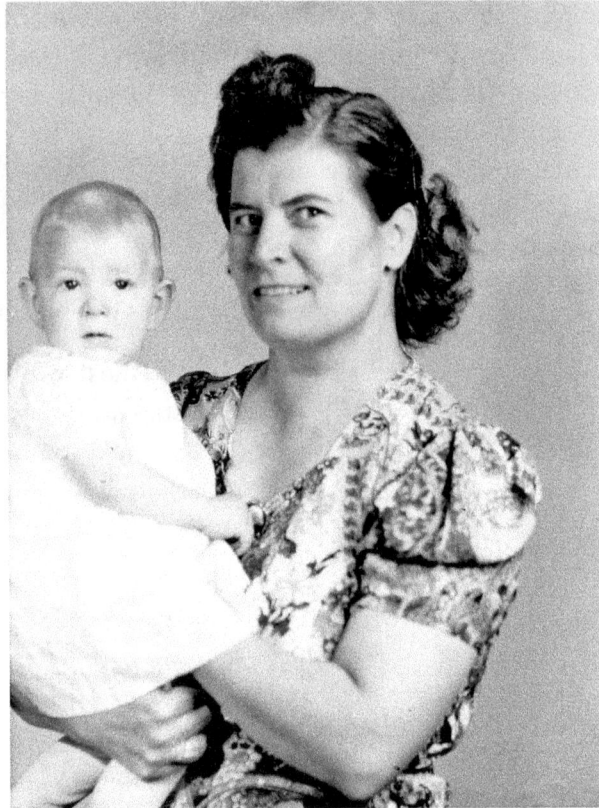

My Mother with my youngest brother, John Foster. John was born November 2, 1941.

Walter Thomas on Dime. Lidy Hot Springs. 1943.

I don't think Walter knew the location of the keys for the commas or periods. That gave the letters more of the flavor of the rural environment. Those of us on the ship particularly enjoyed those letters that covered a sequence of events.

May 21, 1943, Winsper, Idaho -- *"School is out thank goodness I passed isnt that surprising. The old ford is still running good having a little truble keeping it in gas though sence gas rationing."*

"...Neil was staying with me last week we went out to the big hill last night seen one Bobcat five rattle snakes...."

"Robbin isnt going to have a colt this year she has a lot of life and is sure fat Daddy is going to sell Buster about four people want him he sure has a lot of life now he pranced and rared up on his hind leges all the way out to deep creek with me the other day."

"Business isnt so good this year too many young men gone to the war."

"Lynn was home last week he was asking all about all you kids. You know you guys never was home long enough for me to find the wrong side of you you sure have a good reputation every body in the country knows you and asks about you. Sure is nice to have a bunch of brothers that every body thinks a lot of it helps the reputation of the rest of the family too...."

May 22 -- *"Well today Daddy and I went over to the Lodge he harrowed while I cut spudes.... Milk nine cows now about $28.00 a week of cream. Sold two Pigs the other day got $35.00 a peace for them they were just seven months old...."*

May 23 -- *"Went to the Lodge today befor noon Daddy finished harrowing and sold buster for $60.00 I cut spudes.... The saddle horse got out and run off I left the gate open when I got the cows...."*

May 24 -- *"What'a day I and Daddy planted spudes till i'm SICK of them came home and milked then caught old Dime and learned him to jump then went swimming and now am going to bed Daddy doesn't feel too good got a prety bad cold...."*

May 25 -- *"Mother and Henry bought a cow and a calf today for one hundred a piece they are broke to milk but you cant milk them they are so hard. I hased cows today up on Bblue Ccreek had a duce of a time caught one fish but didnt look for any more. I dednt have no saddle to ride got mad and was running Dime through that big sagebrush after a cow when I cough my foot in a sagebrush and I got sent a rolling I finnaly got the cow though. I had to get off at the spring and fix the water on my way back my horse run off and left me afoot with a cow to drive from the upper spring...."*

May 26 -- *"Same old thing today milked cows and planted spudes me and paw are on the lift today the spud planter keeps breaking down.... John Foster fell of the bed just now he done about everything today ate the chickens clabored milk drank the pigs swill waded in the ditch pulled fethers out of the gobbler dumpted ashes in my bed broke his dish at the table and what not?????? Well no excitement today so I guess i'l quite."*

May 27 -- *"I planted spudes while Daddy stayed home and irrigated Mother and Henry went to town and helped brand their bucks. They hauled the cows they bought down here...."*

May 29 -- *"...Today we planted spudes while Mother cought eleven fish they were big ones we will finish planting spudes tomorrow thank goodness. Bought three new parts for the spud planter and it wont plant... it went on the bum today so we* *planted by hand Steve was telling us how to fix it and Daddy told him all we needed to do was jack the middle of it up and put a new in there."*

Jun 3 -- *"Well we finnished planting spudes today...."*

The squadron breathed a sigh of relief when Walter finished planting potatoes. Someone said, *"I wish he would quit planting spuds and send us more of those beef steaks. And, I mean real beef... not the horse meat they served us when we were in Newfoundland!"*

While Walter and Dad were busy trying to grow more potatoes, agricultural scientists back home were also busy trying to find better ways to preserve and transport the crop to those of us in the service. Dehydration of potatoes was in its infancy during WWI. But in the last two years of WWII, the US dehydrated and packaged 20 million bushels of potatos.[6] Food shortages in Europe raised the demand for potato flour to 10 times the normal US output.

Powdered potatoes may have been OK for the Europeans, but those of us in the Service complained about as much about powdered potatoes as the cooks did about the old kind that required peeling. This was part of the power, peel, and politics of the potato. In VT-4 we were darned glad to see Walter shift to a more glamorous subject.

Jun 3 -- *"Went to the falls [Idaho Falls] yesterday I bought a new pare of shoes. It snowed here yesterday and is still colder than a bugger. The water master turned our water out today. Got to brand the rest of the calves soon maybe tomorrow. Daddy and I are going to round up all of the stray horses and tin can them they keep all of the feed ate off so the milk cows dont get any. We are milking 12 cows now get about thirty gallons to a milking. I have got to irrigate tomorrow so no branding."*

Jun 6 -- *"Had a dance last night [at Lidy*

Hot Springs] not a very big crowd they left about five thirty this morning I went to the Lodge today and irrigated...."

Jun 11 -- *"Painted the ford yesterday you ought to see it blue finders gray body black trimmings green on the cover over the moter it runnes better sence I painted it...."*

Aug 29 -- *"Well Daddy and I went to the Lodge today we branded colts. Billy helped me ride we didnt get all of the horses.... I rode that bronc of mine he lasted all day but just as we hit the upper spring four head split away from the bunch I took after them I ran them about two miles up a one way trial couldnt get out of it to head them finally when I reached the top I gave my horse a kick he got about even with them and gave out he came to a big rock and ensted of jumping it he stoped and wouldnt go a step fauther I unsaddled him and let him rest pretty soon he came up to me and started pushing me toward home with his nose so I saddled him up and caught up with Bill the other bunch had got clear of the sight we brought them in and coraled them when daddy seen them he said that we had brought every horse but the right ones... that goes to show what a lot of encouragement you get for trying."*

All the ranchers on Medicine Lodge Creek ran horses on the open range during the Great Depression. The range was vastly overstocked and the ownership of the horses depended to a degree on who helped with the fall roundups. It was always good to be represented when the horses were corralled to claim a share of the "slicks" or unbranded colts. Uncle Henry always knew which colt belonged to which mare and which stallion was the likely parent.

With the passage of the Taylor Grazing Act in 1934, the era of the free range ended. Grazing allotments were established and everyone had to go to town to put in a claim for a share of the open range. Allotments were supposedly based on historic grazing use. Our family had to take severe cuts in both horse and cow herds because Dad was not as aggressive as some of the newcomers to the area. He hated to *"deal with the Federal government."*

Most of the surplus or trespass horses on Medicine Lodge were rounded up and trailed over the divide to the cannery in Butte, Montana. I remember Mother sitting on the corral fence and saying as Dad helped cut out the horses that had to go. *"Oh, Dan,"* she would say, *"Do you have to sell that beautiful bay mare and colt?"* But, she knew they had to go. The horses sold for $10 a head -- the same for a mare with colt at her side.

Our family still had 30-40 head of horses when WWII started. I claimed several of these and I wanted Dad and Walter to take good care of them. Many of those missed in the fall roundup would likely winterkill in the high ranges up around Black Mountain. I kept writing the folks that *"I wish I could help ride for those lost horses on Deep Creek."* I could always write about horses even though I could not say much about our Navy activities.

At the time of the fall roundup, Dad, Mother, and Walter named the new colts that might turn out to be saddle horses after aircraft carriers while Byron and I were in the Navy. On the ranch we now had a "Ranger" and a "Kasaan Bay." The Navy censors prevented us from revealing the names of the ships where we served in the Pacific or we probably would have had horses named "Essex" and "Bunker Hill."

Both Ranger and Kasaan Bay were geldings. I guess the folks did not realize that Navy ships always carried the female identification. *"The Bunker Hill recovered her aircraft and she set a course for the Philippines."*

Aug 29 -- *"...I and Bill rode deep creek yesterday we left the horses in the corral last night those dirty sportsmen had season oppened on chickens the hunters went through there at daylight this morning and left the corral gate open let the horses out on the hay and in the grain Daddy was sure mad by the time we got over there the sage chickens were all killed and the men had gone I wish we had of cought them in there we would have sure fixed them."*

Aug 30 -- *"...I sure wanted to go to school [in Montana]... but Daddy said I had to stay home and help with the work."*

Aug 31 -- *"Went to the rodeo at the Falls... Dad, mom, William, the cook, and I left at six o'clock with four head of calves in the wonderful trailer we bought from Den Sullivan... I had brought the calves from Blue Creek that morning."*

"We got down this side of Roberts a ways and lost a front wheel on the trawler lugges stripted out... along came Harold decided he couldnt help us so the way he went and took the cook with him... the rodeo was to start at eight thirty and it was eight now me and Daddy got the wheel on the best we could and started off again had to go affual slow got to the Falls at nine thirty I got out and went to the rodeo while Daddy was unloading the cattle I got to see most of the rodeo but Daddy and mother didnt get to go."

Sep 1 -- *"The coyotes are starting to come in again this year like they did last year we havent been able to get shells for the rifle yet but if we do the coyotes better run cause I emproved my aim this sommer and I think I can hit them Well the load of grain is comming so Id better quit for today."*

Sep 2 -- *"...We are having a Dance Sunday starting at Midnight wish you were here to help tend bar or help get my courage up enough to go dance you guys*

Our ranch on Medicine Lodge in the winter. Undated photo.

Daniel (left), Walter, and Byron at the bar at Lidy Hot Springs, 1936. My family ran
Lidy Hot Springs for most of the years from 1934 to 1946.

never had much courage that way either from what ive seen and heard The old ford sprung a leak in the water pump I put some iron cement on it hope it stops the leak well got some Geemonetry to do so will close."

Sep -- *"...Say I sure wish you were home so you could learn me how to hunt I had to go to school when Antelope season was open so I went hunting the other day saddled up old Dime and got that hunting knife you sent me and your old thirty-thirty and headed up over the hill went out the head of the spring and over the cedars and into Blue Creek while I was ridding up Blue Creek canyon I came face to face with a Buck and a Doe deer I hopped off old Dime yanked the gun out of the schabbard and let fly at the buck went over him throwed another shell into the chamber and let fly again hit a rock about two inches over his front sholders he dodged behind a cliff and was out of sight I glanced up on the hill and there stood the doe I thought I had good aim on her so I fired and when high.... I started cussing and headed after her the hill was afful rocky and it took me quite a while to get up it when i reached the top I could'nt see a sign of her there were a lot of little draws that she could have gone up I could'nt see her tracks so I headed up the lickiest one.... Which was of course the wrong one... I told Daddy I wouldnt be gone long so I started for home when I got to the upper spring there were three head of antelope going out of water I stoped and got off they heard me so they stopped too they were a long ways away but I thought I'd take a shot at them any way I amed a little high and let drive at the buck there was a rock right in back of him and I hit it I don't think I hit the antelope but he started run-*

ing and ran south around the hill the other two went north I stood and watched and a little while later I saw him go between a draw and up the hill toward the other two he wasnt limping or any thing so I guess he wasnt hurt although I would have liked to stalked him."

"Well that ended the hunt as usual I came in home with out any thing Daddy said other people get antelope but none of us kids ever did and probably never will could'nt even get a coyote last winter"

It seemed to me that Walter's image was coming through to the squadron as that of an unappreciated laborer, while Dad seemed to be a slave driver. Perhaps this sense of guilt on my part prompted me to write the letter reproduced on the next page to my Father in recognition of his 48th birthday.

This nostalgic letter to my Dad reflected my desire to get back to the ranch after the war. I wrote, *"I'm getting additional pay for sea duty -- about $15 a month.... I only had to pay $7 income tax for 1942. I can probably send some money home... invest it in cattle or sheep because I have a feeling money won't be worth much after the war...."*

At the time this letter was written, no one realized that the government policies of price support and the accelerated demand for agricultural products due to the war created an artificial situation that could not last during the peace. Our ranch and many others were soon in a state of collapse.[7] As former Secretary of Agriculture Orville L. Freeman stated: [8]

"Throughout World War II and the Korean conflict, the farmer produced to intense demand and reaped fair returns and grateful recognition. But the technological advances that enabled him to meet the wartime demands betrayed him once the emergencies were over."

TORPEDO SQUADRON 4
****

August 28, 1943

Dear Dad,

I suppose that you are wondering why this letter is written and addressed specifically to you. Well, the occassion is your approaching birthday. I have taken the privelege to deviate from the customary "Dear Folks" to pay my respects to you alone. This is only an inadequate effort to show you that I am thankful for the many things you have done for me. I know that I speak for not one, but six boys, when I say that we are honored to have you as a father.

You know, every so often, during periods of inactivity, I get terifically homesick--for you, and mother, and the ranch--and I began remeniscing. Certain instances become outstanding, and always you are present as a part of the picture.

I can see you leaning against the Round Corral fence while the herd of horses that Daniel and I had just brought off Deep Creek restlessly mill around. You calmly chew on a stem of alfalfa as Daniel and I, all het up inside, talk profusely about the possibilities of making a good saddlehorse out of Dixies' new colt. You say we aught to halter-break Babe's yearlin', or advertise that stray black mare because she has been with this bunch since last fall. In the excitement I drop Dime's reins and he walks sidewards as he drags them over to the manger. You cuss as one of the geldons kicks with both hind feet at a young stud and William gets too close. Then there is lots of confusion as Daniel and I try to rope the colts we have to brand. After we just about run them down and maybe accidentally catch one or two you take the lasso rope and finish up. Then there is the smell of burning hair and possibly warm blood if a two year old stud happens along. Finally we start the remainder of the herd back to Deep Creek on a high lope so the bay mare won't lead them out in the lavies. Then we unsaddle and go to the house where we finish the discussion of horses with Mother and Henry.

That night we are pretty darned tired and we dread the thought of milking those few cows. But with your iniatitive we all chip in and it really wasn't so bad after all.

When haying season comes around you again lead the way. Stelzer was right when he said you raised yourself a hay crew. We make short work of that Reno contract despite that old broken down derrick and the wind, and that roan stud that no one could bridle but you. You let Frank gyp you on the hay measurement, but then you always gave the other ranchers the best deal because you were easy to get along with.

There were numerous times following a long night at Lidy's when you let us boys sleep in while you milked and done the chores all alone. You went out and harnessed up and fed the stock during those winter blizzards when we were in school. You did all the hard work on the Fourth and 24th and at those little rodeos we put on while the rest of us had fun. These are only a few of the things that make us indebted to you as the best father in the world.

Well, Dad, I guess you know that all this adds up to me wishing you a happy birthday this year and many years to come.

Your Son,

Gerald

P.S. I am enclosing a little check and you can buy your own birthday present. Give my regards to the rest of the family.

Ens. G. W. Thomas
Torpedo Squadron Four

Gerald's letter to his Dad. August 28, 1943.

Chapter 16 | A Question of Security

"We will track you down... even if the war is over!"

After remaining in the area east of Luzon for about a week, the **ESSEX** returned to Ulithi for more permanent repairs and for R&R for the crew. R&R at Ulithi meant Mog Mog, one of the 40 islets that make up the atoll. When Ulithi became a Navy base, Mog Mog was transformed into a recreation center. There was an officer's club, an enlisted men's club, and of course beaches. The 200 or so native people had been evacuated to a safer location.

Capture by the Japanese

During this period, as the Pacific campaign intensified, all hands in Air Group 4 were assembled in the Wardroom for a special briefing on security. One of the ship's officers introduced an Army intelligence officer to conduct this briefing.

The intelligence officer stated that on one occasion a Naval pilot had been shot down during a strike, ditched near one of the islands, and was captured by the Japanese. During the interrogation that followed, the captured pilot supposedly revealed the D-date and H-hour for the invasion of one of the Pacific targets.

"This classified information in enemy hands cost the lives of hundreds of Allied troops," he said. The intelligence expert then threatened all of us with the statement *"If any of you are captured by the Japanese and, if under interrogation, you reveal any information about the location or planned action by Allied forces in the Pacific, we will track you down and prosecute you, even if it takes ten years after the war is over!"*

He repeated this statement several times so that we could not forget. And he may have accomplished his objective. However, these threats made all of us very angry. Here we were out in the mid-dle of the ocean trying to fight the enemy and now we were threatened by our own people.

At the time of this briefing, we had received very little advice on how to resist revealing information when subjected to physical abuse. For myself, I wondered just how long I could hold out under torture. Could I comply with the strict orders to reveal only my name, rank, and serial number?

During WWII even the experts knew very little about brain-washing techniques or truth serums. We only knew that the Japanese tortured and mistreated POWs. The details of the Bataan Death March, which began on April 9, 1942, were not revealed until after the Japanese surrender. There were, however, credible stories coming from neutral sources which prompted President Roosevelt to issue a statement on April 21, 1943, about criminal responsibility.

"This Government has vigorously condemned this act of barbarity in a formal communication sent to the Japanese Government. In that communication this Government has informed the Japanese Government that the American Government will hold personally and officially responsible for these diabolical crimes all of those officers of the Japanese Government who have participated therein and will in due course bring those officers to justice." [1]

This set the course for the postwar trial of war criminals in Japan.

Aboard the **ESSEX**, we kept hearing stories about the pilots and crew members who were shot down and captured by the enemy. Every pilot agreed, *"If we are hit, try to stretch the flight path to reach the water! Keep away from shore! Maybe*

Aerial view of Mog Mog Island, Ulithi Atoll, Caroline Islands. 1945.

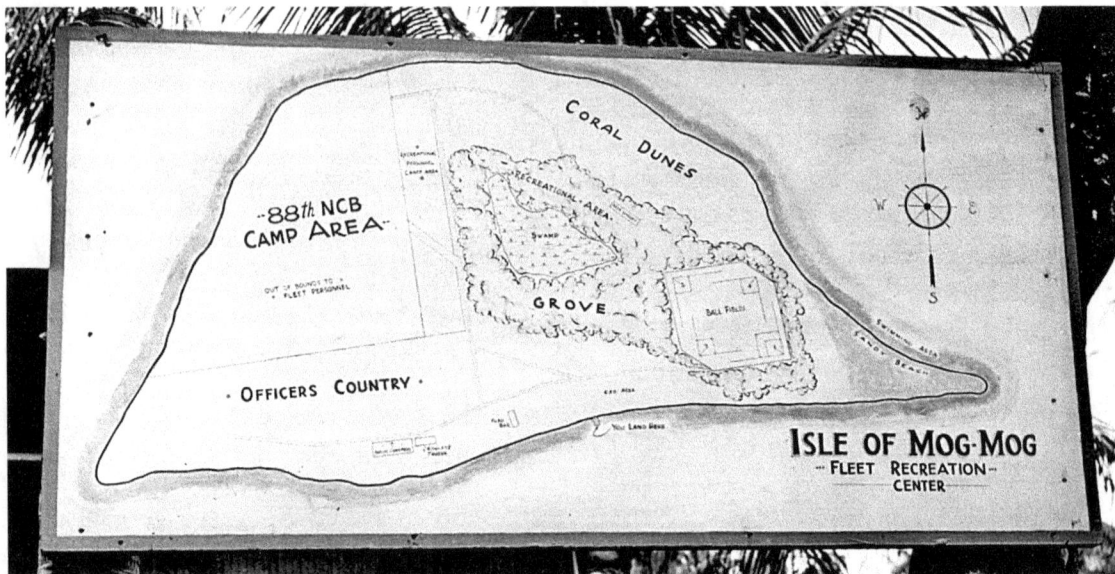

Map of Mog Mog posted outside of Officer's Club. December, 1944.

a friendly rescue sub or picket destroyer will get a position report on the downed flyers and attempt a rescue."

Some of the details of Japanese torture were reported by Robert Sherrod, correspondent with **Time** and **Life**. He called this section in his book "A Study In Depravity." [2] Sherrod's comments were based upon the Proceedings of a Military Commission on War Crimes convened by US Pacific Fleet on Guam in 1946, which cited several cases of confirmed torture, body dissection, and cannibalism by the Japanese on Chichi Jima.

> *"Not only had American prisoners on Chichi been tied to stakes and bayoneted, but... a Japanese officer had ordered his medical officer to remove an American flyer's liver, which was served at a sake party."*

> *"On 4 July 1944, a Naval aviator who parachuted during the second carrier raid on Chichi was captured... interrogated... and bayoneted to death."*

> *"...it had been determined that the eating of prisoners was a stimulant to morale...."*

The records show that no word of these atrocities ever reached the Japanese people. It is hard to estimate the value of complete control of the press to a nation dedicated to an all-out war.

Not too long after this major security briefing, our commanders developed a much better approach to the protection of classified information. This technique was simple and straightforward: Don't tell the pilots and crew of the strike groups anything that they don't need to know to carry out the mission of the day -- no future plans, no D-Day information, no fleet tactics.

Most of us were happy to see the policy change, although in some cases, a little more information might have helped with survival if we had been shot down over enemy territory.

Censorship

Since the Navy worried a great deal about security -- particularly the position, composition, and tactical plans for fleet operations, we were subjected to rather strict censorship and security regulations. We had several examples of "Promulgation of Deck Court" for smoking while the "Smoking lamp was out" or otherwise breaking blackout rules. Other security restrictions were also imposed on us.

Implementation of the rules of censorship for outgoing mail was the responsibility of the officer component on the ships. We each took our turn checking the letters to make certain that no information was leaked that had value to the enemy. Wardroom discussions revealed that some officers cut heavily into the letters they were assigned. Some even cut out personal or sexual references intended only for wives or sweethearts back home. I let those kinds of comments stand and concentrated more on locations, ships, or planes. As for my own letters, I took the easy way out.

July 27, 1943 -- *"Dear Walter, am I happy!! Just got back to blank, USA, from a long and tedious session on the blankety-blank sea between the coast of blank-blank and blank, where we spent most of our time in the harbor between blankety cruises. Sure is good to be back on good old terra firma, USA once more -- and the change in climate does remarkable things for a person. Makes a fellow feel like a good turn at the pitchfork, or maybe a session at cultivating spud. And would I like to climb on the top rail of the round corral and look over that bunch of horses you brought in from Deep Creek!!"*

"...But before you start meeting the trains and busses, I had better tell you that I won't be able to make Idaho this time since me and the Admiral aren't very chummy as yet. Should get three days tho -- maybe time enough for me to look up Delbert in Maryland. Hope so anyway.

He said my last letter to him was cut to ribbons by the censor so don't know what I said but reckon I'm okay, which is true."

It was two months after the Norway strike before I felt free to talk about my tour of duty on the **RANGER**. OPERATION LEADER took place October 4, 1943, and my letter to my folks dated Dec. 5, stated *"Since this letter won't be censored I can tell you of my activities for the past four months...."*

Officer's Club on Mog Mog. It had formerly been the island's boys' school. 1945.

Chapter 17 | Support for Mindoro Occupation

"The Captain shot down a Jake for the first kill on December 14."

As Task Force 38.3 was refueling and returning to Ulithi, Cdr Klinsmann prepared comments and recommendations on our operations in the Leyte-Luzon area. He emphasized the following points: [1]

- *"Intense and accurate... antiaircraft fire is a primary problem. Smoke screens might help."*
- *"AA fire increases after the first planes are committed in the dives."*
- *"Since our losses are steadily increasing... the primary target VF must be the AA installations."*
- *"More VF are needed to reduce AA fire so that the VB and VT can concentrate on their targets."*
- *"Rocket projectiles were used for the first time by our Hellcat pilots and the results were not very satisfactory."*
- *"More varied and wider dispersal of Japanese aircraft, together with improved camouflaging presents an increased problem in locating these planes."*

Klinsmann's memo may have helped increase the number of VF, but the major concern of the ship's command was protection against Kamikazes: *"Because of the suicide tactics of the Japanese, the composition of Air Group 4 was changed to include a greater number of fighter planes."* [2]

This change also included a reduction in the number of TBMs. Our squadron was reduced from 18 to 15 planes. This left us with a surplus of pilots, so we transferred three of our new replacements back to Guam -- O'Brien, Zook, and Pletts. These three had been on very few combat flights with VT-4. Gray and Cannady had joined Torpedo 4 at the same time. According to Bill Cannady, our Exec saved him from a similar transfer.[3]

*"I owe Hamrick a lot because the next time we came back into Ulithi they cut back one more and I was the excess pilot. I had my orders to leave. At noon that day I went down to lunch and had my gear all packed and on the quarterdeck. I was waiting to go up and see P. J. Davis and I thought, **'Oh, you're supposed to go up and see the skipper and nothing happens.'** Then suddenly over the bullhorn I was told to go to Hamrick's stateroom. I went in there and saw him and he apologized for the fact that P. J. couldn't see me because he was in the briefing for the next big mission. Ham said there was no reflection on me -- they were going by the numbers, and I had to be dumped. I told him that I understood and we shook hands and I saluted him and walked out, and I got about 20 feet out of his stateroom and he said, **'By the way, if you miss that barge at 1330, I don't know what we can do. I guess we'll have to keep you as excess complement because we're leaving at 1400.'** With that I went down and got my gear off the quarterdeck, went down into the chief's quarters at the rear end of the ship, and sat there until the Task Force cleared the nets out of Ulithi. Then I went back up into the Ready Room. I was still a member of Torpedo Four -- thanks to Ham."*

While we were in Ulithi, the US Pacific Fleet was strengthened by the addition of a British Pacific Task Force with 4 carriers, 2 battleships, 5 cruisers, and 15 destroyers. This strike group was under the command of an individual whose name was familiar to Air Group 4 -- Admiral Sir Bruce

Grumman F6F-3 Hellcat. Unidentified pilot. May, 1943.

Fighting 4 pilots scramble for their Hellcats for the strike on Luzon,
December 14, 1944. *USS ESSEX*.

Fraser. The Brits were assigned to the overall command of Admiral Spruance.[4]

Task Force 38.3 moved out of Ulithi on December 11, 1944. TF38.3 was now under the Command of Admiral F. C. Sherman, who was on our ship. We were in company with the *TICONDEROGA, SAN JACINTO, LANGLEY, NORTH CAROLINA, WASHINGTON, SOUTH DAKOTA, SANTA FE, MOBILE, BILOXI, OAKLAND,* and 14 destroyers.[2] The next day we joined up with TG 38.1 and TG 38.2 to form Admiral Halsey's powerful Third Fleet.

Under Halsey's overall command we steamed into position to launch strikes against Luzon. The primary concern now was the support of the occupation of Mindoro.

Fighter Sweeps -- December 14-15, 1944

The carrier was in a position on December 14, about 150 miles east of Luzon, to maintain continuous fighter cover over Japanese airfields on Luzon and to cover the US invasion forces now landing on Mindoro. The first two fighter sweeps of the day were launched at 0700. Twelve Hellcats were under the command of the VF-4 skipper, Lt Cdr K. G. Hammond, and 12 were under the command of Lt H. T. Houston. These groups flew through a heavy overcast to hit Baler, Carbanatuan, Tarlac, and Lingayen airfields.[5]

Lt L. M. Boykin led another fighter sweep, launched at 0923, against these and other fields on Luzon. No planes were encountered in the air, but several were destroyed on the Japanese air bases.

The next fighter sweep on December 14 was lead by Lt G. M. Harris, Jr. The 6-plane group concentrated on Lingayen airfield. After the attack, Ens R. T. Snider's F6F Hellcat developed an oil leak: [5]

"The oil pressure in the plane flown by Ensign Snider decreased and finally the engine froze. He made an excellent water landing and managed to get in his raft. His scalp was lacerated on the gun sight when impact was made with the water. Ensign Snider stated that his shoulder straps were not locked. His pair leader, Lt(jg) Ginther promptly reported the water landing and remained overhead until relieved by a CAP section from the USS TICONDEROGA. The landing occurred at 1500 (I) 40 miles west of the disposition. Ens Snider was picked up by the USS THATCHER at 1630."

Without any rest, the VF-4 skipper, K. G. Hammond, was ordered to lead his second strike of the day *"to investigate a report of an enemy convoy"* off the coast of Luzon. The 6-plane division "spotted a DD, DE, FTB, and a lugger at Latitude 15° 38' N, Longitude 119° 50' E, course 180°, speed 10 knots." [5]

During the bombing and rocket attacks on the convoy, Lt Cdr Hammond observed a Jake (Aichi E13A seaplane) about 2,000 yards north of the convoy. As he pulled out of his dive, he headed for this enemy plane, attacked from 5 o'clock above, and fired into the engine. As a result, VF-4 reported that *"The Captain shot down a Jake for the first kill on December 14"* [6]

The next day two VF-4 strike groups were launched at 0640. Targets for Strike Able were air fields on Luzon, while Strike Baker was ordered to Salvador Island, south of Santa Cruz, to attack a Japanese personnel landing ship (LSM). They left the ship *"dead in the water."* [5]

"While recovering from this third attack northwestward from the ship, Lt(jg) Watson sighted two Zekes (Mitsubishi A6M 'Zero' fighters) at 1500 feet northwest of Salvador Island on a southerly heading. The Zekes were flying in column and Lt(jg) Watson made a flat side approach on the leading Zeke and closed to a no deflection shot from astern. Hits were observed in the Zeke's fuselage, and its belly tank was ignited. As the Zeke nosed over, Lt(jg) Watson found that the second Zeke was on his tail. He immediately broke off the attack and

Intelligence photo taken by Fighting 4 of southern Luzon coast.
December 15, 1944.

Curtiss SB2C Helldiver. Undated photo.

turned away. In the meantime, Lt Tutwiler, who had followed Watson down in the attack on the ship, observed the encounter and made a high side run on the second Zeke which broke off its attack on Watson and turned into Lt Tutwiler's attack. The opposing aircraft fired on each other in this head-on encounter and Tutwiler could see his tracers entering the Zeke's engine. The Zeke pulled away and was last seen, losing altitude, toward a wooded area near the beach."

The **ESSEX** launched 6 more Hellcats, led by H. T. Houston, later in the forenoon of December 15. The purpose, again, was to sweep and patrol airfields on Luzon. At Tarlac field, the group destroyed two Tojos (Nakajima KI-44 fighters) and damaged airport facilities. They also burned a fuel dump near Lingayen airstrip. This softened the Japanese defense for the coordinated attack scheduled the next day.

Lingayen Airfield, Luzon -- December 16, 1944

The next major strike for Air Group 4 took place on December 16, 1944. On this date Cdr Klinsmann led a morning flight of 8 VF, 14 VB, and 14 VT on a strike against Lingayen Air Field and installations.

Upon reaching the target, VF remained as high cover while VB and VT attacked. Targets were assigned to VB and VT in that order, and upon completion of the attacks, VB and VT were escorted to the east coast of Luzon and were then detached to return to base as there had been no enemy aircraft opposition in the area. VF were ordered to remain over the area as a combat air patrol.

The Torpedo 4 tactical organization was as follows: [7]

Strike Able - December 16, 1944

P. J. Davis, Jr. (pilot)
　R. F. Gray and N. J. Schmolke (crew)

C. N. W. "Scott" Vogt
　Leo E. Halvorson and R. E. Kelly

Strike Able - December 16, 1944 (continued)

G. M. "Buck" Barnett (downed, hydraulic leak)
　C. W. Lathrop and C. Christopher

W. F. "Willie" Walker
　S. A. Hastings and G. F. Zeimer

Page P. Stephens
　A. Beard and Andy "Marge" Mocsary

Vernon A. Landre (returned, oil leak)
　A. "Tony" DeCenso and Charlie C. Statler

Gerald W. "Jerry" Thomas
　J. E. Holloman and Don H. Gress

R. M. "Hoppy" Hopfinger
　F. W. Wilson and A. W. Yarman

B. R. "Trex" Trexler
　C. W. Barr and J. W. Aldrich

G. M. Bell
　A. J. Tankard and R. R. Pittman

Robert F. "Bob" Ruth
　J. F. "Forrest" Ballard and C. L. McConnell

L. C. Gray
　J. E. Ganley and H. R. Green

Ed S. Binder
　W. D. Jenkins and R. D. Biddle

G. D. "Mak" Makibbin
　R. B. Montague and R. Campbell

W. H. Cannady, Jr.
　E. A. Shirley and J. C. Gerke

Those of us in Torpedo 4, after hearing about the effective fighter strikes the two previous days by our trusty Hellcats, expected a milk run to Lingayen. We climbed above the cloud cover, approached the target at 10,000 feet, made glide bombing runs at "red-mark" speed, and pulled out at about 1200 feet.[7]

"The first division overshot, bombs falling in the dispersal area north of the runway, on the beach, and in the water."

"The second division attacked the barracks west of the runway. One bomb

dropped by Lt(jg) Thomas was seen to hit one of the buildings in the area, while the damage by the other bombs was unobserved."

"The third division dropped on the runway and the two maintenance shops northwest of the runway. One hit was scored by Ensign Bell on the eastern-most end of the maintenance shops destroying the eastern end of the building. Three bombs cratered the northern edge of the runway. The remaining bombs fell in the dispersal areas north of the runway."

"The fourth division dropped on the runway with three bombs cratering the runway near the center and the remainder falling in the dispersal area to the north."

The dive-bombers, due to consistently heavy losses to antiaircraft fire, tried different tactics for this strike. Instead of preceding the Avengers, they followed us. And, rather than roll over into the typical near-vertical dive, they used glide-bombing tactics similar to the typical VT runs. They dove out of the sun to minimize exposure. As a result, all of the Helldivers got back to the **ESSEX** without losses.[8]

The combined efforts of VF, VT, and VB left the Lingayen airstrip badly cratered and the support facilities with severe damage.

A midday fighter sweep, led by Lt W. W. "Dub" Taylor, followed our coordinated attack. The 8-plane group of Hellcats attacked previously damaged ships and again hit Tarlac, Lingayen, Rosales, and Carbanatuan fields. This flight lasted nearly 5 hours, and: 5

*"At 1700 (I) Lt(jg) Watson was forced to make a water landing when his fuel supply was exhausted. He got clear of the plane but had difficulty in breaking out his life raft and abandoned it. Watson was supported by his life jacket while his pair leader circled the position until a DD, the **USS Ingersoll**, picked him up at 1710."*

Lt(jg) Leonard A. Watson was unhurt and the **ESSEX** brought him back aboard two days later -- just in time to save him from the discomfort of riding out a major Pacific hurricane on the destroyer Ingersoll.

A Torpedo 4 Avenger gets a wave-off returning from the December 16, 1944 strike on Lingayen. **USS ESSEX**.

Chapter 18 | Flying Conditions Average

"Ensign Allander got vertigo in a cloud and was last seen spiraling down in his plane."

Operations vs. Combat

One thing never seemed to change during our service on three aircraft carriers -- that was the weather summary. The teletype in the Pilot's Ready Room may have given details about the heavy overcast, freezing rain, and high winds, but invariably the concluding statement was *"Flying Conditions Average."*

We finally learned to send a pilot out to the flight deck to check. Buck Barnett was a likely candidate since he was our "night-flying expert." And he would report back *"Can't see the other end of the flight deck for the fog, wind nearly blew me off the flight deck, but the teletype is correct, flying conditions are average!"*

The records show that Torpedo 4, like most of the squadrons in WWII, lost more men in so-called "operations" than to "combat," and weather was a big contributor. Official Navy reports classified the losses of pilots and crew as either "Losses in Combat" or "Losses Operationally." Why did the military tell the relatives back home that so-and-so was killed in training or lost in an operational accident as opposed to killed in action? Either way you are dead as a result of the war.

The way the losses were reported was bound to have a psychological impact on the family back home. Operational deaths would always seem so unnecessary. Both of the first two skippers of Torpedo 4 were lost to weather or operations. Yet, their deaths were just as noble as those individuals shot down by the Nazis or the Japanese.

Routine carrier takeoffs with a heavy load of armament were always questionable. From the cockpit, even though we checked the instruments, we learned to listen for the slightest change in the sound of the engine which might reveal a loss of power. And we always welcomed the "moderate winds" which increased the air flow over the flight deck. Five to 10 knots made the difference between a comfortable takeoff and "sweating it out."

Carrier landings were more dangerous than takeoffs. This process required a team approach. The pilot did his best to get "into the groove" as he started the final turn to line up with the flight deck. Then in those final few seconds, we shifted our trust to the Landing Signal Officer. The LSO was always an experienced pilot. He had flown most, if not all, of the planes he was guiding. He knew how to read the speed of the plane from its attitude. And, most importantly, he learned through experience the characteristic approaches of the different pilots. Nevertheless, there was always a sigh of relief when we "caught a wire."

But while the carrier launch and recovery took the lives of many Navy pilots, our worst adversary was the weather. Granted, we had undergone a modest amount of instrument training; not nearly enough in our opinion. However, our problem was trying to combine formation flying with instrument flying -- trying to keep our eyes on the instrument panel without chopping off the wing of our section or division leader. And some pilots were lost because they couldn't combine "dead reckoning" navigation with formation flying. If they became separated from the group in a cloud, they might not know their latitude and longitude.

Typhoons Take Their Toll

In the Pacific our two carriers were in and out of several typhoons. Only one of these received exceptional notoriety. Sometimes called "Halsey's Typhoon," this storm took place while we were

Torpedo 4 Exec Lt Hamrick takes off as waves break 80 feet over the flight deck. *"Flying Conditions Average."* **USS ESSEX**. February 22, 1945.

Torpedo 4 Avenger gets the "cut" signal from the Landing Signal Officer. **USS ESSEX**. February 9, 1945.

supporting the Philippine operations. A complete report on the nature of this storm and the fleet operations at the time is contained in Capt C. Raymond Calhoun's book **Typhoon: The Other Enemy**.[1]

On December 16-18, 1944, the **ESSEX** (Flagship of TG 38.3), along with the rest of TF 38, was caught in one of the most severe typhoons on record. Three destroyers, the **HULL**, **MONAGHAN**, and **SPENCE**, were sunk with 778 men killed. Virtually all ships in the Task Force sustained damage -- and many planes on the carriers were torn loose from their tie-down lines and sent crashing across the flight and hanger decks. The final count was 146 aircraft lost or destroyed by the typhoon.[2]

The **ESSEX** log records the events as follows:[3]

- *"Dec 17 -- Fueling at sea in area about 500 miles E of the Philippine Islands."*
- *"1325 -- Set course to westward to escape an approaching typhoon."*
- *"Dec 18 -- Riding out a second typhoon, which had appeared 250 miles to the SE in area about 250 miles E of the Central Philippines."*
- *"Dec 19 -- Fueling and receiving replacement aircraft in an area about 250 miles E of the Central Philippines."*
- *"Launched an afternoon search for straggling ships and survivors of ships that foundered during typhoon."*
- *"Dec 20 -- Operating in TG 38.3 proceeding to search for survivors of vessels that foundered during the typhoon."*
- *"In late afternoon set course for initial launching point for continued strikes against Luzon."*
- *"Dec 21 -- Operating in TG 38.3 proceeding to fueling rendezvous and searching for typhoon survivors en route. Strikes cancelled because of weather."*
- *"Dec 22 -- Fueling at sea in area about 400 miles E of the Central Philippines continuing search for typhoon survivors. In late afternoon set course for Ulithi Islands."*
- *"Dec 23 -- Steaming in TG 38.3 en route Ulithi Islands."*

Because of the extreme weather conditions during this typhoon, it was virtually impossible to launch planes to aid in the search for survivors until December 19. In the meantime, the destroyers and the DEs that were on the scene did what they could to rescue men from the turbulent waters.

Admiral Halsey, who was on the New Jersey, later wrote in his autobiography:[4]

"No one who has not been through a typhoon can conceive its fury. The 70-foot seas smash you from all sides. The rain and scud are blinding; they drive you flat-out, until you can't tell the ocean from the air. At broad noon I couldn't see the bow of my ship, 350 feet from the bridge... this typhoon tossed our enormous ship as if she were a canoe... we could not hear our own voices above the uproar."

Repercussions from this fleet disaster reached Admiral Nimitz and went on to the Washington bureaucracy. There seemed to be plenty of blame to go around, but the focus of the concern was on the decisions of Admiral Halsey and his aerological advisors. A Court of Inquiry was called in January, 1945. Some of their conclusions were:[1]

- *"The fleet movements directed by Admiral Halsey after the advent of bad weather were logical, but he should have ordered special weather flights and weather reports from ships to cover the critical area from which no weather reports were being received...."*
- *"...The aerological talent assisting Admiral Halsey was inadequate."*
- *"...with regard to the damage and losses suffered by the MONTEREY, COWPENS, SAN JACINTO, CAPE ESPERANCE, ALTAMA-HA, NEHENTA BAY, and KWAJALEIN (and most of the other ships), the court was of the opinion that the ships were handled... in an acceptable manner... damage was directly attributable to the storm."*

The Court made recommendations about ship design and stability, weather forecasting, and:[1]

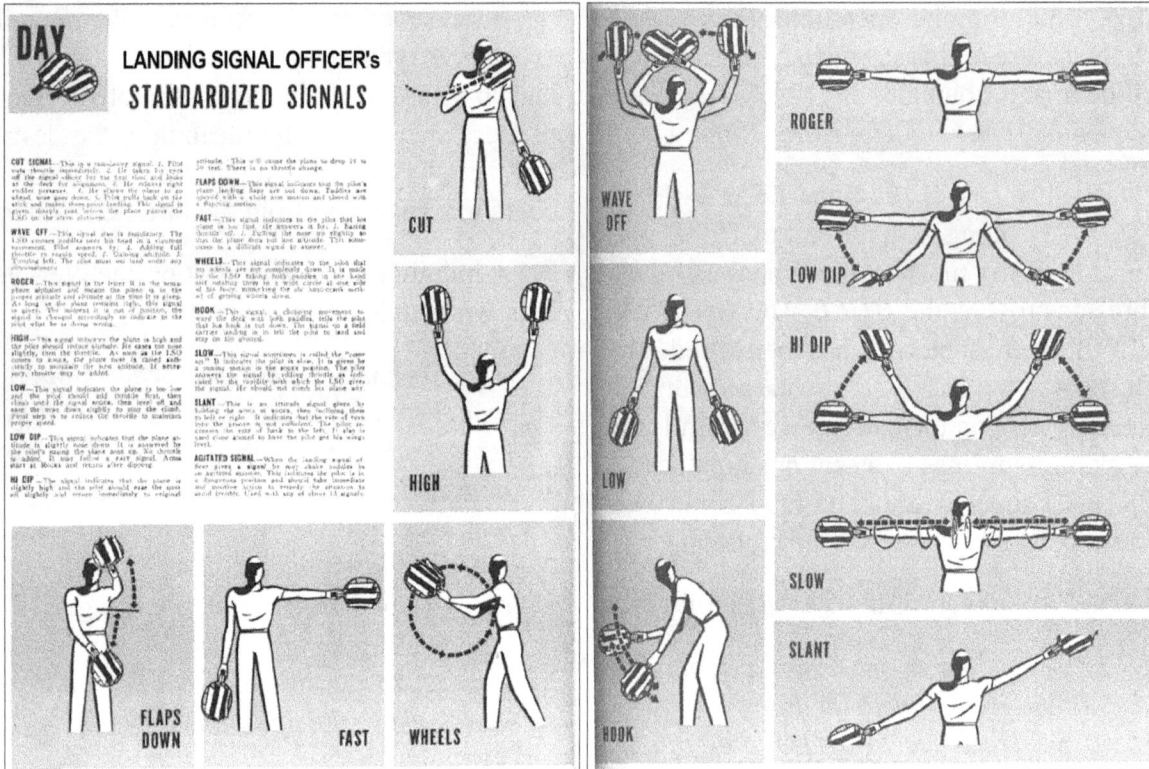

1945 chart showing the Landing Signal Officers' daytime signals.

Photo of arresting wire No. 1, *USS RANGER*. When a plane's tailhook snags the wire, it pulls out, and hydraulic cylinders attached to each end of the wire absorb the energy necessary to stop the plane. October, 1942.

"That weather ships should be stationed in the area; and at least two planes daily be assigned as weather reconnaissance planes to cover sectors where unusual weather was suspected."

This meant that some of our planes would be launched and recovered under situations that could not be labeled as "Flying Conditions Average." On one such occasion, our Executive Officer, Lt Hamrick was launched as waves were breaking over the flight deck, 80 feet above the water. Ham stated: [5]

"I took off right through the spray. The bow hit the water and was coming up. It sort of tossed me in the air. I fluttered around a bit before I got going. They sent us on a search for storm survivors."

"The landing was rough. I came around on the approach too high. But the signal officer kept me up there. He was watching the stern go up and down. When he "cut" me I dove for the deck because I thought it was a long ways down. But it was coming up fast! I rared back on the stick. We hit solid... broke both front tires!"

Another typhoon "almost as destructive as the Kamikazes" hit the US Fleet off the coast of Okinawa on June 5, 1945. This typhoon inflicted severe damage to 4 battleships, 8 carriers, 7 cruisers, 11 destroyers, and a host of auxiliaries.[6]

Unidentified destroyer sinks during "Halsey's Typhoon." December 18, 1944.

ESSEX crew rush to tie down an F6F Hellcat during a storm. June, 1944.

Fighting 4 Hellcat looses six rockets during rough landing on *ESSEX*. December 19, 1944.

Chapter 19 | Marines Replace Dive Bombers

"Millington claimed the first kill by CV-based Marines during WWII."

After the typhoon and fueling at sea the ***ESSEX*** moved into Berth 14 at Ulithi. Shore leave was authorized to Mog Mog on Christmas afternoon. Crewmen, as usual, were confined to the fenced-off area and beer was rationed. Officers were issued rum and coke, and someone broke out the dice for diversionary crap games.

That night there was a big fight on the dock between two air groups. Several of us ended up in the water. This was not the first or last scrap between ship's personnel on Mog Mog. Usually no one knew who started the ruckus.

Shakedown for the Marines

On December 28, 1944, two Marine fighter squadrons replaced the VB-4 due to consistently heavy losses of the SB2C dive-bombers. VMF-124 and VMF-213 were the first Marine squadrons to augment carrier air groups during World War II.[1]

Bombing 4, the "Top Hatters," were transferred to Guam. The torpedo pilots hated to see them go. We had a lot of close friends in VB-4. Some were regulars at our poker tables. We respected the dive bombers because their missions and responsibilities were similar to our own.

The personnel component of the Marine Squadrons as they boarded the ***ESSEX*** was:[2]

	VMF-124	VMF-213
Officers, Naval Aviator	23	22
Officers, Ground	3	2
Enlisted, US Navy	60	60
Total Strength	86	84

The plane component for the ***ESSEX*** was now 36 Corsairs, 55 F6F Hellcats and 15 Avengers.

The Marine pilots soon discovered that carrier operations were more difficult than land-based flights. Two pilots and three F4Us were lost in the first two-day shakedown. Records from the archives show the following planes lost: [3]

- Dec 30, 1944 -- one F4U crashed on takeoff.
- Dec 31 -- one F4U crashed on takeoff and one F4U crashed approaching flight deck.
- Jan 3, 1945 -- one F4U lost at sea.
- Jan 7 -- five F4Us lost at sea.
- Jan 16 -- one F4U lost at sea.
- Jan 21 -- one F4U lost at sea.
- Jan 25 -- one F4U forced down in enemy territory.
- Mar 1 -- one F4U lost -- pilot bailed out.

Besides the Marine F4Us that were lost, there were many damaged, with frames buckled, during hard landings on the ***ESSEX***. Watching the launch and landings of the Marine Corsairs was a great pastime for pilots and crews not scheduled for the flights. We could anticipate that someone would get in trouble almost every day.

At the time of reporting to the ***ESSEX***, each Marine pilot had an average total of 400 hours flight time in the Corsair. Also the pilots had only about 12 carrier landings. Carrier qualifications had been conducted in the San Diego and Hawaiian areas aboard the ***USS SARATOGA, USS MACASSAR STRAITS*** and ***USS BATAAN***. [2]

"Despite the care exercised by the Air Department in allowing all safety margin possible, three accidents occurred in two days time, all undoubtedly due to pilots lacking familiarity with the airplane in its

Bombing 4 (VB-4). *USS RANGER*. October 1, 1943.

VMF-124 and VMF-213. *USS ESSEX*. March 5, 1945.

Lt Thomas J. Campion (VMF-124) crashes off the starboard bow of the *ESSEX*. The accident was caused by climbing too steeply and turning to the right too soon. December 30, 1944.

Lt Campion´s plane sank extremely rapidly. The tail is visible here.

The belly tank of Lt Campion's plane explodes. Lt Campion did not survive the accident.

Marine Corsair making its landing approach to the *ESSEX*.
December 30, 1944.

higher loading condition (full ammunition and full belly tank). Two of the accidents were fatal, one spinning in on takeoff, the other on approaching for a landing. The third pilot was recovered." [4]

The Corsair was a good carrier-based plane, but it took good pilots and much practice to compete with our Navy F6F Hellcats. The Marines believed that the F4U could not carry a 1000-pound bomb from the flight deck, but later experience indicated this could be done.

Lt Col William Millington was in command of VMF-124 and Major David E. Marshall commanded VMF-213.

Millington claimed the first kill by CV-based Marines during WWII. Later when Cdr Klinsmann was shot down during the strike on the Pescadores, Millington became our Air Group Commander, the first Marine to command a Navy Air Group.

Mistaken Identity -- January 12, 1945

The *ESSEX* official *"Report of Circumstances Surrounding Shooting Down of Friendly B-24 Over Camranh Bay, French Indo-China, during South China Sea Sweep of the Third Fleet"* outlines reports from the Marine pilots, B-24 sightings by VF-4 Hellcat pilots, various endorsements and gun camera film.* [4]

Interrogation of F6F pilots from VF-4 after the incident revealed the following sightings of B-24-type aircraft on January 12, 1945:

TCAP #1 -- *"At 0815 one silver-color B-24 was sighted at 9500 feet... presumed to be friendly."*

Strike #1 -- *"At 0845 a single B-24 was sighted at 12000 feet... presumed to be friendly."*

TCAP #3 -- *"At approximately 1435 (I) four B-24s were sighted at 7000 feet... F6Fs observed bomb splashes in the water offshore."*

"Between 1445 and 1500 a CAP was vectored out to two B-24s 25 miles west of force at 7500 feet...."

CAP #4 -- *"CAP closed near enough to identify a bogey as a B-24."*

Photo Mission #2 -- *"At 1730, one B-24 was sighted...."*

Most of the F6F pilots stated that insignias on the B-24s were not visible and that some of the Liberators were camouflaged. Also, some Navy planes were fired on when they approached the B-24s. Evidently, there was no radio communication with the Air Force planes due to different frequencies.

It would be easy to understand why the China-based Army gunners would open fire on the Navy fighters, especially since they were not forewarned of the surprise carrier-based attack on French Indo-China. Excerpts from the official report follow: [4]

"At 1850 on 12 January 1945, while on CAP #5, Capt Edward P. Hartsock, USMCR, 1st Lt George Parker, USMCR, and 2nd Lt Herbert Libbey, USMCR, shot down a four-motor, reddish-brown colored patrol bomber (later identified by photos as a B-24) over the French Indo-China coast near Camranh Bay. The plane was unmarked except for camouflage paint and responded to questioning maneuvers and signals with gunfire only."

"...the bogey began firing furiously at our CAP from waist gun positions. Hartsock and Parker were on the bomber's starboard side, above and slightly aft, while Libbey was abeam of Hartsock on the bomber's port side. Hartsock waggled his wings, and pressed his "C" channel button (not being sure of the type of plane), but heard nothing and received continuous fire from the bomber. As it turned toward him and Parker, diving for the overcast, Hartsock made his decision to attack."

"...Hartsock and Parker attacked in overhead passes, both scoring hits which seemed to cause smoke. Libbey, attacking in a high side run, concentrated in a long burst on the port inboard engine, flamed it and exploded the bomber which then disappeared, smoking, into the overcast."

"...Immediately after shooting down the subject plane the three F4U pilots participating in the engagement identified it (in a report of VHF) as an Emily."

*"Upon returning to the **ESSEX**, these pilots reported to the ship's ACI Officer and expressed their concern over the exact identity of the plane they had destroyed. They stated that upon first sighting the subject plane they thought it was a flying boat but that upon closing each of them noted twin tails and general resemblance to a B-24. However, the lack of any insignia and hostile actions of the subject plane caused them to attack."*

"...On 13 January, 1945, development of the film from the gun cameras of the F4Us proved conclusively that the subject plane was a B-24."

This unfortunate incident served as a lesson to us all. It pointed to the importance of further ID training and it recalled the times our own ships' gunners had fired at our own planes returning from strikes. We were all vulnerable to mistakes.[4]

*"Much later, it became known that the B-24 had radioed its base that it was under attack by US Navy aircraft. Why the Liberator should have opened fire on planes it recognized as friendly remains a mystery. And while the tragedy caused considerable grief, there were no recriminations. Correspondent Robert Sherrod, aboard the **ESSEX** at the time, overheard one major say,* **'I'd have done the same thing. If anybody shoots at me, I'm going to shoot back. I expect the other fellow to know his recognition as well as I do. There are ten lives in a B-24, but it can cause a thousand deaths aboard ship if there are Japs in it.'**"

As the Marine pilots gained experience, all members of Torpedo 4 looked forward to seeing the beautiful inverted gull-winged F4U Corsairs flying cover for our strikes. In time the Corsair pilots also agreed to carry a heavy bomb load and competed favorably with the old reliable Hellcats. Thus, the F4U became a multipurpose, carrier-based combat plane. Capt W. J. Bedford of VMF-124 stated in his journal, *"Navy seems glad to have us aboard and are cooperating in every respect."* [3]

During the remainder of our tour of duty on the **ESSEX**, Marine fighters were credited with 10 Japanese aircraft shot down, 16 destroyed on the ground, and at least 11 ships damaged by bombs or rocket fire. The loss of 8 pilots and 17 Corsairs, half of the original complement, demonstrated both the risk and the determination of the Marines.

Chapter 20 | Forbidding Formosa

"...we added five names to our list of MIAs."

The *ESSEX* was underway again on the 30th and we spent New Years Eve, 1945 at sea *"steaming in TG 38.3 en route to fueling rendezvous."* [1] We were headed for a new target -- Formosa. This would give us an opportunity to test out the new TBM-3cs that were delivered to the *ESSEX* from a jeep carrier.

The few days that we spent en route to Formosa provided the only opportunity to expose the new Marine pilots to carrier operations. As noted in the prior chapter, we lost the first corsair on December 30 when Lt Campion crashed on takeoff.[2]

The next day we lost two more F4Us -- one went in the drink as it cleared the flight deck and one spun in coming up the groove. One pilot was rescued, but Lt B. W. Bennett was never spotted after the crash. Lt Col Millington, Commander of VMF 124 admitted: *"Numerous problems were experienced in the process of familiarizing the Marine pilots with carrier doctrine and procedure."* [3]

Watching these Marines adjust to carrier operations made many of us wish we had the dive bombers back. After the next series of strikes, even Millington stated, *"It is believed that had VB-4 been aboard for this operation, damage to enemy shipping by this [air] group would have been higher."* [3]

Formosa Airfields -- January 3, 1945

The major purpose of the carrier-based air strikes on Formosa was to destroy ships or airfields that might be used to counter the upcoming invasion of Luzon by Allied forces.

Formosa was a new name added to our strike vocabulary. The island was strategic to Japan as a source of valuable supplies and as a launch site for naval operations. The name of the Island was changed to Taiwan (Republic of China) when Chiang Kai-Shek and his followers were forced off the Chinese mainland by the Communists after WWII.

As viewed from the cockpit, Formosa was about 225 miles long and 60-80 miles wide. Threatening sea cliffs, forming vertical walls, faced the Pacific side. Rough, forested mountains, reaching heights of nearly 13,000 feet, would tend to negate the forced-landing option and would make any bail-out dangerous. In the prestrike briefings we were advised that the "wild savages" called Saiban, because of their hate for the Japanese, might give downed airmen the only possible chance for evading capture and torture.

The weather was bad as the *ESSEX* moved into launch position on January 3. In spite of these overcast conditions, the carrier launched a predawn strike force of 8 Hellcats and 8 Avengers.[4]

"The proposed target was Kagi airfield which was providing strategic support for the Japanese operations in the Philippines."

"Upon departing base the flight encountered extremely adverse flying conditions, the overcast being solid from 700 feet to above 10,000 feet. In climbing through this overcast VF became separated from VT, and some VF and VT became separated from their divisions."

The only planes that emerged through the overcast for the rendezvous were 7 Hellcats and 4 Avengers -- not a very effective strike group. Nevertheless, under Cdr Klinsmann's direction, the group attempted to spot Kagi Airfield through the occasional openings in the cloud cover. The strike

Marine Corsairs warm up prior to strike on Formosa. This was the first action for carrier-based Marines during WWII. ***USS ESSEX***. January 3, 1945.

Torpedo 4 Avenger over Formosa. January 4, 1945.

group finally located an airfield that: [4]

"VT insisted was not KAGI but KO-KAN, while VF were just as insistent that the field was KAGI."

"Commander Klinsmann's division acted as high cover while the other division, led by C. A. Shields, preceded the VT in their dives. Thereafter, the group commander's division strafed KOBI to the North."

This was another one of those frustrating days for Torpedo 4. Our planes were loaded with 100-pound fragmentation bombs.

Effective with this strike, all Avengers were ordered to carry only one crew member instead of two. This change was made for three reasons:

- Japanese fighters seldom made underside runs, so the belly gunner was not needed.
- Crew members in the belly were not protected from flak by armor plate.
- Radios were more sophisticated and did not require extra attention by the radioman.

With a one-man crew it was still necessary for the turret gunner to arm the bombs and set the intervalometer (a device for automatically taking pictures at timed intervals).

Makibbin and I continued to carry a second crewman designated as a photographer due to our special training at the aerial photo school in Harrisburg, Pennsylvania.

The VT-4 tactical organization consisted of: [4]

Strike -- January 3, 1945

P. J. Davis, Jr. (pilot) (did not attack targets)
  N. J. Schmolke (crew)

C. N. W. "Scott" Vogt
  R. E. Kelly

G. M. "Buck" Barnett (did not attack targets)
  C. Christopher

W. F. "Willie" Walker (did not attack targets)
  G. F. Zeimer

Strike -- January 3, 1945 (continued)

Page P. Stephens
  Andy "Marge" Mocsary

J. E. Hewitt
  L. P. Shuman

Gerald W. "Jerry" Thomas
  Don H. Gress and R. B. Montague

R. M. "Hoppy" Hopfinger
  A. W. Yarman

P. J.'s division went one way into the soup, and Page took our 4-plane division on a different path. P. J., Buck, and Willie did not reach the target and Scott Vogt got separated in the overcast, eventually joining a 7-plane Avenger group from the *TICONDEROGA*.

The *TICONDEROGA* group chose the harbor installations at Suo as an alternate target.[4]

"Lt(jg) Vogt dropped twelve 100-pound GP bombs on an oil storage at SUO, scoring hits."

Page led our division across Formosa toward Kagi airfield. However, the weather was so bad we couldn't find Kagi, so we bombed Kokan through a hole in the clouds. Our task was to crater the runway to prevent Japanese planes from taking off en route to Luzon.[4]

"All bombs were observed to hit on the large aiming point. In view of the small number of planes dropping, it is held unlikely that the object was totally achieved."

Anti-aircraft fire was moderate as we went into the glide bombing attack. During the dive the hatch flew off the turret of one of the Avengers and tore a hole in the stabilizer.

After the run, Hoppy, Ed Hewitt, and I joined up with Page below the clouds and climbed back through the mist on a southeasterly course. When we broke out on top we were surprised to see bursts of Ack Ack around us *"which trailed fairly accurately, suggesting radar control or at least radar tracking."* [4]

Eiko Airfield, Formosa. Note bomb-drop pattern following strike by Avengers
from the **USS ESSEX**. January 4, 1945.

Marine Corsair returning from strike on Formosa. **USS ESSEX**. January 4, 1945.

Radar-controlled AA fire was a new experience for us. Don Gress, in my turret, shouted *"Ack Ack on our tail!,"* so I took evasive action. I had told Don earlier to alert me -- especially if the bursts were close to our tail. The first bursts were usually behind the plane. Then they moved forward to the lethal position unless we took immediate violent maneuvers.

Cdr Klinsmann had ordered all torpedo planes to return to base while his division made a strafing run on Kobi airfield. The CO then located Kagi, but the weather closed in before he could attack.

Fighter Sweeps -- January 3, 1945

The **ESSEX** launched two additional F6F fighter sweeps and one Marine F4U strike group on January 3. One of the Fighting 4 groups was dispatched to Okinawa and the other two sweeps were sent over Formosa.

The first VF-4 sweep was launched at dawn with Skipper Hammond as leader. Because of the extreme weather conditions, Hammond's flight was forced to stay close to the deck for most of the 340-mile outward leg. Upon reaching Okinawa, Hammond split the flight into two parts and conducted simultaneous attacks on Naha and Yontan airfields. They burned at least 5 aircraft at Naha and seriously damaged two SDs off shore. Anti-aircraft fire was "intense." [5]

"Lt H. T. Houston was hit and compelled to make a water landing. He was observed in a life raft, and the group stayed over him until gasoline inadequacy forced its return to base. However, rescue facilities which investigated the area could find no trace of him, and it is believed he drifted to shore and was captured."

(Forty years after the war I learned that "Hubbie" Houston had been taken prisoner and had endured terrible treatment in several Japanese POW camps. In spite of several attempts, I was unable to arrange an interview with him.)

The next Hellcat sweep, led by Lt Keers, was sent over Formosa, but the weather was so bad only one plane got through to attack. This plane, piloted by Ens Wright, got separated and joined up with an attack group from VF-44.

In addition to the two VF-4 sweeps, the **ESSEX** launched a fighter sweep of Marines in their new corsairs. This was the first action for carrier-based Marines during WWII. Lt Col Millington led the group of seven F4Us over Formosa. [6]

"...to provide fighter cover for VT-4 torpedo bombers and strafe Kagi Airfield, destroying 10 t/e [aircraft] on the ground and one Nick or Fran airborne, credited to Millington. A train and other installations were also strafed."

Unfortunately, 1st Lt Robert W. Mullins was lost on this Formosa sweep. Capt William J. Bedford in his journal recorded: [7]

"[Mullins] became separated in the soup. He was nowhere in sight when the main group broke out about 800 feet over water. He was later heard transmitting by Navy pilots. He was lost, no homing radio, no receiver, no compass. ...hit by AA evidently. CAP attempted to locate him and lead him home with no success."

Kagi, Formosa -- January 4, 1945

In spite of the bad weather, the **ESSEX** launched a strike group at about 0700 hours on January 4. The assignment again was for the 12 Avengers, loaded with 100-pound GP bombs, to crater the airfield at Kagi. Eight Hellcats were to provide escort in case of enemy planes.

The strike group split into two groups and broke through the overcast at 8,000 feet. They reassembled above the clouds and made a slow climb to 14,500 as they proceeded toward the target. [4]

"KAGI airfield was overcast and could not be located and Commander Klinsmann

ordered VT to attack an airfield believed to be EIKO. VF remained as high cover during the attack and rendezvous, and escorted VT from the target area and returned as a target CAP."

The VT-4 tactical organization for the strike was: [4]

Strike -- January 4, 1945

P. J. Davis, Jr. (pilot)
  N. J. Schmolke (crew)

W. J. Hopkins, Jr.
  Stan W. Coller

Will S. Souza
  T. R. Sims

L. A. "Cozy" Cole
  N. H. Knox

Ed S. Binder
  W. D. Jenkins

H. J. Deimel
  C. L. Ely, Jr.

G. D. "Mak" Makibbin
  R. Campbell and R. B. Montague

W. H. Cannady, Jr.
  J. C. Gerke

B. R. "Trex" Trexler (returned to base)
  C. W. Barr

G. M. Bell (downed, radio trouble)
  J. F. "Forrest" Ballard

L. C. Gray (downed, fouled flaps)
  J. E. Ganley

E. A. "Ted" Newell
  W. J. Lace

Pilots reported that the Eiko airfield appeared to be in the final stages of construction, but serviceable at the time of the strike. VT-4 planes did a good job of cratering the runways and rendering damage to airport support facilities.

While the torpedo planes were returning to the

Essex, Hendricks' fighters came into the same general area, and[5]

> *"...found an opening in the cloud cover through which to attack Tsuina airfield. Due to weather conditions, the group could not safely observe all of its results, but claims three aircraft probably destroyed and some buildings seriously damaged by bomb and rocket hits. No airborne planes were sighted."*

The next major fighter sweep of the day consisted of 19 Hellcats led by Lt Cdr K. G. Hammond, the Skipper of VF-4. Five planes from this group had to return to the carrier due to "mechanical discrepancies." The remaining 14 headed for Okinawa -- another assigned target for the **ESSEX**. The fighters made runs on Yontan and Naha airfields, reporting that *"the operational aircraft observed the day before had been removed or concealed."* (4) In addition, the strike group strafed two FWDs entering Nago Bay, and they caught fire. The Hellcats also seriously damaged two trawlers outside Naha.

The Marines saw their second day of action when Captain E. P. Hartsock led an 8-plane F4U sweep over central Formosa. *"The area was covered with a solid, low overcast which they could not pierce, and no enemy planes were encountered."* [6]

One of the Marine pilots, 1st Lt Donald R. Anderson, flying combat air patrol, crashed into the ocean and was not picked up, *"...cause undetermined."* [6]

At the end of the short shakedown and the first two days of combat in the Formosa-Okinawa area, Air Group 4 could count relatively few successes. The weather had created more problems than the enemy. And we added five names to our list of MIAs -- Marine Lts T. J. Campion and B. W. Bennett, Navy Lt H. T. "Hubbie" Houston, and Marine 1st Lts R. W. "Moon" Mullins and D. R. Anderson.

Chapter 21 | More Strikes on Philippines

"We lost the VF-4 Skipper and 3 Marine pilots, Jan. 6-7, 1945."

January was producing a lot of bad weather and green ink for the pilots of AG-4. Green ink was used in our log books to denote strikes; red ink meant night operations.

Busy schedules meant an increase in complaints. This was a good time to contrast our treatment on the three carriers. The quality of Navy meals was one popular topic of contrast. The food on the *ESSEX* was vastly inferior to that on the *RANGER* or *BUNKER HILL*. Scuttlebutt placed the blame on the ship's supply officer. He wanted the high command to know that he could feed the crew on less -- or maybe he was trying to promote the war effort. We enjoyed coffee and cinnamon toast on the *RANGER* but, even coffee was rationed for flight crews on the *ESSEX*. It became a custom when we dropped anchor in Ulithi to take a short R&R to Mog Mog, and then head for a different ship in the harbor for some decent food. Our next stop in Ulithi would be no different.

The *ESSEX*, however, was not headed back to Ulithi where we could get a good steak. Rather, we were scheduled for more strikes on northern Luzon.

In the meantime our carrier was steaming from Formosa to an attack position off northern Luzon. On January 5, Statler recorded that *"several Jap planes were around the Task Force."* [1] We were constantly harassed by these Japanese bogeys.

More than 50 kamikazes were active against the Naval units carrying MacArthur's troops headed for Luzon. The escort carrier *OMMAN-NEY BAY* was sunk by a suicide plane on Janu-ary 4. On the 5th, kamikazes flew into the cruiser *LOUISVILLE*, CVEs *MANILA BAY* and *SAVO ISLAND*, one destroyer and one destroyer escort. Before the landings on Luzon, scheduled for January 9, Japanese suicide planes had struck two more CVEs (the *KADASHAN BAY* and the *KITKUN BAY*), sunk three minesweepers in Lingayen Gulf, and damaged 2 battleships, 2 cruisers, 2 more destroyers, one APA, and another minesweeper. [2]

"It was blood-curdling to watch a plane aim relentlessly at your ship, its pilot resolved to blast you and himself to hell." [3]

Convoy as Alternate Target -- January 6, 1945

Our first major strike on January 6 was focused on clearing northern Luzon of aircraft and rendering the fields inoperable. The *ESSEX* launched nine F6Fs and 15 TBMs with Aparri airfield as the preferred target.

"The airfield and area assigned to this group was closed in by the weather. Upon orders from Commander Klinsmann the group proceeded westward and crossed the coast near Laoag to attack shipping reported there...." [4]

The AG-4 flight found some excellent targets just west of Laoag. Boykin's fighter division attacked 3 Sugar Charlie type vessels. Otto Klinsmann's Hellcats made strafing and bombing runs on two medium AKs or AOs. Some of the VF then went south to Currimao, exploded a small ammunition ship, and strafed a freighter west of Cabucao. Fighters reported light-to-medium AA fire. [4]

Japanese ships disguised and hiding along the shoreline west of Lapog.
January 6, 1945.

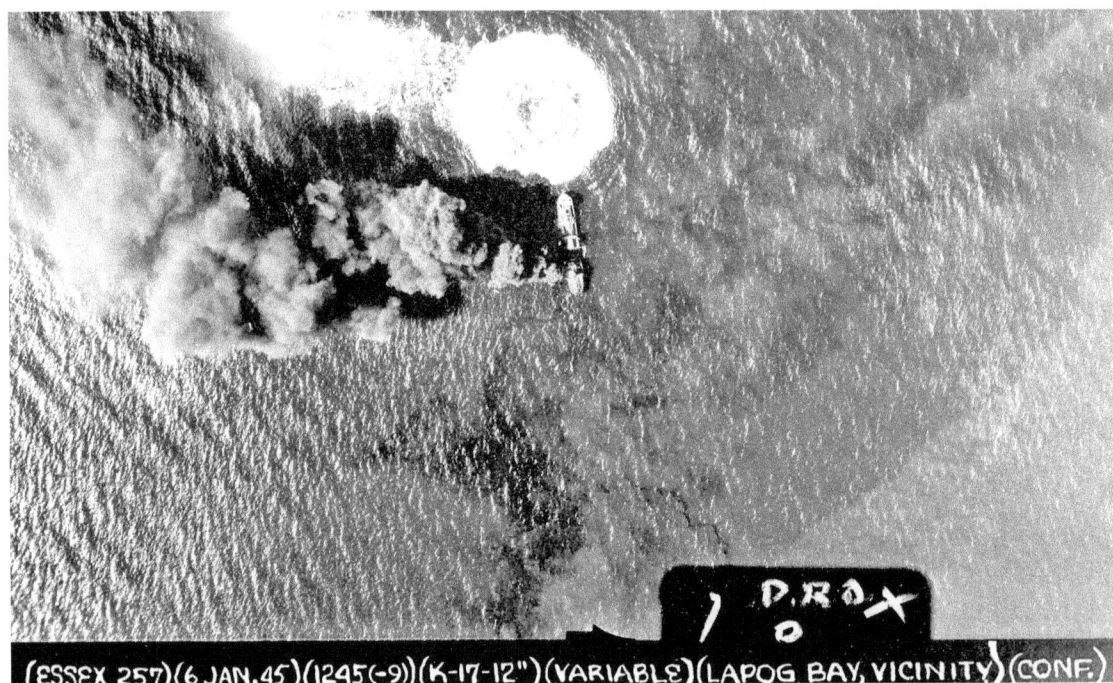

(ESSEX 257)(6 JAN.45)(1245(-9))(K-17-12")(VARIABLE)(LAPOG BAY, VICINITY)(CONF.)

Japanese ship under attack by Torpedo 4, west of Lapog. January 6, 1945.

The tactical organization for Torpedo 4 for this strike was: [4]

Strike -- January 6, 1945

Lee L. "Ham" Hamrick (pilot)
  W. M. Hardin (crew)

Don A. Henry
  E. A. Shirley

Felix E. Ward, Jr.
  Don M. Applegate

E. A. "Ted" Newell
  W. J. Lace

W. J. Hopkins, Jr.
  Stan W. Coller

Will S. Souza
  T. R. Sims

L. A. "Cozy" Cole
  N. H. Knox

B. R. "Trex" Trexler
  C. W. Barr

G. M. Bell
  A. J. Tankard

Robert F. "Bob" Ruth
  C. L. McConnell

L. C. Gray
  J. E. Ganley

Ed S. Binder
  R. D. Biddle

H. J. Deimel
  C. L. Ely, Jr.

G. D. "Mak" Makibbin
  R. Campbell and R. B. Montague

W. H. Cannady, Jr.
  J. C. Gerke

Since Aparri field was ruled out as a target because of weather, the torpedo planes were ordered to attack a convoy previously attacked by other planes from Task Force 38.[4]

"One FTC, 2 SBs, and 5 SDs were found still afloat and underway, scattered along the northwest coast of Luzon close to shore between Darrena Point and Vigan. VT each made 3 individual 35-40 degree glide-bombing attacks on the ships, dropping four bombs per run. The ships attacked by VT were the FTC, 2 SBs, and 1 SD."

"While very many damaging near misses were scored, several direct hits furnished the main contribution to the destruction of the ships attacked."

"Lt Hamrick, leader of the flight, scored two hits amidships on the FTC near the mouth of the Abra river on his third run setting the ship afire."

"Lt(jg) Souza and Lt(jg) Henry each scored two hits on the SB later shown burning."

"An SB was hit by Lt Newell on his third run and by Ens Bell on his second run."

"A camouflaged SD was hit by Lt Trexler and Ens Deimel, each scoring one hit. All four of the ships attacked were heavily strafed by the wing guns of all the VT."

The Japanese ship that Cannady picked out for his bombing run was almost below him. Consequently, his dive was too steep.[5]

"I was forced to make about a 4-G pullout. As we leveled out over the water, the plane lurched. I looked in the mirror, and my gunner, J. C. Gerke, was wiping his forehead. I wondered why. Then I saw the tail of my plane -- the left elevator and stabilizer were gone! Only about 2 inches were left hanging out from the fuselage. No wonder Gerke was shaking his head."

"I was plenty worried because we had a long haul back to the carrier. I did not call in an emergency because the plane seemed to be flying OK. Later, I got chewed out because I did not alert the carrier to

Japanese ships under attack by Torpedo 4 at Lapog Bay. Note the near perfect smoke ring caused by one of the bombs. January 6, 1945.

my condition. I was flying one of those new TBM-3es that had been flown aboard as replacements."

The first strike group from the *ESSEX* had imposed serious damage to a number of Japanese ships. Returning pilots also had enthusiastic praise for the AG-80 **TICONDEROGA** strike in the same area; *"An effective dive bombing attack... with spectacular explosions."* [4]

A 12-plane fighter sweep, launched from the *ESSEX*, arrived near Laoag shortly after the departure of Torpedo 4. This group of Hellcats was under the leadership of Lt Cdr Hammond. *"With their rockets, bombs and .50 calibers they claimed four vessels destroyed and three seriously damaged."* But this was a sad day for "The Red Rippers" as the debriefing report shows. [4]

"During the attack intense light and medium AA fire was experienced from batteries along the shore. In the second attack Lt Cdr Hammond's plane was mortally damaged by heavy AA in the engine and empennage. Lt Laird's plane received a 20-mm shell aft of the cockpit which did considerable damage."

"As the flight rendezvoused out to sea from Darrena Point Lt Cdr Hammond reported that his oil pressure was decreasing rapidly and that he was going to try to make the Lingayen Gulf area. As he made his way south the planes in the flight joined up on him. When about 8 miles southwest of Vigan Lt Cdr Hammond turned his plane into the wind for a water landing when his engine froze. The landing was made in a slightly nose down attitude and without dropping the belly tank."

"At the moment of impact there was a flash believed to have been caused by the explosion of the belly tank and the plane skipped or cartwheeled. The plane sank in a matter of a few seconds and the only trace

on the surface was an oil slick and part of the belly tank. The aircraft circled the area for 20 minutes but nothing was observed on the surface in the area."

Marine units from VMF 213 and 124 were also launched from the **ESSEX** on January 6. Major W. E. Crowe led a fighter sweep directed at Aparri, but diverted to secondary targets due to weather. The Corsairs strafed some small merchant ships and warehouse facilities at the mouth of Aparri River but clouds obscured the results. No airborne enemy aircraft were encountered. [6]

Aparri Airfield -- January 7, 1945

For the second time, the assigned mission for *ESSEX* planes was to knock out all enemy airborne aircraft and any aircraft found at Aparri airfield.

"Eleven VF and 12 VT were scheduled, all VF and 11 VT rendezvoused and proceeded to the target area in a slow climb to 11,000 feet at 145 knots true airspeed."

"Upon reaching the target area one division of VF remained high as cover, and the remaining divisions ordered to precede the VT in a rocket and bombing attack. VF divisions took turns acting as cover while remaining divisions made rocket and strafing runs...." [4]

The Torpedo 4 tactical organization was as follows: [4]

Strike Able -- January 7, 1945

P. J. Davis, Jr. (pilot)
  N. J. Schmolke (crew)

C. N. W. "Scott" Vogt
  Leo E. Halvorson

G. M. "Buck" Barnett
  C. Christopher

W. F. "Willie" Walker
  S. A. Hastings

Page P. Stephens
  A. Beard

Strike Able -- January 7, 1945 (continued)

J. E. Hewitt
  C. W. Lathrop

Gerald W. "Jerry" Thomas (returned to base)
  J. E. Holloman and R. B. Montague

R. M. "Hoppy" Hopfinger
  A. W. Yarman

B. R. "Trex" Trexler
  J. W. Aldrich

G. M. Bell
  R. R. Pittman

Robert F. "Bob" Ruth
  C. L. McConnell

H. J. Deimel
  L. S. Leach

Shortly after I became airborne, Gress and Montague called me on the intercom to report a gas leak. I was forced to jettison my bombs and return to the carrier after the remainder of the strike group had been launched. My return meant that photographic coverage of the strike would be limited. The other Avengers, with Davis leading, climbed to 11,000 feet and proceeded to the target in stepped-down diamond formations.[4]

"VT attacked Aparri airstrip from east to west, pushing over from 9000 feet and employing glides ranging from 35 to 45 degrees. Average speed in glide was approximately 310 knots indicated. Practically all bombs dropped hit the runway and severely cratered it. The strip was left entirely unserviceable, at least temporarily. During the attack VF heavily strafed dispersal areas adjoining the runway, the revetments at the west end of the runway, and the silent antiaircraft positions flanking the strip."

The strike group reported two probable Zekes and one twin-engine bomber among the five aircraft on the ground. Two wrecks or dummies were also reported.

A fighter sweep led by Boykin arrived at Aparri shortly after the strike group. These Hellcats also attacked the field and support facilities. *"Tutwiler noticed an SB anchored in the river nearby and dropped his bomb on it, scoring a hit."* [4]

This was the worst day to date for the new Marine pilots. Capt W. J. Thomas led a target CAP, consisting of eight F4Us, toward Aparri in *"exceptionally foul weather in which the flight became separated, and three members, apparently lost, are reported missing in action, and two others were rescued after forced landings when their fuel became exhausted. Thomas, alone, found Aparri Airfield and strafed it."* [6]

The three pilots who got lost in the overcast and crashed at sea were:

- 1st Lt Robert M. Dorsett
- 1st Lt Daniel K. Mortag
- 2nd Lt Mike Kochat

The two pilots who ditched were 2nd Lt Robert D. Green and 2nd Lt William H. Cloward. These Marine pilots were rescued, after about one hour, by the destroyer, *USS COTTON*.

One of our Torpedo planes, evidently damaged by AA fire, had trouble with the approach and landing. This Avenger crashed into the barrier and was so badly damaged that it had to be pushed overboard. When word spread that there was no room on the hangar deck for repairs, one of our mechanics jumped into the cockpit and quickly disconnected the clock. The TBM was shoved off the fantail and hit the water on its back. The extended wheels reminded me of a dead duck with feet in the air. In a few seconds, the TBM sank and the ship sent word to the fleet commander to order a replacement.

Clark Field--January 7, 1945

In spite of the bad weather, with five planes from the *ESSEX* already down, another strike was launched at 1300 hours. This strike consisted of nine Hellcats and nine Avengers. A new target was assigned -- Clark Field on Luzon. Under Cdr Otto Klinsmann's leadership, the target was located.[4]

"VF were ordered to attack, followed immediately by VT. Commander Klinsmann led his division down from 12,000 feet, attacking from south to north, pulling out at 3,000 feet, and followed VT in another strafing run from north to south."

VF bombed, rocketed, and strafed enemy aircraft at the field. Tonys, Sallys, and unidentified T/E bombers were observed.

The Torpedo 4 tactical organization was: [4]

Strike Baker -- January 7, 1945

Lee L. "Ham" Hamrick (pilot) (returned to base)
  W. M. Hardin (crew)

Don A. Henry
  A. G. Schiesz

Felix E. Ward, Jr.
  C. J. Warrington

Vernon A. Landre
  A. "Tony" DeCenso

E. A. "Ted" Newell
  D. E. Venderville

W. J. Hopkins, Jr.
  R. E. Simendinger, Jr.

Will S. Souza
  T. R. Sims

L. A. "Cozy" Cole
  N. L. Shiverdecker

Ed S. Binder (downed, gas leak)
  R. D. Biddle and W. D. Jenkins

W. H. Cannady, Jr.
  J. C. Gerke

Lt Newell assumed the lead of the Torpedo squadron when Ham's propeller started "surging," and he was forced to go back aboard.[4]

"Nine VT took off and rendezvoused without incident, but Lt Hamrick returned to base shortly after takeoff because propeller was surging. Lt Newell then assumed lead of the VT."

The strike group *"proceeded to target area at 12,000 feet at 150 knots indicated."* As the flight approached Clark Field, 2 Oscars and 2 Frances attacked the torpedo planes. Three of our turret gunners, Warrington, Simendinger, and Venderville, claimed hits and damage to one of the Frances. This damage was confirmed, but no kill was credited to VT-4 crewmen.

The attack on Clark Field was made from northwest to southeast.

"...pushing over from 10,000 feet. VT acquired an average speed of 330 knots in glides varying from 30 to 40 degrees. Two VT dropped on the wooded dispersal area between runways #1 and #2, 2 VT dropped on the barracks immediately west of runway #2, and 4 VT attacked the revetment area between runways #1 and #3. Of the last 4 VT, one was unable to get his bombs to release over target and later jettisoned them over water. In all 32 clusters were jettisoned, including those mentioned above and those of the pilot returning to base early."

"Antiaircraft fire over the target was intense, and though none of the VT were hit, several aircraft of Task Force 38 flying low over target were observed to be shot down." [4]

Deck crew examine chart of operations painted on island bulkhead of *USS ESSEX*.
January, 1945.

Mail being transferred from an unidentified destroyer to *USS ESSEX*. March 29, 1945.

Chapter 22 | US Landings on Luzon

"Mr. Cole ordered me to jump.... Thank God, Mr. Cole didn't leave the plane."

Torpedo Four had a one-day break from strike assignments on January 8, while the **ESSEX** was refueling and receiving replacement aircraft. We brought aboard two new torpedo pilots and two air crewmen for VT-4 and several Marine and fighter replacements.

I wrote home to Walter, *"Say Bud, isn't it just about time you turned out one of those typing masterpieces? Golly, all the fellows are wondering what happened to you -- Has Ranger bucked you off again?"*

January 9, 1945, was D-Day for the US Invasion of Luzon. Task Force 38, Halsey's Third Fleet, supported the invasion with air attacks on Formosa and Luzon. Admiral Kincaid's Seventh Fleet, with some 600 vessels of which 18 were Escort Carriers (CVEs), was more directly involved in close Naval coverage for the troop landings.

> *"Some sixty-eight thousand Americans began clambering ashore on the vulnerable Lingayen beaches in what became the largest United States land campaign of the Pacific War. More American forces were engaged on Luzon than in either Africa or Italy."* [1]

During the invasion, the Japanese flew many Kamikaze one-way missions against the landing fleet, sinking one escort carrier, the **OMMANNEY BAY**, and damaging several other ships of the Third Fleet.

Einansho -- January 9, 1945

The first strike assignment for the **ESSEX** air group on "D-Day - Luzon" was launched at 0715. There were 15 Avengers and 9 Hellcats scheduled with the charge.[2]

> *"...to destroy air facilities at enemy fields in west central Formosa. Because of the thick overcast extending from 700 feet to 8000 feet this flight was unable to locate fields in the assigned area and therefore attacked a more southerly location, Tainan (EINANSHO) airfield. This target was covered with three cloud layers; bases at 12,000 feet; 7000 feet and 4000 feet respectively...."*

The Torpedo 4 tactical organization consisted of: [2]

Strike Able -- January 9, 1945

P. J. Davis, Jr. (pilot)
   R. F. Gray (crew)

C. N. W. "Scott" Vogt
   R. E. Kelly

G. M. "Buck" Barnett
   C. Christopher

W. F. "Willie" Walker
   G. F. Zeimer

Page P. Stephens (downed, no hydraulics)
   Andy "Marge" Mocsary

Vernon A. Landre (downed, gasoline leak)
   Charlie C. Statler

Gerald W. "Jerry" Thomas
   J. E. Holloman and R. B. Montague

R. M. "Hoppy" Hopfinger
   A. W. Yarman

Lee L. "Ham" Hamrick
   R. A. Trembley

Don A. Henry
   E. A. Shirley

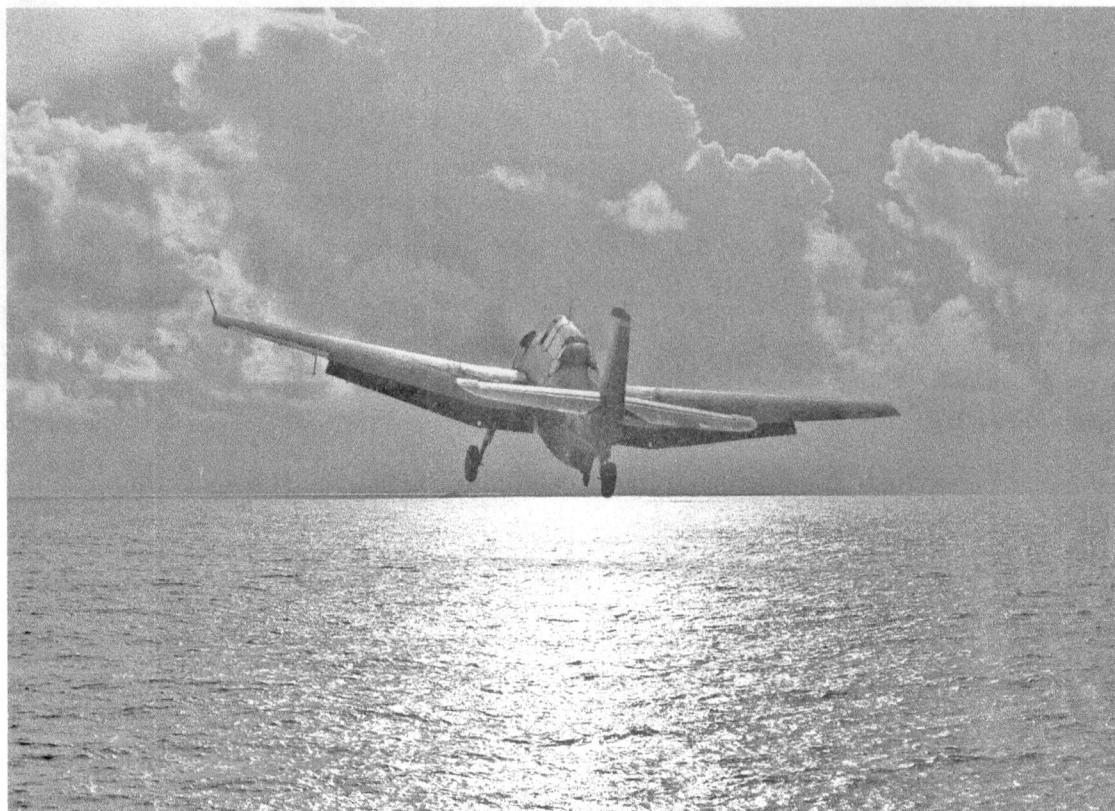

Torpedo 4 Avenger takes off from *USS ESSEX*. Undated photo.

20 mm anti-aircraft battery in action against Japanese aircraft.
USS ESSEX. March, 1945.

Strike Able -- January 9, 1945 (continued)

Felix E. Ward, Jr.
  Don M. Applegate

J. E. Hewitt
  L. P. Shuman

Ed S. Binder
  W. D. Jenkins

H. J. Deimel
  C. L. Ely, Jr.

Robert F. "Bob" Ruth
  C. L. McConnell

The 13 Avengers that got off the deck rendez-voused without incident and proceeded to the target area with the Hellcats as escort.[2]

"Though the assigned mission was to crater the landing ground at Kagi airfield on Formosa, the only break in the overcast was in the vicinity of Tainan and the flight chose Einansho (Tainan) airfield as the alternate target."

"VT attacked Einansho airfield from northeast to southwest pushing over from 8000 feet just below a solid overcast and conducted a glide-bombing attack through the undercast at 1500 feet. Glides varied from 30 to 45 degrees and average speed acquired in glide was 310 knots indicated. One VT pilot failed to drop and was instructed not to return singly and make a run on the field because of the intensity and accuracy of the antiaircraft fire; his bombs were jettisoned over water."

"Anti-aircraft fire came not only from the air field but from the countryside all along the flight path on approach to and retirement from target and from a DD at Tainan."

Seven of the Hellcats that escorted the Avengers to Einansho swung south over the Formosa East Coast. Outside Takao harbor, they spotted a large concentration of Japanese shipping.[2]

"Attacking through a barrage of heavy and medium AA from the destroyers, the VF strafed both warships as well as the tanker. Results were not fully observed."

A separate strike group of 11 Marine Corsairs was also dispatched to south central Formosa.

No airborne opposition was encountered but the flight strafed 18-20 aircraft on the ground at Kaputsua airfield. By this time the Marines had agreed to carry 500-pound bombs on their F4Us. These were dropped through the overcast over Tochein Harbor, resulting in at least one fire.[3] For the first time, all Corsairs returned to the ***ESSEX***.

Toyohara Airfield -- January 9, 1945

The second major strike of the day for the air group was launched at 1241 hours. This strike consisted of 12 F6Fs and 12 TBMs, but only 9 TBMs made the target. The weather was still bad and the assigned target, Kagi airfield, Formosa, was covered with clouds. [2]

"The group turned north, seeking better weather and a feasible target. When in the vicinity of Toyohara A/F the weather opened up and presented excellent opportunities for attack...."

The Torpedo 4 tactical organization consisted of: [2]

Strike Baker -- January 9, 1945

P. J. Davis, Jr. (pilot)
  N. J. Schmolke (crew)

G. D. "Mak" Makibbin
  R. Campbell and R. B. Montague

W. H. Cannady, Jr.
  J. C. Gerke

Page P. Stephens
  Andy "Marge" Mocsary

B. R. "Trex" Trexler (downed, tail chewed up)
  C. W. Barr

G. M. Bell
  R. R. Pittman

Strike Baker -- January 9, 1945 (continued)

Will S. Souza (downed, engine cutting out)
  T. R. Sims

L. C. Gray
  H. R. Green

E. A. "Ted" Newell (returned to base)
  D. E. Venderville

W. J. Hopkins, Jr.
  Stan W. Coller

Gerald W. "Jerry" Thomas
  J. E. Holloman

L. A. "Cozy" Cole
  N. L. Shiverdecker

Our Skipper, P. J. Davis, led the 9 Avengers that were able to rendezvous after the launch. Due to the overcast we were forced to join up at a low level, and then climb as a formation through the soup. We had to reach about 17,000 feet, on oxygen, to clear the Formosa mountains and the thick cloud layer. Kagi airfield was ruled out by the Air Group Commander.[2]

"Through a break in the undercast, Toyohara was spotted and VT attacked the airfield from southeast to northwest pushing over from 10,000 feet. VT employed glides varying from 35 to 45 degrees and acquired an average speed of 290 knots in glide."

"...the cratering was as effective as could be expected. One of the 500-pound GP bombs dropped by Ensign Bell struck a single-engine aircraft parked on the landing area and demolished it. Stray bombs fired unidentified buildings in the hangar-barracks area immediately west of the landing area."

"VT rendezvoused just west of Toyohara Satellite airstrip and proceeded toward base. Over the mountains VT became separated in the clouds and returned to base in scattered groups but without incident. From the eastern side of Formosa to the task force, the clouds were solid from 8000 feet down to 500 feet, with general rain squalls throughout the area."

I was not alone in expressing relief when the carrier came into view. We were darned glad to get back to the carrier without any losses, although three Torpedo 4 Avengers had been hit with anti-aircraft fire. We were fortunate that our Avengers seldom caught fire, could absorb AA damage, and still fly back to base.

Cozy Cole was flying one of the TBMs that got hit. Ack Ack knocked the glass out of the canopy cover. His crewman, Shiverdecker, stated: [4]

"Mr. Cole ordered me to jump. I saw all those trees and canyons down below, so I delayed the bail out. Thank God, Mr. Cole didn't leave the plane. Our radio went out, so some fighters picked us up and escorted us back to the carrier. We ran out of gas taxiing to the elevator."

The weather on Formosa had certainly not been cooperative. But then, while it restricted the effectiveness of our attacks, it also limited the ability of the Japanese airmen to support the Luzon landings. We had only one report of encounters with enemy airborne aircraft by VF-4 on January 9.[5]

"Burnett and Zdancewicz, on a search to the north, surprised a Val by itself, and quickly set it afire. Hecklers tried to convince them it was a Jap cadet on his first flight."

Chapter 23 | The South China Sea

"The combined effect of the VT and VF attacks was devastating."

Task Force 38 Takes a Risk

After these last strikes on Formosa, Admiral "Bull" Halsey made the decision to take TF-38 into the South China Sea. This was a high-risk move, creating much discussion and wonderment among our pilots. The Admiral was evidently looking for a major part of the Japanese fleet, including two aircraft carriers. We were headed for Camranh Bay, Saigon, and Hong Kong. Robert Sherrod, *Time* magazine correspondent, came aboard the *ESSEX* to follow the action. Sherrod reported.[1]

"The venture into the South China Sea was as audacious as it was unlikely. Who ever heard of taking all your ships into a pond surrounded by Kamikazes on four sides? If the enemy had a fanatical bone in his body, now was his chance to throw himself at his tormentor. If he was looking for targets here they were -- 11 carriers, 6 battleships, 13 cruisers and 48 destroyers, plus a night-carrier group (2 carriers), and, of all things, a fragile tanker force whose sinking would leave the whole fleet helpless."

Our task force moved through Bashi channel into the South China Sea at night on January 9. Admiral Halsey wrote that *"...it is hard for me to realize that we slipped past the Japs."* [2] As was his custom, Halsey flashed a message over the teletype to the Ready Room, where we were being briefed with maps and data on French Indo-China: "WE MAY HAVE A GOLDEN OPPORTUNITY TOMORROW TO COMPLETELY ANNIHILATE AN IMPORTANT ENEMY FORCE. YOU ALL KNOW THAT IS WHAT I EXPECT OF YOU. GIVE THEM HELL. GOD BLESS YOU ALL. HALSEY." [1]

As TF-38 was moving into the South China Sea -- a noteworthy event for the Navy -- MacArthur's soldiers went ashore at Lingayen Gulf. The Army issued a big news release on January 10, 1945.[3] The 15 ships that were sunk by Halsey's planes while we were in the South China Sea did not command the attention of General MacArthur's accomplishments. This was another example of the effectiveness of the General's public relations staff.

Those of us on the flight line were not familiar with the intricacies of the decision-making process; nor were we in on the inside discussions or conflicts between the various levels of command. Through scuttlebutt, however, we heard about the differences of opinion between Admiral Nimitz and General Douglas MacArthur. We also knew that each time the Navy made a major attack that might get publicity back home, General MacArthur countered with some kind of publicity stunt. MacArthur was always wading ashore, recapturing lost ground, or reporting other major victories to command the attention of the American press.

Within the Navy itself, we devised ways to complain about our circumstances and the lack of attention to the risks we were undertaking by the High Command. For example, one of our favorite songs was as follows:

They sent for MacArthur to go to Talagi
but General MacArthur said no.
He gave as the reason,
It wasn't the season,
Besides there was no USO.

Bless them all, bless them all.
Bless the long and the short and the tall.
Bless all the admirals in COMAIRSOPAC.
They don't give a damn if we never get back.
So, we're saying good-bye to them all....

Stills from film taken by R. B. Montague of torpedo strike by Thomas on a tanker. Still 2 shows the torpedo hitting the water (Thomas' plane circled). Still 7 show's Thomas' plane flying over a Japanese cargo ship (see below), which opened up on the Avenger with AA.
Cap St. Jacques. French Indo-China. January 12, 1945.

The Japanese cargo ship overflown by Thomas following the successful torpedo drop on the tanker. Photo by J. E. Holloman.
Cap St. Jacques. French Indo-China. January 12, 1945.

And so on. This was one way to let off some steam after we returned from a strike. Someone also composed an apropos song about Navy pilots entitled, "I Wanted Wings." This was also a favorite.

I wanted wings till I got the goddamn things,
Now I don't want them anymore!
They taught me how to fly, then they sent me here to die,
I've had a belly full of war.
You can save those Zeros for the goddamn heroes,
Distinguished Flying Crosses do not compensate for losses.
Brother, I wanted wings till I got the goddamn things,
Now I don't want them anymore.

I'll take the dames, while the rest go down in flames,
I've no desire to be burned.
Air combat's called romance, but it's made me wet my pants,
I'm not a hero I have learned.
You can save those Mitsubishis for the goddamn sons of bitches,
Cause I'd rather date a woman than be shot down in a Grumman.
Brother, I wanted wings till I got the goddamn things,

Now I don't want them anymore.
I don't want to die in a goddamn PBY,
That's for the eagers, not for me.
I'll not trust my luck to be picked up by a Duck,
After I've crashed into the sea.
Oh, I'd rather be a bellhop than a flyer on a flat top,
With my hand around a bottle not around the goddamn throttle.
Brother, I wanted wings till I got the goddamn things,
Now I don't want them anymore!

Torpedos in Saigon Harbor -- January 12, 1945

There was very little time for singing songs or playing poker on the evening of January 11, 1945. After chow, we had to report for briefings, distribution of Chinese currency, and other last minute preparations. January 12 was to be the first carrier-based naval air strike against French Indo-China (South Vietnam).

General Quarters was sounded at 0655. Night fighters from the *ENTERPRISE* and *INDEPENDENCE* were already out on a search for Japanese ships along the Indo-China coast.[1] They reported no enemy shipping in the Camranh Bay area. In the meantime the Free French underground radioed that there was plenty of shipping in the Saigon River, including a cruiser. The *TICONDEROGA's* strike force sank a convoy composed of 2 large oilers, 2 medium oilers, and 3 destroyer escorts.[3]

The *ESSEX* launched Marine Corsairs for Combat Air Patrol over the Task Force early in the morning. Later in the day, VMF 124 and VMF 213 participated in fighter sweeps over Saigon and attacks on several airfields as well as shipping along the Saigon River.

The primary morning strike group launched from the *ESSEX* included 12 Hellcats, loaded with rockets and 1000-pound bombs, and 14 Avengers loaded with torpedoes. Our target was enemy shipping and shore installations along the Saigon River near Cap St. Jacques. Commander Klinsmann was designated as target coordinator.

"On the way to the target the flight observed planes from the USS TICONDEROGA and other ships in the task force attacking a convoy between CAPE PADARAN and PT. KEGA. The group commander checked with the target coordinator and upon being informed that no help was needed, he continued on to the assigned area. Before arriving the flight had the report of the target CAP, and they were ordered to meet the incoming flight and strafed DEs and other ships firing while strike group delivered attacks." [3]

The twelve TBMs from VT-4 rendezvoused at 1000 feet and proceeded toward Saigon at 0800. We were led by P. J. Davis. The Torpedo 4 tactical organization was: [4]

Strike Able -- January 12, 1945

P. J. Davis, Jr. (pilot)
R. F. Gray (crew)

C. N. W. "Scott" Vogt
Leo E. Halvorson

G. M. "Buck" Barnett
Joseph C. Cohen

Photo shows masts of tanker sunk by Thomas and cargo ship under attack.
An VT-4 Avenger is visible in the upper right. Cap St. Jacques in the
background. January 12, 1945.

Another view of the sunk tanker and cargo ship. Cap St. Jacques. January 12, 1945.

Strike Able -- January 12, 1945 (continued)

W. F. "Willie" Walker
S. A. Hastings

Ed S. Binder
W. D. Jenkins

H. J. Deimel
C. L. Ely, Jr.

G. D. "Mak" Makibbin
R. Campbell and R. B. Montague

W. H. Cannady, Jr.
J. C. Gerke

Page P. Stephens
A. Beard

Vernon A. Landre (downed, tail chewed up)
A. "Tony" DeCenso

Gerald W. "Jerry" Thomas
J. E. Holloman

R. M. "Hoppy" Hopfinger
A. W. Yarman

Robert F. "Bob" Ruth
C. L. McConnell

As we approached the coast of Indo-China, we were directed to attack shipping at Cap St. Jacques.

"A convoy was intercepted which consisted of two FOX TARE BAKERS and one SUGAR ABLE preceded by several escort vessels... VT crossed Cap St. Jacques peninsula southeast to northwest then cut back for advantageous attack position initiating the attack from NNW to SSE."

"Torpedoes were dropped at 250 feet altitude, average speed of aircraft being 250 knots indicated. Dropping range was short but sufficient for torpedoes to arm. The first division attacked a FOX TARE BAKER and the torpedoes of Lt Davis, Lt(jg) Vogt, and Lt(jg) Barnett found their mark; the fourth torpedo hooked left." [3]

With Hoppy on my wing, I swung south in order to get a better torpedo run on a 10,000-ton tanker. Our approach was ideal in spite of the distraction of antiaircraft fire. I released my torpedo, turned to avoid the tanker, and flew directly over a Fox Tare Baker. I dipped up and down in evasive action. I could see the gunners on the ship shooting at me. Just as I cleared the ship, Holloman took a picture, and the ship exploded from someone else's torpedo.

"Holloman called to say that the tanker we had attacked also had exploded. **"Turn back, turn back,"** *he shouted,* **"I can get a good picture!"** *I turned only to find that the AA fire had intensified and I was now a lone target, so I told Holloman,* **"The heck with the pictures! We're headed out to sea!"**

This was one of the best torpedo attacks for VT-4 of the entire war. We went in slow -- around 250 knots -- and dropped at about the right distance from the ships. All of our fish ran true, with only two missing good targets. The operations report, prepared after our return to the **ESSEX** states.[3]

"The torpedoes of Lt(jg) Thomas and Ens Hopfinger struck the SUGAR ABLE, while the performance of a third torpedo fired at this ship was unobserved. The second FOX TARE BAKER received three torpedoes dropped by Lt(jg) Makibbin, Ens Deimel, and Ens Cannady; the performance of a fourth torpedo dropped on this ship was unobserved. Lt(jg) Binder, noting that all the larger vessels were under attack, proceeded southward a short distance and dropped on a DE scoring a hit. All of the ships attacked by VT were sunk...."

"During the attack VT were met with intense antiaircraft fire from the escort vessels and from the hills near the targets...."

"The combined effect of the VT and VF attacks was devastating. When the **ESSEX** *planes retired, all ships had been sunk or beached...."*

Japanese ship sinking after being struck by a VT-4 torpeodo.
Cap St. Jacques. January 12, 1945.

Chapter 24 | Saigon Takes Its Toll

"Suddenly, the executions stopped. Two Americans remained alive -- Ens Quinn and Vincent Grady."

The **ESSEX** launched Strike Baker at 1330 on January 12, 1945, to attack enemy air facilities, shipping, and shore installations in Saigon Harbor. The admiral wanted to make every minute of our stay in the South China Sea as effective as possible.

Robert Sherrod, *Time* magazine correspondent, was on board to record fleet action. He chose to make the flight with Torpedo 4 to gather firsthand information for his report. We all thought he was crazy to take this unnecessary chance, when interviews with the returning flyers would have sufficed. But Bob Sherrod had been on other dangerous missions during his excellent coverage of the war in the Pacific and he didn't seem concerned. We checked him out with a life jacket and parachute harness, and placed him with an experienced pilot, Lt B. R. Trexler. Also accompanying us on this strike was 2nd Lt Hal Goodwin, the Marine groups' Public Relations Officer. He flew with the strike leader, Lt Hamrick.

This strike group consisted of 14 Avengers and 12 Hellcats for escort. Lt L. M. Boykin led the first VF division with Lt N. P. Byrd, Jr., and Lt W. W. Taylor leading the other 4-plane fighter divisions. All F6Fs were loaded with 1000-pound bombs.

The VF-4 planes rendezvoused with the VT-4 flight and with TBMs and F6Fs from the **USS SAN JACINTO**. Because of a low overcast extending from the task force disposition almost to the coast, the group flew at 1000 feet until about 5 miles from the Asiatic mainland, then climbed to 14,000 feet.[1]

"On the way to the target area, pilots saw many burning ships along the French Indo-China coast from Camranh Bay to Cap St. Jacques."

"When the flight reached the harbor area in the Saigon River east and southeast of Saigon, pilots saw a light cruiser lying on its side in shallow water. This ship [was] sunk by an earlier TF-38 attack."

Five Hellcats from Boykin's Fighting 4 group dropped their 1000-pounders on a large AK which was already burning. Taylor scored a direct hit and there were several other damaging near-misses. *"One bomb fell close aboard an AO in the same vicinity."*

*"One division of the 12 **ESSEX's** VF also strafed oil storage tanks, causing fire (and) thick black smoke to rise from at least two such installations...."* [1]

Marine Corsairs were also called in for this strike against Saigon. They scored direct bomb hits on a Fox Tare Charlie and a Sugar Charlie Able. The Fox Tare Charlie sank. VMF 124 *"probably destroyed or damaged 20 planes on the ground."* [2]

The Corsair flown by 2nd Lt Joseph O. Lynch, VMF-124, was hit with small-arms fire, causing engine failure.[1]

"He made a successful landing three miles west of Trang-Bang, French Indo-China... and was last observed, apparently uninjured, standing on the ground next to his plane.... It was impossible to conduct rescue operations due to the active antiaircraft positions, however, Lt Lynch is reported in friendly hands.

Lynch was picked up by a native policeman who smuggled him to a French colonial outpost. There he met up with the Don Henry, also downed

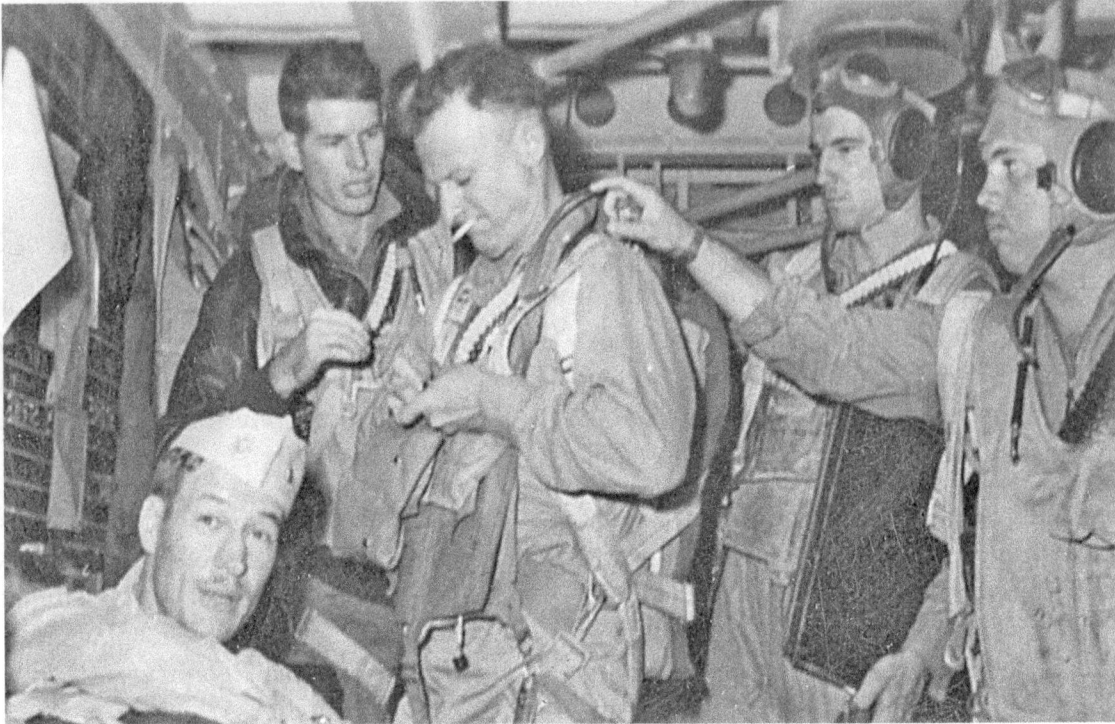

Lt Hamrick helps *Time* correspondent Robert Sherrod adjust his parachute for Saigon strike. W. J. Hopkins and F. H. Bissell look on. Thomas looking at the camera. January 12, 1945.

Torpedo 4 strikes crosses shoreline on its way to Saigon strike. January 12, 1945.

that day.[4]

VMF-213 attack groups, led by Lt Col Millington and Major Johnson, strafed Bien Hoa and Long Trank Airfields and several ships. One ship took a direct hit by a Corsair carrying a 500-pound bomb.[2]

The 14 torpedo planes from the *ESSEX* were led into the Saigon area by Lt Hamrick. The VT-4 tactical organization was: [1]

Strike Baker -- January 12, 1945

Lee L. "Ham" Hamrick (pilot)
  W. M. Hardin and H. L. Goodwin (crew)

Don A. Henry
  E. A. Shirley

Felix E. Ward, Jr.
  C. J. Warrington

J. E. Hewitt
  C. W. Lathrop

F. H. Bissell
  W. H. Moore

E. A. "Ted" Newell
  W. J. Lace

W. J. Hopkins, Jr.
  R. E. Simendinger, Jr.

Will S. Souza
  T. R. Sims

L. A. "Cozy" Cole
  N. H. Knox

B. R. "Trex" Trexler
  C. W. Barr and Robert Sherrod

G. M. Bell
  A. J. Tankard

Keith Gardner
  W. A. DeYoung

L. C. Gray
  J. E. Ganley

Vernon A. Landre
  A. "Tony" DeCenso

Since Vernon Landre was cancelled from the morning flight because another plane chewed up his tail during the taxi, he was reassigned to Strike Baker. All TBMs were loaded with four 500-pound bombs.[1]

> *"...VT went inland and approached the city of Saigon from east northeast and initiated their attack from that direction. VT pushed over from 8500 feet and acquired an average speed in glide of 290 knots indicated while employing glides of 40-55 degrees. Though there was damaged shipping at Saigon, all ships attacked by VT were previously undamaged."*

> *"Lt Hamrick, while in a glide on an FTC (not shown on chart) in the river above the city, found himself in an unfavorable position for attack. Observing an oil storage concentration across the river, he pulled out and released his bombs on the storage at 1000 feet in a 10-degree glide. The oil storage blew up, the explosion rising above the altitude of the plane."*

Pictures of these oil storage tank explosions were widely circulated in later press releases. Ham stated: [5]

> *"When I dropped my wing to go into the dive, I was past my target. I spotted a dozen oil storage tanks up to the north of us -- so I circled and dropped my four 500-pounders on them. What an explosion! The marine correspondent, Goodwin, who was in the belly, was firing that little .30 caliber machine gun between picture taking. He started shouting, **"I blew up the tanks! I blew up the tanks with my 30!"** Of course, he was disappointed when he found out it was our four bombs that did the job, and not his peashooter."*

The rest of Hamrick's group also gave a good accounting of themselves. Ens Hewitt and Ens Bissell selected a Fox Tare Baker, which was tied up 200 yards up Arroyo L'Avalanche from the Saigon River. One of Hewitt's *"500-pound GP bombs hit*

Torpedo 4 strikes approaches Saigon. January 12, 1945.

Burning oil tanks. Saigon. January 12, 1945.

Japanese ships burning and sinking after Torpedo 4 attack.
Saigon River, French Indo-China.
January 12, 1945.

Another shot of the burning oil tanks. This photo was widely published in the
United States. Saigon. January 12, 1945.

A light cruiser lies capsized beside a supply pier. Jean-Claude Surleau states that this was the
French light cruiser *Lamotte Picquet*.[4] Why was it attacked? To my knowledge, none of our pilots
knew there were any "friendlies" in the area. We assumed all ships were Japanese or Japanese
controlled. (Wikipedia states the ship was disarmed and abandoned.) Saigon. January 12, 1945.

directly amidships. Ens Bissell, attacking the same ship, also scored one hit amidships."

Other sections of the debriefing report state: [1]

"Lt(jg) Ward and Ens Landre attacked a FOX BAKER at Saigon immediately below the confluence of Arroyo L'Avalanche and the Saigon river. Lt(jg) Ward placed one bomb directly amidships and Ens Landre put one on the stern. The remainder of their bombs fell in the adjoining Saigon Navy Yard and Arsenal and fired several unidentified buildings."

"Ens Bell dropped on a SUGAR ABLE, underway and heading downstream, straddling the ship. One of the bombs was a damaging near-miss, and though debris was seen to fly from the ship with the bomb explosion, no smoke or fire was seen."

"Ens Hopkins attacked a FOX TARE BAKER, underway and heading downstream, scoring two hits, one on the bow and one on the #2 cargo hatch. Lt(jg) Souza hit the next ship down the river, a FOX TARE CHARLIE, with one 500-pound GP bomb directly amidships."

"Three VT attacked the FOX BAKER, underway and heading upstream, which was the ship next in line down the river. The first of Lt Trexler's widely spaced bombs struck the ship aft of the superstructure while one other fell in the water and the remaining two fired two or more warehouses across the river. Ens Cole and Ens Gray missed."

"Lt Newell dropped on a FOX ABLE, stationary and heading downstream, scoring a hit with one of his bombs on #4 cargo hatch. Ens Gardner, attacking the same ship, missed."

Time correspondent Robert Sherrod summed up the results of our strikes, *"By any accounting*

12 January, 1945, must be regarded as one of the great days of the US Navy." [3]

Fate of Don Henry and E. A. Shirley

The next part of the official report is subject to controversy. This concerns the fate of Lt(jg) Don Henry. The debriefing report states:

"As aircraft retired, Lt(jg) Henry called the flight leader stating that he had not released his bombs and requested permission to make another run. The flight leader suggested a target, but his message was not acknowledged. No more was heard from the plane. (Note: On return to base a TBM from another carrier joined up making correct count. Hence, plane was not noted missing until well after departure from target.) It is not known what target Lt(jg) Henry attacked."

Since Ham was leading this TBM flight, I asked him to describe what happened. He stated, *"D. A. called and said his bombs did not release, and he was going back. I told him not to go back -- to wait for fighter cover! But, he broke off anyway and went back toward Saigon. We never heard any more but, I assumed he dropped and rejoined the group."* [5]

Allowing ample time for Don Henry to return to the carrier, the **ESSEX** made contact with the other carriers in TF-38 to see if Don had landed on another ship. No reports were received and no one saw Don after he left the VT-4 formation, nor was fighter cover provided for his return to Saigon.

There were some strange circumstances surrounding this incident. Both Don and his crewman, E. A. Shirley, had taken extra survival kits and extra guns aboard the TBM. Was this a premonition, or had they made other plans?

VT-4 pilots and crew made comments after the Saigon strike about the unusual precautions taken by Henry and Shirley. Hamrick stated: [5]

"You know, D. A. had gathered up his coins and his bridge cards. He was going to teach the French how to play bridge when he went down. He was prepared with extra survival gear. But, I was afraid if D. A. was caught by the Japs he would try to fight his way out."

T. R. Sims, one of Souza's crewmen, also noted: [6]

"There were five or six of us playing poker in the back of the Ready Room. Shirley came up the night before that strike and asked how much silver we had. He said, **'They don't take paper money over there in case you get shot down. I want all of the silver you can give me.'** *So we must have given him 40 or 50 dollars worth of silver. He said,* **'Because I'm not coming back.'** *Those were his exact words.* **'I'm not coming back from this trip."***

When we reached the States in April of 1945, I went home on leave. Jean Ellis, my fiancee, and I went to see Don Henry's Father, Claude. He was a farmer near Drummond, Idaho, and was Don's closest living relative. My intent was to assure him that Don was in the hands of the Free French in Indo-China and had a good chance of getting back to the States.

Jean stayed in the car while I went to the door of the farmhouse. When Don's Father opened the door, I told him that I was from Torpedo 4, and I wanted to talk to him about Don. Before I could say more, he started cursing.

"Who in the hell is this guy Hamrick? Let me show you a letter he wrote about Don. I'll be damned if I can understand how anyone could write this kind of a letter. He says, **'We all envy Don because he went down in an area where there was a good chance for survival.'** *How could anyone say he 'envied' a man shot down in enemy territory, a thousand miles from our nearest land base in China?"*

Claude Henry kept on ranting about Ham's letter. I was so taken aback that I didn't know how to respond. What Ham was trying to say was that if Don had to go down, French Indo-China was better than most other places where we were headed -- Tokyo, for example. Ham was trying to be encouraging; instead, his intent was misunderstood.

It became obvious that my trip to Drummond to reassure the family was not going to succeed. I returned to the car, reported to Jean the unexpected response to my visit, and we drove back home disappointed.

When Ham heard about my meeting with D. A.'s Father, he said, *"That was a poor choice of words on my part. I did not realize they would not understand. I'm sorry."*

No further word was received about D. A. Henry until the war ended. In December, 1945, I picked up a copy of the *Idaho Falls Post* and saw Henry's picture.[7] The article stated that when Don found that his bombs had not released he:

"...radioed for permission to fly back over the target to see if the bombardier could get the bombs to release. Permission was granted and when they returned all enemy fire was concentrated upon them resulting in their being shot down. Lt Henry made a perfect landing in a small clearing in the jungle, but discovered that their bombardier had been killed by enemy fire."

The Idaho Falls paper further stated that the family had been notified that Don had been killed by the Japanese, when he and an Army sergeant were *"betrayed in their hiding place by the French Indochinese."* We heard that Don had pulled a gun, and the Japanese patrol shot him on the spot. *"Sgt Quinn was taken prisoner and just recently returned to the US, where he told his story to Navy personnel, who informed the family about how their son met his death."* This article stated that *"Lt Henry was killed on April 26, 1945."* He was awarded the Air Medal posthumously. Don had received the DFC for earlier strikes.

Since Sherrod was on this flight, he took a special interest in trying to trace the events that led to Henry's capture and death. He concluded that Henry, after several weeks, joined up with 6 crew members of a PBM, which had made a crash landing 26 January, 1945, at Quong Ngai: [3]

> *"...somehow they found their way to the primitive Moi village of Pletonang, in the mountains north of Saigon. There on the morning of 12 March 1945, two months to the day after Lt Henry was shot down, they met their fate at the hands of a cruel and remorseless enemy.... After accepting their surrender the Japanese commander ordered them to kneel, tied their wrists together, shot them in turn, then kicked each backward into a shallow grave."*

More recently, I have learned that an American, Martin L. Mickelsen and a Frenchman, Jean-Claude Surleau (who was in Saigon at the time of the Air Group 4 strike) are conducting research on the Saigon strikes of January 12, 1945, with particular attention to the fate of those airmen who were shot down. Task Force 38, as a whole, lost 16 planes -- two from the **ESSEX**.

Mickelsen located Lt Lynch's Escape and Evasion (E&E) Report, which was filed after Lt Lynch returned to the States through Kunming, China. (Lt Lynch, VMF-124, was shot down on the same strike, as already noted.) Lynch met up with Don Henry while being protected by the Free-French, but was later separated. In the report, Lynch reports that Henry's crewman Shirley had not been rescued, due to a language confusion problem: [4]

> *"The thumbs-up signal has a different meaning in this vicinity, in that instead of meaning that 'everything is all right,' they count on their fingers and mean the 'count of one.' This has caused confusion and in one instance resulted in the death of a TBF radioman. The latter instance occurred when a TBF pilot, who crash-landed near Saigon, misunderstood the signal of his native rescuers, thinking that they meant ev-*

erything was all right and that they would take care of his plane, and when he nodded his head, they thought that to be the case, all the time escorting him away from the scene of the crash. After a lapse of time, when they realized their misunderstanding, they returned to the scene, but too late. The Japs had been there and the radioman's body was found a short distance from the plane."

During his research, Martin Mickelsen located Ens William A. Quinn, who was with Don Henry at the time he was killed by the Japanese. (The Idaho Falls news article erroneously reported that a Sgt Quinn was Don Henry's radioman.) Ens Quinn was one of 2 survivors of a crew of 11 Navy reconnaissance fliers shot down off the Indo-China coast on January 26, 1945. Quinn's account of the fate of Don Henry follows (as recorded by Mickelsen): [4]

> *"Don told Quinn that he had been burned waiting for Shirley to jump out of the plane. He did not know Shirley had not jumped since he was struggling to keep the plane under control. Don was badly burned. He was placed in a house on the outskirts of Saigon by the Underground, then sneaked into the hospital to be patched up."*

> *"Don Henry was escorted by the Free French to a hideout in the mountains where he joined 9 other Americans (including Quinn) and 3 Frenchmen. Quinn and Henry were in the same hut when the Japanese attacked. "Don attempted to run away, went out (the) door, hit in leg, tried to run back asking Quinn to help him. Henry was wearing a white undershirt -- an easy target in the moonlight. Quinn was wearing a black sweater. Don was killed by many hits to his white undershirt. Quinn was hit in the leg."*

> *"The remaining Americans had to surrender. They were tied up and forced to sit. The Japanese tried to interrogate them in broken French and Japanese -- trying to find out who they were and how they got*

there. The Japanese started a fire with the contents of the huts, tore off the bamboo door and threw it on the fire."

"The Japanese commander paced back and forth, interrogating them for about an hour. Suddenly, without warning, the Japanese took someone from the other end of the line to the side of the hut and beheaded him. Then they took Tommy. Tommy screamed, "No! No!" Shouting and screaming the men were decapitated one at a time. Quinn tried to get up -- screaming and crying. He was hit in the back of the neck with a rifle butt." ("Tommy" in this recounting remains unidentified.)

"Suddenly, the executions stopped. Two Americans remained alive -- Ens Quinn and Vincent Grady. Quinn learned later that the Japanese beheaded two Americans for every Japanese killed in the surprise attack. The two survivors were sent to a prison camp in Saigon and were released after the Japanese surrender. Quinn brought back this story and stated, **'Don was a hero!'**"

The French report concerning the fate of Lt(jg) D. A. Henry, as translated by Mickelsen, states: [4]

"...The seventh (Lt Henry) injured with grave burns was assigned for six weeks at Mytho then to a plantation at Loc Ninh. He found a glorious death in the month of April, 1945, fighting at the side of the French resistance. Finally the body of E. A. Shirley, found among the debris of his machine, was previously interred at the French cemetery of Saigon.

Leo S. Leach, VF-4, a good friend of Henry's told me:

"E. A. Shirley was from my hometown, Syracuse, New York. I started 3 times to see his parents on my 30-day leave, but was too much of a coward to see them. One day they came to my house to visit me. I would say they were a very brave set of parents. We had a very long talk and I went to their house for dinner. After a number of years, Shirley's remains were transferred from India to the family plot in New York."

Don Henry's remains were returned after the war and re-buried in Ashton, Idaho.

Author visiting Don Henry's grave. Ashton Cemetery, Ashton, Idaho. July 1, 2007.

Chapter 25 | Air Group Commander Lost: Pescadores

"...about to be hoisted aboard he lost his grip on the ring, floated clear of the bow and sank.... Commander Klinsmann's loss is unexplainable... unwarranted."

It had been three days since the strike on Saigon. No further word was received about Don Henry or Shirley. Squadron members went ahead with the inventory of their gear and Ham was assigned the duty to notify the relatives back home.

The weather turned bad in the next several days with rumors of an impending typhoon. Nevertheless, on 15 January 1945, the **ESSEX** received orders to launch a strike group against prime shipping targets in Takao Harbor, Formosa.

Twelve Avengers, with an escort of 9 fighters, were launched with instructions to rendezvous below the cloud ceiling of 800 feet and proceed to target.

Cdr Klinsmann led the group, flying the lead Hellcat. All but two of the fighters were loaded with bombs or rockets. The other VF in Klinsmann's division were flown by Martin, White, and Maikowski. Lt Blackwell led the second fighter division, which included Olson, Garrigan, Hinrichs, and McBee.[1]

After flying through very undesirable weather conditions, the attack group reached Takao Harbor, only to find it closed in by clouds. Cdr Klinsmann then ordered the flight to proceed to the Pescadores Islands, where shipping had been reported. Ample targets were found in Mako-Ko, and targets were assigned to VT and VF by divisions. The weather here was also very bad. The tactical organization for VT-4 was: [1]

Strike -- January 15, 1945

Lee L. "Ham" Hamrick (pilot)
  R. A. Trembley (crew)

Keith Gardner
  P. J. Wilson

Strike -- January 15, 1945 (continued)

Felix E. Ward, Jr.
  Don M. Applegate

J. E. Hewitt
  L. P. Shuman

E. A. "Ted" Newell
  W. J. Lace

F. H. Bissell
  W. B. Cook

Will S. Souza
  T. R. Sims

L. A. "Cozy" Cole
  N. L. Shiverdecker

B. R. "Trex" Trexler
  J. W. Aldrich

L. C. Gray
  H. R. Green

Robert F. "Bob" Ruth
  C. L. McConnell and R. B. Montague

G. M. Bell
  R. R. Pittman

Upon arrival at the Pescadores, the flight found two warships (a destroyer and its escort) and three or four AKs or AOs. The DE was anchored and the DD was underway. Anti-aircraft fire was "most intense" from shore installations and from the ships, particularly the DD and DE.

"The low cloud cover compelled VT pilots to employ very shallow glides, greatly reducing the accuracy of the drops. Lt Hamrick scored with a hit directly amidships on the Fox Tare Baker. Ens Gardner placed one bomb on the stern of the same

Captain Gordon Rowe pins the Air Medal on Cdr George Otto Klinsmann in recognition of his actions during the OPERATION LEADER strike on Norway. April 18, 1944. *USS Ranger*.

Cdr Klinsmann (center) discusses December 15, 1944 strike on Luzon
with Rear Admiral Forrest Percival Sherman (right). Others unidentified. *USS ESSEX*.

ship. Lt(jg) Ruth hit the Fox Baker amid- ships with a 500 pounder. There were many near misses, none of which appeared to be damaging, on all four of the ships attacked. The DD appeared to be burning on depar- ture, probably as a result of VF attack." [1]

After Cdr Klinsmann assigned VT targets, he led his own division in a rocket and strafing attack, and sent Lt Blackwell's division against ground in- stallations at the Naval Base at Mako.[1]

"Commander Klinsmann picked the DD as a target for his division scoring two rocket hits himself just aft of amidships on the DD from reports of others on the flight. Lieutenant White fired his rockets at the largest of the AKs, a probable SB. Lieu- tenant White saw his rockets hit about 50 feet to port of the vessel. Ens Hinricks [sic] aimed his half-tonner at another AK but missed. A small harbor craft was strafed vigorously by a single VF without obvious effect."

"Immediately after this attack, Com- mander Klinsmann's plane was seen cov- ered with oil from an AA hit probably in the oil line. This necessitated immediate return to the ship without further observ- ing results. Lieutenant Blackwell's division, which had been attacking shore installa- tions at Mako, was ordered to escort the VT. Commander Klinsmann's division, plus Ens Olson, started back toward base."

"Because of the clouds the flight soon lost sight of land. Lieutenant White, Lt(jg) Maikowski, and Ens Olson broke off from the others and flew toward Formosa... to check their position against known land."

Due to low oil pressure from the AA damage to his Hellcat, Cdr Klinsmann decided to make a water landing near the two dispatched US picket destroyers, *"...rather than depend on his plane fly- ing the additional 50 miles over very rough seas."* The remainder of the combat report states:[1]

"...His wingman, at his request, went over the forced landing check off proce- dure and got a 'thumbs up' on each item. Both DDs were informed of the unpending [sic] water landing and were standing by to effect the rescue. The Commander made a perfect water landing, was observed to abandon and clear his plane before it sank. Lt(jg) Martin, the group commander's wingman, had experienced engine trouble on the return flight and as the two DDs had the Commander in sight, and the view of the Commander's apparent good condition and position for a quick rescue by either of the DDs, the wingman departed for base upon receiving a wave of one hand from him indicating that the Commander was able to take care of himself from then on."

"One of the DDs reported having Com- mander Klinsmann in sight, successfully throwing him a life line with a life buoy ring attached, and as he was pulled along- side and about to be hoisted aboard he lost his grasp on the ring (the DD having just enough stern way on for steerage), floated clear of the bow and sank before the DD could position itself again. The DD report- ed that neither Commander Klinsmann's life jacket nor life raft were inflated."

There was great sadness aboard the **ESSEX** when the rest of Air Group 4 heard about the loss of our friend and Commander. Otto had been with us since the early days on the **RANGER**. He was a good pilot; respected by the dive bombers because he first led their "Top Hat" squadron; supported by VT-4 because he knew how to bomb; and acknowl- edged by his fellow fighters in VF-4 because he readily adapted to the Hellcats and never hesitated to lead his group into the most intense action.

John Selka, who served as Otto's plane captain, stated, *"He was a wonderful man, a great leader; a gentleman. He treated everyone, including enlisted men, like his own family."* [2] His Chief Yeoman, Don Anderson, added:[3]

"I share the same feelings about George Otto Klinsmann. He was always thinking of his people, his pilots, his crewmen. I was his chief yeoman, and he was like a father figure to me. After the debriefing reports were checked by the ACI officers, I had the job of typing them and turning them over to Cdr Klinsmann. I was so busy typing reports for Otto that I rarely got ashore for R&R."

There was no panic about Otto's ditching. It was easy to see why he would not bother to inflate the rubber raft -- besides it wasn't that easy to release and inflate. Also, to inflate the life jacket too soon could be cumbersome, so he probably thought that was not necessary in spite of the rough seas. There was one complicating factor -- Otto carried extra gear that might have contributed to his drowning. Don Alexander stated.[3]

"I'm not talking about one or two pounds! He had a couple of extra boxes of shells in his flight-suit pockets -- and extra survival equipment. If he went down over land he wanted to be able to survive. This extra weight certainly would inhibit his ability to stay afloat."

Nevertheless, none of us could understand why the rescue destroyer did not send some seamen overboard to assist with the rescue. When I went down the next day, several men jumped into the rough seas to help me reach the lines dropped over the side. As the operations report states, Cdr Klinsmann's loss was *"unexplainable... unwarranted."*

"Plane Down" -- a watercolor by Douglas Raymond Cahoon, VF-4, the artist of our group. Doug was lost on a strike on Okinawa on March 1, 1945, the last combat mission of Air Group 4.

Chapter 26 | In the Drink

"On what was to prove the longest and least profitable combat flight in the history of the squadron."

January had been a hectic month for Torpedo 4. We had taken part in strikes every few days with breaks only for refueling or short stops at Ulithi Lagoon. Many of the pilots and crew were suffering from combat fatigue. When we reached the Ready Room about 6:30 am on January 16, 1945, we heard the weather reports and the strike plans, and were less than enthusiastic.

As we went through the briefing, we were conscious of the loss of our Air Group Commander. No one could replace Otto. He had been a steady and reliable leader as far back as our service on the *RANGER*.

The senior officer in the Air Group was a Marine -- Lt Col W. A. Millington. He was named Acting Commander of Air Group 4 for this strike and later took over formally as Commander.

The scheduled targets on January 16 were shipping and installations on the island of Hainan, China -- an outbound flight of more than 400 miles. We were to join other planes from Task Group 38.3 under the overall command of Admiral "Bull" Halsey. All of the torpedo planes from the other two carriers (*SAN JACINTO* and *LANGLEY*) were equipped with wing tanks but, for some unknown reason, the *ESSEX* did not have wing tanks aboard for our Avengers. Even rough calculations plainly indicated that the Torpedo 4 planes would have difficulty stretching the gas supply to reach the proposed targets. Any deviation from the flight plan, or interruptions by attacks from Japanese fighters, would mean close calls for VT-4.

A heavy overcast delayed the launch until 0805. At that time, eight Hellcats, under the leadership of Lt G. M. Harris Jr., and 10 VTs, under the leadership of P. J. Davis, were launched into the

mist. Attempts to rendezvous under the overcast were futile, so we climbed into the clouds more or less as individual planes.

The Torpedo 4 tactical organization consisted of: [1]

Strike Alpha -- January 16, 1945

P. J. Davis, Jr. (pilot)
  N. J. Schmolke (crew)

C. N. W. "Scott" Vogt
  R. E. Kelly

G. M. "Buck" Barnett
  C. Christopher

W. F. "Willie" Walker (water landing)
  G. F. Zeimer

Page P. Stephens
  Andy "Marge" Mocsary

Vernon A. Landre (returned to base)
  Charlie C. Statler

Gerald W. "Jerry" Thomas (water landing)
  Don H. Gress and R. B. Montague

R. M. "Hoppy" Hopfinger (returned to base)
  F. W. Wilson

Ed S. Binder (water landing)
  R. D. Biddle

H. J. Deimel
  L. S. Leach

Three fighters called in to the ship for permission to return to base due to mechanical difficulties (Kelley, Sikors, and Callen). Ens Landre and Hopfinger, from VT-4, also returned to the ship. It appeared that I would have to "down" my plane when it failed to turn up full RPMs at the takeoff spot, but I decided to chance a borderline power setting so I took off and tried to join up with Stephens under the cloud layer.

About this time, the ship directed all VT-4 planes to join the Air Group 44 leader, who was to serve as target coordinator. He reported that he was at 6500 feet above the overcast and would wait for VT-4 planes there.[1]

The 10 TBMs that got off the flight deck began to climb through the overcast, but there was no way we could hold our formation. Therefore, we split off in various directions and climbed through the soup individually -- always hoping that we could avoid midair collisions.

After about 15 minutes, eight of the ten planes had rendezvoused, joined the Air Group 44 leader, and proceeded on base course. The other two planes, failing to rendezvous, returned to base, jettisoning their bombs before landing aboard. Our debriefing report continues: [1]

"After about 20 minutes on base course, Lt Davis suggested a new heading, computed from the wind given by the ship for that altitude (6,000 feet) just before takeoff. At this point, Lt Davis was given the lead. Approximately 85 miles from the task force, the overcast cleared. From then on ceiling was unlimited, visibility 10-15 miles."

"ETA for landfall passed and land was still not in sight. Thus, the pilots knew that the wind and ship's point option data had been incorrect. When landfall was made, the formation was uncertain as to its exact position. This landfall was later identified as Becassines Point on the Liu Chow Peninsula, some 50 miles due north of the HOI HOW area, the intended target. Lt Davis then set a course of due south, but after a few minutes the Air Group 44 leader directed a heading of 240 degrees true and the formation assumed that heading. The flight made landfall on Hainan Island just east of Lin-Kao."

At this point, I deviate from the official report to give my own impressions. It should be noted that our skipper, P. J. Davis, had to sign the official report, and, therefore, his own bias is evident in this, as well as other combat reports. Fortunately, Lt Lou Gardemal, our ACI officer, was also present during the pilot briefings, and he moderated the final version.

When VT-4 planes made landfall, P. J. Davis misread the map and took a wrong turn. The correction ordered by Air Group 44 leader from the *LANGLEY* was also in error. Consequently, we lost valuable time and expended part of our gas supply trying to locate the designated target. Also, we experienced light ant-iaircraft fire at certain locations on Hainan, just enough to keep us uncomfortable.

Japanese Zeros were reported attacking some of the task force planes, although neither Don Gress, my turret gunner, nor I saw any enemy planes.

As we were crossing Hainan Island, P. J. Davis called the Air Group 44 target coordinator and told him that we were getting low on gas and needed an immediate target assignment.[1]

"The formation then wandered around at 10,000 feet in a generally west and west-southwest direction waiting for the assignment of a suitable target. At this point Ens Walker reported a low gas supply. After about 20 minutes of such wandering, the Air Group 44 leader ordered an attack on what he supposed to be a seaplane base."

As the report indicates, we dropped our bombs in a glide-bombing mode on this so-called "Sea Plane Base." By the time I made my run, the place was reduced to rubble. I dropped anyway, since I could not return to the ship with armed bombs aboard. Each of the VT-4 planes was loaded with four 500-pound, general-purpose bombs.

After the attack, the return flight carried us over a Japanese airfield (identified later as Ting On). When Ed Binder (with R. D. Biddle as gunner) dropped his "hung-up" bomb on the field, I thought, *"I have just enough gas to make a decent approach to that airstrip, and maybe I should. I will never make it back to the Carrier!"* But, I decided I could reach the US Submarine dispatched near land to pick up survivors, or perhaps the picket destroyer, which, although a long way from us, was at least 50 miles closer than the ***ESSEX***.

As we started our over-water return leg, I heard Willie Walker call the skipper again. *"I'm out of gas. I'm going down!"* P. J. Davis did not acknowledge.

The VHF Channel we were using was cluttered with calls from desperate pilots from other squadrons -- some had been hit with AA fire, some by Japanese planes, and others were low on gas. I broke in with a call to our Skipper, *"Willie is going down -- send in a position report!"* No answer. I called our fighter cover leader with the same message. Still no answer.

I thought, *"Surely someone will drop back and circle Willie."* I then called the code name of the picket destroyer with Walker's latitude and longitude. No answer -- only cluttered airways.

Disgusted with our Skipper, our fighters, and everyone in general, I dropped out of formation to circle Willie's plane as he started a dead-stick water landing. I thought, *"This mission is all fouled up. It will serve them right if they lose the whole damned squadron!"*

So I decided, since I was also about out of fuel anyway, to land beside Willie. There was a big splash as Willie's plane hit the water -- but it appeared that he and his crewman, G. F. Zeimer, had survived the crash. The combat report states: [1]

> *"At a point approximately 45 miles from STRIKE PICKET No. 1, Ens Walker was forced to make a water landing at 1413 (Item) because fuel was exhausted. Though the accompanying TBMs from the other carriers had wing tanks (and those of VT-4 had not), none remained to circle over-*

head. Lt(jg) Thomas, not having enough gas to complete the flight to base, elected to circle the spot to report the position of his downed squadron mate and to assist in bringing the DD to the scene."

As I circled Walker's downed plane, I heard P. J. Davis call the *ESSEX* and report that he was over the picket destroyer. He requested permission for the group to make a direct approach to the carrier due to fuel shortage (normally a circle around the picket was required for the Task Force to make certain the planes were ours and not Kamikazes). I thought, *"If our other planes are already over the destroyer, perhaps I have enough fuel to reach it, even if I can't make the carrier!"* [2] Consequently, I took a heading toward the picket. I switched several times to empty tanks in the hope of getting a few more miles from the engine. The gauges were accurate. That TBM would not run on fumes!

In a few minutes, it became obvious that the fuel remaining in my Avenger would not carry me to the rescue destroyer. I called my crew on the intercom, *"Prepare for a water landing. Jettison hatches. Montague, you climb out of the belly and sit backwards in the second cockpit. Pick up any extra survival kits you see and get ready to abandon ship!"*

Hurriedly, I pulled out my plotting board and made a quick calculation of our location. I called the code name of the rescue destroyer. This time the airwaves were clear and I received a Mayday acknowledgment.

D. H. Gress was in the turret, facing backwards. He was a regular member of my crew and I had confidence in his ability. R. B. Montague, on the other hand, was a ship's photographer and this was only his fourth hop with me.

My fuel gauge indicated that I had enough gas for a power-on landing. I looked down at the wind streaks and wave action to get the wind direction and velocity, extended the tail hook to get a feel for the water, and made a full-stall landing.

My Pacific crewmen, Don H. Gress (left) and John E. Holloman. Undated photo.

Our squadron photographer, Robert B. Montague. Following our rescue, Robert was transferred
out of the squadron. I didn't see him again until a Torpedo 4 Reunion in 2005. Undated photograph.

This ended a 6.5-hour flight in my TBM-3. The splashdown was not much harder than a normal carrier landing, although the plane was completely submerged for a few seconds.

Montague and I jumped out on the right wing as the plane came to the surface. We pushed the large raft that was stored in the fuselage over to Gress, but he was washed off the wing before he could get it inflated. Montague and I inflated a small raft, then we, too, were washed off the wing. As we floated under the tail of the plane, I thought it would drag us down as it sank. While I was fighting to get clear of the plane, Montague was taking pictures with a small camera that he had managed to salvage (see photo).

In a few seconds the plane sank, and we were all alone in the South China Sea in the one-man raft. We had lost one paddle, but we had extra survival kits. The surface of the sea was smooth, but the swells were more than 30 feet high. At the tip of the swells, we could see for miles -- at the bottom of the swells, the sea seemed to close in on us.

The rescue destroyer was nowhere in sight. It was lonely, and I was disgusted -- too disgusted to worry about sharks or long-term survival.

Montague and I kept searching the rough seas for Don Gress. He was nowhere in sight. I thought we had lost another damned good crewman. Don described the problem when he talked to me later.[3]

"Jerry, I can recall your question over the intercom before we went down, 'What would you rather do, land on the island or go out to sea?' I said, 'Go out to sea.' I was scared to death of getting into Japanese hands."

"I never did see you fellows. I was on one side of the plane, and you were on the other. I didn't think we were ever going to get that life raft out. It was hung up. When it finally came out, the line was wrapped around my leg, and I nearly drowned. When I finally got the raft inflated, I did

not have the strength to get in. I hung on a while, then finally was able to crawl over the edge. I laid on the bottom of the raft until I was rescued. My God, I was so sick!"

Later that afternoon Montague and I spotted a destroyer coming toward us. It turned out to be a new ship, the **USS SULLIVANS**. This destroyer was named after the five Sullivan brothers who were lost when the US cruiser *JUNEAU* was sunk by the Japanese on November 15, 1942. The ship was new to the Pacific theater.

The destroyer came up to our rubber raft, the crew tossed over some rescue nets, and a few seamen jumped into the ocean to assist us aboard. I was so grateful to be picked up that I gave away all my extra survival gear to the crew -- even the kit containing Chinese and Japanese money. I kept my .38 and shoulder holster, however.

Montague and I immediately asked about Don Gress. The ship had already spotted him and, in a few minutes, we brought him aboard.

I then asked one of the officers if they had picked up Willie Walker. The answer was, *"We have picked up several other survivors, but we do not have a position report on Walker."* They asked me to come up to the bridge and look at some maps with the captain. Since my plotting board was in the plane at the bottom of the ocean, I had to calculate from memory the approximate location of Willie's splash site.

The ship's captain then directed the **SULLIVANS** to the area that I designated. We made several circles and finally located Walker and Zeimer just before dark. They had two rubber rafts lashed together and appeared to be in good shape. We found them only minutes before the task force was directed out of the China Sea.

Ens Walker's version of the water landing follows: [4]

"It was more of a dip-bombing operation than a glide-bombing attack. We turned back east to go home. Of course, I

Photo by Robert Montague of our Avenger's tail just before it sank. January 16, 1945.

Thomas being transfered from **SULLIVANS** to **ESSEX** by breeches buoy. Ensign
Deimel and Hopfinger in background. January 17, 1945.

knew I wouldn't make it. I had to discuss a crash landing with my gunner somewhere near the East Coast. He didn't particularly like the idea, and I wasn't overly fond of it myself. We had been briefed that there would be a rescue submarine off the coast. We were taking the chance that we would be picked up by them. We did know that the fleet would be leaving the South China Sea late that afternoon or that night. We thought there might be a chance to get back aboard."

"We proceeded on and on and on until I had burned all but a little gasoline in one of my tanks. I couldn't go any further, so I made a water landing. My water landing wasn't very good, although it was planned well. I had my tail hook down but there were big, huge swells. I just tipped one of them; that kind of messed me up, and I just collapsed right into the other swell. The plane didn't have any gasoline, so it just bounced up like a cork but water came up over the hatches."

"We got a little hasty in abandoning that airplane. We both had on our seat packs. We stood on the wing and inflated the large raft. Somehow Zeimer slipped off the wing and got separated. He pulled his chute pack and got in the small raft. He would be inside of one swell, and I would be inside of another, but he rowed toward me, and I rowed toward him, and finally we got together. He transferred over to the big raft with me. The small raft was pulled in tow, and we proceeded on."

"It started getting late, and we started getting cold; we were both just shivering. Four F6Fs flew over. I took my .38, loaded one with tracer-and-ball and fired it; I guess they didn't see it, because they just kept on going. I thought that might be our last chance. Just before dark, I happened to look over my left shoulder and there was

this huge destroyer right up above me. I didn't know it if was Japanese or American -- friend or foe. They came alongside and threw a cargo net over the side, and we climbed aboard very happily. They gave us dry clothes and a place to sleep."

*"One thing that was said before we landed, **'When the first one goes down, we will all make a mass water landing.'** I thought, **'Here I go. Everyone is going to come join me.'** Jerry circled, but I didn't blame anybody because I thought if you had the fuel, go as far as you can."*

"My head was throbbing a little when they finally picked me up. I did not heave. Zeimer was sick, sick, sick. He blamed the dye marker for making him nauseated."

The Marine fighters on the strike also suffered from fuel shortage. Capt Bedford, VMF-124, wrote about the day's events: [5]

"I had 160 gals gas -- Wasty had 120 gals. Nip and tuck, so we took right off for the fleet."

"Weather scrummed up so we let down thru overcast and proceeded to base at 2,000 feet. Homing beacon not heard. Were on course 1 hr. 10 min. when my compass gave out, turned the lead over to Wasty. Still 50 min. to go -- had 30K headwind."

*"Worst feeling in the world -- no signal as yet on homing and gas down to 80 gal. Visibility about 3 miles. Chewing chatter on radio as planes reported dropping in the drink all around us. TBF's and F6F's out of gas. I could see we four landing in the drink ourselves. Just then Marshall got a homing signal and he took lead -- shortly afterward we all received it and 5 hrs and 5 min. after taking off -- I kissed those oily pine planks of ye flight deck of the **USS ESSEX**."*

Ens William F. Walker. *USS ESSEX*. Undated photo.

Lt Edward S. Binder. *USS ESSEX*. Undated photo.

Shortly after my rescue by the *SULLIVANS*, I was offered a shot of "medicinal whisky" and a bowl of canned peaches. That night I got seasick. A bad storm was brewing and the destroyer rolled so radically that I could not stay in my bunk. That night and the next day I spent about as much time on the deck of the sick bay as in my bunk, with constant dry heaves and the worst headache I can remember.

Don Gress said, *"They gave me clean clothes. I was rather hungry so I went through the chow line. By the time I got through the line, I just looked at that food and dumped it in the bucket. Never did sit down with it. I thought we were on that destroyer for several days."*

I, too, thought we were on the *SULLIVANS* for several days, but Air Sea Rescue records show a transfer to the *ESSEX* in the evening of the second day.[6] The *SULLIVANS* had picked up a number of other pilots and crew during that South China Sea operation; several were wounded. The captain finally received permission in spite of the rough seas, to transfer us to the *ESSEX* for better medical care. Statler recorded in his journal.[7]

"Jan 17, 1945: Very rough seas. Decision made to transfer several pilots and crew members picked up by Destroyer Sullivans to the ESSEX but experienced difficulty shooting a line across and sending them over in a breeches buoy. Dunked Thomas in water but all transfers successful. Spent the day trying to refuel, but had little success due to bad weather."

A few minutes after I was transferred to the *ESSEX*, I was offered dry toast. My seasickness moderated in a few hours. I was accustomed to the roll of the carrier but not the roll of the destroyer. I was glad to be back on a more stable platform -- particularly since Task Force 38.3 was leaving the South China Sea and heading into a "Monsoon with high seas."[8]

Upon my return to the *ESSEX*, I learned that all Torpedo 4 personnel had been accounted for.

The report on the third plane that went "in the drink" states: [1]

"From the picket to the task force, a distance of 50 miles, approximately, the formation strung out considerably. Somewhere in this area Lt(jg) Binder ran so low on gas that a water landing was made at 1443 (Item). Lt(jg) Binder and his crewmen were picked up by the USS CALLAHAN."

"Jolly Ed" Binder had R. D. Biddle with him as turret gunner. His other crewman, Don Jenkins, was scheduled to go but, *"I had laryngitis and couldn't utter a sound so Biddle had to take the assignment. He took the rifle we always carried and it went down with the plane. The highlight of my tour in the Pacific was the Tokyo strikes -- but, routine flying with Mr. Binder provided all the excitement I ever needed."*[9]

Pilot debriefings state that *"many small buildings were set afire and were burning furiously as aircraft departed [from the target]. Film which would have identified target better were [sic] lost aboard a TBM which was forced to make a water landing."* The film referred to was in my plane. When we made the water landing, Montague abandoned all photo equipment, except his hand-held camera. Only one photo from this camera, showing the tail of our plane as we drifted away from it, was clear.

The confidential report to our higher levels of command on the January 16 strike started with the statement, *"On what was to be the longest and least profitable combat flight in the history of the squadron...."* The seven of us that tasted the salt water of the South China Sea on that day would tend to agree with this conclusion.

One of the more appropriate comments as I was brought back aboard was made by our Executive Officer, Lee Hamrick.[10]

"Jerry finally got to go swimming in the South China Sea. You know, we had to send a keg of ice cream over to the destroyer for

every crew member they picked up and returned to the Carrier. Our major concern was, 'Do we have enough ice cream to reclaim all of these guys?'"

A Touch of Hong Kong -- January 16, 1945

While the rescue of the Torpedo Four crew members from the South China Sea was taking place, the ESSEX launched twelve F6F Hellcats, loaded with 1000-pound bombs, for a high-speed strike on Hong Kong Harbor. This was the first carrier-based strike on Hong Kong, and no one knew what to expect from fighter opposition or AA fire. No specific targets were assigned, but the group was advised that Japanese shipping was in the area.

This fighter sweep was under the command of Lt W. W. "Dub" Taylor. The three divisions rendezvoused and departed for Hong Kong at 1610 hours, broke through the overcast at about 3,000 feet, and flew toward the target at 16 - 20,000 feet.

The group sighted several ships in the Hong Kong Harbor. Dub Taylor's division pushed over from 15,000 feet in a 60-degree glide bombing run.[11]

"Barrage-type heavy AA was thick and concentrated at this level and at two lower levels. Lt Taylor released his half-tonner at 5,000 feet, aiming for a large AK, possibly a Fox-Tare-Baker, between Hong Kong Island and the southern extremity of Kowloon peninsula. Lt(jg) Lepp aimed at the same vessel, while Ens Fewell sought to hit another large AK in the same vicinity. Lt(jg) Rhodes's bomb hit and exploded within the Royal Navy Yard."

"The undiminishing and accurate AA fire and the high hills on Hong Kong Island necessitated a pull-out at 4,000 feet and speedy retirement to the south, and results were not observed. It was believed, however, that Lt(jg) Rhodes's bomb landed well within destructive radius of important Navy Yard installations and caused serious damage there."

The Second Division, led by Lt(jg) T. J. Graham made a high-speed, high-angle run on ships in the same area of Hong Kong Harbor, *"...through clouds of AA fire."* Graham overshot the ships lying in the harbor and saved his bomb for another target -- a lighthouse, radio-radar installation and possible AA or CD emplacement on a small island in the Potoi group south of Hong Kong.

Ens Gustafson dropped his bomb at a third AK in the harbor, while Lt(jg) Guyles scored a bomb hit on the Royal Navy Yard. Ens Sarris's bomb was aimed at one of the AK. The speed of retirement prevented observation of results.

Lt Smith's division, using the same tactics as the other eight VF in the flight, bombed the Cosmopolitan Dockyard on the west side of Kowloon Peninsula. All bombs were soon to land within destructive radius of shore installations, and a column of black smoke was rising from the area as the VF retired.

Fortunately, all 12 Hellcats got in and out of the area without loss to AA fire. Some comments from pilots on the Hong Kong flight are significant.[11]

Lt Smith: *"If we had been told our exact objective, we would have been able to instigate a much better attack, much safer for the pilots and therefore probably much more accurate."*

Lt(jg) Rhodes: *"Because of the short notice pilots received before executing this attack, maximum effectiveness could not be attained.* **TICONDEROGA** *planes attacked just prior to us and were receiving heavy AA up to 15,000 feet, well concentrated and accurate. Several ships were noted in the harbor. Two had been set afire. Altogether, four huge fires were noted."*

Lt(jg) Guyles: *"Hong Kong is well guarded by AA. Guns are in a circle around the harbor. Fire comes from all sides. Even the smallest islands appeared to hold AA guns."*

Marines Sweep Hainan -- January 16, 1945

On the afternoon of January 16, the **ESSEX** launched Strike Baker, consisting of 7 Corsairs flown by pilots of VMF 124 and VMF 213. These F4Us, under the leadership of Capt W. J. Bedford were instructed to make a sweep over Hainan.

The Marines were each carrying two 250-pound bombs. The group made bombing and strafing runs on ships found near Point Sifa and in Yu Lin Kan Bay. Several enemy ships were damaged by the F4Us.

As the flight proceeded toward Gaalong Point, it was attacked by Japanese Zekes. Lt Strimbeck was heard saying, *"They're shooting at me! There are nine Zekes!"* [2]

Unfortunately, Lt Strimbeck, at the time of the attack, did not jettison his belly tank. He was also still carrying two 250-pound bombs. The War Diary states: [2]

"Lt Wastvedt slid out to starboard so they could start a section weave, but Lt Strimbeck (apparently excited) turned away from him in a tight 180-degree turn, leaving the enemy with a perfect no-deflec-

tion shot. The Zeke hit his belly tank, and Strimbeck's plane immediately burst into flames. The pilot bailed out and was seen parachuting downward."

Capt Bedford in his journal records: [5]

"Feel terribly tired and half sick. Geo. (Strimbeck) violated all our training by turning away from Wasty when attacked -- if he had scissored I feel that he might still be here."

A rescue sub was vectored to the location of the downed pilot. There were no reports on a later rescue.

The remainder of Capt Bedford's flight engaged the Zekes. Reynolds *"got on the tail of one Zeke, saw hits travel up the back of the fuselage, and believes he may have damaged the tail controls or killed the pilot.... He last saw the Zeke descending on one wing, but not necessarily out of control... cannot be listed as a probable."* [2]

The Marines characterized the flak as heavy along the entire coastline from Samah Bay to Cape Bastion, and the ships were putting up *"moderate and accurate automatic AA."*

Inventory form signed by Thomas for his downed Avenger. The plane and engine are written off separately, each for one dollar. In theory Thomas was responsible for paying the two dollars.

Marine Corsair landing on the **USS ESSEX**. January 1, 1945.

Chapter 27 | From the China Sea to Formosa

"Medals are at present unavailable in the combat area."

Bad Weather and Bogeys -- January 17-21, 1945

If historians were to rely on the brief impersonal comments contained in the official ships' logs, we would know very little about the war in the Pacific. For example, Torpedo 4 ditched three planes in the South China Sea on January 16, and the *ESSEX* brought the seven airmen from those planes back aboard the next day, January 17. The ship's log merely states *"Fueling at sea and receiving replacement aircraft in Area 200 miles west of Luzon."* [1] No mention is made of the personnel transferred back aboard. Charlie Statler's journal is more succinct. [2]

Jan 17, 1945 -- *"Very rough seas. Decision made to transfer several pilots and crew members picked up by Destroyer SULLIVANS to the ESSEX but experienced difficulty shooting a line across and sending them over in a breeches buoy. Dunked Thomas in water but all transfers successful. Spent the day trying to refuel, but had little success due to bad weather."*

Jan 18 -- *"We went through a typhoon last night. Weather still very bad."*

Jan 19 -- *"Beautiful weather.... Finished refueling."*

Jan 20 -- *"Started through the channel at approximately 1130. Jap snooper planes reported several times. GQ sounded at 1715 when 15 Jap planes were spotted -- 11 were shot down. (They were Nicks, Nells, Lilys, Bettys, and Helens).... At approximately 0200 Condition One was sounded. There were two snoopers at 30 miles. They faded shortly."*

As Task Group 38.3 was moving through Balingtang Channel, Tokyo Rose reported that the American Fleet was *"bottled up"* in the South China Sea. [3] Of course, these were high risks as Halsey's armada moved within easy reach of shore-based Japanese planes. But TG 38.3 was certainly not bottled up. Also, the carriers were maintaining constant combat air patrols over the fleet.

The *ESSEX* launched both VF-4 Hellcats and VMF Corsairs to serve as patrols. These CAPs were vectored to a number of Japanese bogeys. Brown and Byrd, from VF-4, each shot down a "Nell." [3]

Our Marine Corsairs *"downed eight twin-engine Jap bombers, and one probable, with no losses to ourselves."* [4] Most of these planes were identified as "Helens." Credit for 3 kills went to 1st Lt McGill; and one kill each to 2nd Lt Kehoe, 1st Lt Stallings, Capt Bedford, and 1st Lt Knight. Capt Kersey shot down a "Sally."

Takao Harbor, Formosa -- January 21, 1945

By dawn on January 21, the *ESSEX* was again in position to launch strikes on Formosa and Saki Shima Gunto. We were about 130 miles off the east coast of Formosa when the 0700 flight was launched. The target was shipping reported in Takao Harbor.

Eight VF-4 Hellcats and 10 VT-4 Avengers rendezvoused at 1500 feet and proceeded toward Takao, climbing to 12,000 feet as they approached the target area. The fighters maintained high cover and employed the standard "weave". maneuver.

Antiaircraft fire was "most intense" as the group approached Takao Harbor. Fighters went in first, followed by TBMs in a glide-bombing attack.

Capt Wilbur J. "Gus" Thomas, VMF-213, in Ready Room, plotting navigation data.
Capt Thomas became one the top Marine aces of WWII, credited with 18.5 "kills."
Undated photo.

Marine Corsairs warming-up for takeoff. ***USS ESSEX***. January 25,1945.

The Torpedo 4 tactical organization consisted of: [5]

Strike Alpha -- January 21, 1945

P. J. Davis, Jr. (pilot)
  R. F. Gray (crew)

Keith Gardner
  W. A. DeYoung

Felix E. Ward, Jr.
  C. J. Warrington

J. E. Hewitt
  C. W. Lathrop

E. A. "Ted" Newell
  W. J. Lace

W. J. Hopkins, Jr.
  Stan W. Coller

Will S. Souza
  T. R. Sims

L. A. "Cozy" Cole
  N. H. Knox

B. R. "Trex" Trexler
  C. W. Barr

G. M. Bell
  A. J. Tankard

Robert F. "Bob" Ruth
  J. F. "Forrest" Ballard

L. C. Gray (downed, radio trouble)
  J. E. Ganley

Torpedo 4 approached its targets up the lagoon from southeast to northwest and pushed over from 10,000 feet in 40-degree glides. The official report shows an average attack speed of 305 knots, but several pilots reported passing the "red mark." [5]

"Lt Davis, leading the first division, strung his bombs across two ships, one bomb hitting the stern of a Fox Baker... and another hitting a Sugar Baker... on the stern. The other pilots of this division scored some very near misses on the closely bunched ships, but no damage was observed."

"Lt Newell, leading the second division, strung his bombs across three closely grouped Sugar Bakers..., but the damage inflicted was not observed. The remainder of his division proceeded farther up the harbor to drop on the large concentration of ships. Ens Cole scored a hit with one bomb on the bow of a Sugar Baker...."

"In the third division, Lt Trexler scored with one bomb amidships on a Fox Tare Charlie... and Ens Bell placed one of his bombs amidships on a Sugar Baker.... Lt(jg) Ruth dropped on warehouses. The bomb explosions were observed, and it is certain that several buildings were destroyed and several damaged."

When Bob Ruth and Will Souza got back to the **ESSEX** Ready Room, they were all excited, *"Anti-aircraft fire was far worse than Manila, and, by darn, the puffs were multicolored! What the heck is this? Fourth of July fireworks?"*

We decided later that the Japanese gunners were using a new AA technique. The colored bursts were markers. Instead of firing at individual planes, the gunners were trying to blanket areas in our flight path. This technique was very effective when our planes were forced into a single approach due to limited openings in the clouds or some other feature restricting a varied, coordinated attack.

The TBM damage report after the Takao strike shows major repairs needed for three VT-4 Avengers: (a) wing damage due to TBM crashing into a Hellcat spotted forward, (b) anti-aircraft fire, probably a 40-mm, tore off half of port elevator, and (c) the third TBM was hit with a 12.7-mm projectile, which entered starboard ring cowl and exited exhaust stack.

Back on the **ESSEX**, Statler reported that: [2]

Jan 21 -- *"At 1200 the ship went to GQ. Two planes closed in on our formation. One bomb and one Banzi Boy hit the TI-CONDEROGA. Both of these planes were* *shot down. About an hour later two more planes tried to get in. One was shot down. The other one crashed on the flight deck of the TICONDEROGA. Several men were killed and injured. The TI was pretty badly damaged. The LANGLEY was hit with a dud."*

Capt. Bedford wrote: [6]

"I had just got halfway thru my navigation when we got G.Q. and were ordered to leave Ready Room. The Ti (TICONDEROGA) was short distance ahead and smoking like the devil. She had an enormous fire on her hangar deck. At 1230 we were ordered to return to Ready Room and prepare for take-off. I no sooner got there when our main batteries began blasting away at another Jap diving on the Ti. It was a Kamikaze suicide bomber and he crashed into the base of the super structure. Another huge fire resulted."

Several fighter sweeps were launched from the ESSEX throughout the day. A 6-plane Marine target patrol, under the leadership of Lt Col Millington, bombed Kobi Airfield, a railroad roundhouse, and factories near Shimie.[4]

"One plane flown by 2nd Lt John T. Molan made a forced landing near the base, and (the pilot) was picked up by the USS CAPERTON."

Bedford wrote: *"I circled him... [until a] DD picked him up."* [6]

Two other VMF patrols were sent over Formosa, one led by Capt Thomas and one by Major Crowe. They attacked Tsuina airfield without encountering air opposition. But Capt Thomas's six Corsairs ran into trouble with gas shortages as they approached the ESSEX for landing.[5]

"Returning to base, four planes landed at 1115, and while the other two were in the circle, bandits appeared over the task group. Observing one enemy dive-bomber

diving on the ESSEX, Capt Thomas, who had about 20 gallons left in his tank, poured full throttle and got in one burst at the bandit which was splashed by F6F pilots at the same time. Thomas and Goetz who had been airborne for 6 hours, twenty-five minutes, landed aboard the USS ENTERPRISE completely out of gas and without aid of any signal officers. Later that afternoon they returned to the ESSEX."

The Fighting 4 "Red Rippers" were also busy on January 21 with CAP assignments and fighter sweeps. One division damaged 9 ships and strafed airfield facilities in the vicinity of Miyako Jima. Another group was dispatched to Okinawa, where they attacked airfield facilities.[3]

"At Miyako Jima, Lt(jg) R. W. Ginther was caught in an explosion of his own bomb as he attacked a ship, and was killed."

This report on Ginther provided additional evidence of the determination of the VF-4 pilots to press home their attacks to low and effective levels. But, these mast-head runs increased the danger of flying into your own or your section leader's bomb explosions. Also, the most effective AA fire was from the 20- and 40-mm guns at the low point in the run. Blackwell's Hellcat was also hit by antiaircraft fire.[3]

"...which tore off part of his wing and necessitated a crash landing on board the ESSEX. It was a spectacular crash from which he emerged with superficial injuries."

Toshien Naval Base -- January 21, 1945

Strike Baker for Torpedo 4 was launched at 1400 hours. The target again was Takao Harbor and Toshien Naval Base, Formosa. Five Hellcats were assigned for cover and strafing support.

Of the 12 Avengers assigned to this strike, only 10 were able to rendezvous and proceed to the target.

The Torpedo 4 tactical organization consisted of: [5]

Strike Baker -- January 21, 1945

Lee L. "Ham" Hamrick (pilot)
R. A. Trembley (crew)

F. H. Bissell (downed, damaged propeller)
W. H. Moore

Gerald W. "Jerry" Thomas
J. E. Holloman

R. M. "Hoppy" Hopfinger
A. W. Yarman

G. M. "Buck" Barnett
Joseph C. Cohen

W. F. "Willie" Walker
S. A. Hastings

C. N. W. "Scott" Vogt
Leo E. Halvorson

Vernon A. Landre
Charlie C. Statler

Ed S. Binder
W. D. Jenkins

H. J. Deimel
C. L. Ely, Jr.

G. D. "Mak" Makibbin
R. Campbell

W. H. Cannady, Jr. (returned to base)
J. C. Gerke

During the launch, Ens Cannady hit a VF plane that was spotted forward on takeoff. The pilot circled, jettisoned his bombs, and made an emergency landing aboard. Also, Bissell taxied into another plane on the flight deck and bent his propeller.

After our launch and rendezvous, we joined up with a strike group of 6 VF and 8 VT from the *USS SAN JACINTO* (President George H. W. Bush's air group). Our Hellcats and the *SAN JACINTO* strike force attacked shipping in Takao while our torpedo planes were assigned the Toshien Naval Base. We approached the base from the northeast.[5]

"Anti-aircraft fire at Toshien was comparable to that at Takao. Not only did a large amount of defensive fire come from the ships under attack and from the naval base itself, but also from heavily defended Ape Hill to the south as VT retired. The puffs from anti-aircraft fire were multi-colored...."

"Lt Hamrick dropped his bombs on a large destroyer (possible Terutsuki Class,...). One hit directly amidships by Lt(jg) Thomas, plus several very near misses were scored."

"Three VT attacked a FOX TARE BAKER... which was docked. Though bombs fell very near and all around the ship, no damage was observed. It is believed however, that adjoining installations suffered heavily."

"Lt(jg) Barnett and Ens Deimel dropped on 3 large oil storage tanks in the southeastern section of the naval base. At least one of the tanks was seen to explode, and the others may have been burned out also."

"Ens Hopfinger dropped on a barracks construction in the northeastern section of the naval base. His bombs were seen to explode amid the buildings, and large fires were started."

This official report is fairly straightforward. It certainly does not indicate the high level of excitement we all experienced as we pressed home the attacks. And, as usual, when we returned to the Ready Room, the flight leaders had to sort out the results of the strike. In this case, Hamrick our Exec, and Lou Gardemal our ACI officer, had to confirm the "hits" and make follow-up recommendations. The final citation that I received for the effective run on the Terutsuki class destroyer, after some enhancement by Lou Gardemal, had a more glamorous tilt than the official debriefing report.

"The President of the United States takes pleasure in presenting the GOLD STAR in lieu of a Third Distinguished Flying Cross to

LIEUTENANT GERALD WAYLETT THOMAS

UNITED STATES NAVAL RESERVE

for service as set forth in the following:

CITATION:

For heroism and extraordinary achievement in aerial flight as Pilot of a Torpedo Bomber in Bombing Squadron FOUR, attached to the USS Essex, during operations against enemy Japanese forces in the Formosa Area, on January 21, 1945. A skilled and intrepid airman, Lieutenant (then Lieutenant, Junior Grade,) Thomas braved withering antiaircraft fire to launch a vigorous glide bombing attack on a Japanese destroyer, scoring a direct hit and inflicting

extensive damage on the hostile craft. His superb airmanship, courage, and devotion to duty throughout reflect the highest credit upon Lieutenant Thomas and the United States Naval Service.

For the President,

[James Forrestal]

Secretary of the Navy"

On the few occasions when the ship took time to recognize those individuals who were to receive decorations, a high-ranking officer assumed the responsibility. He read the citation, pinned a medal on our uniform, and promptly requested that the medal be returned. He reused the same medal several times. We were each given a note which read:

"Medals are at present unavailable in the combat area. The Secretary of the Navy has been requested to forward medals, when available, to recipients of awards."

"South China Sea" -- watercolor by Douglas Raymond Cahoon, VF-4.

Chapter 28 | Premonition at Amami O Shima

"I tried to cheer him up but he really had the blues… and he never made it back."

Kikai Jimi -- January 22, 1945

We continued our strikes in the Okinawa area on January 22. At 0650, the ***ESSEX*** launched a flight of 9 F6Fs and 9 TBMs to attack the airfield at Kikai Jima and shipping off the northwest coast of Amami O Shima.

The Hellcats, carrying 500-pound bombs and rockets, made a good accounting of themselves. Lt(jg) Garrison, Lt Smith, Lt(jg) Rhodes, Ens Peters, and Ens Hendricks scored rocket hits on a Sugar Dog-type vessel. Lt Avants also strafed a similar vessel, reporting a major explosion. Returning to the ship at 1105, *"Lt(jg) Rhodes's plane crashed into the final barrier and overturned. The pilot suffered minor injuries."* [1]

The 9 torpedo planes on this flight were assigned to the same targets proceeding to the area at 9000 feet. The Torpedo 4 tactical organization consisted of: [1]

Strike Alpha -- January 22, 1945

P. J. Davis, Jr. (pilot)
  N. J. Schmolke (crew)

F. H. Bissell
  W. H. Moore

G. M. "Buck" Barnett
  C. Christopher

W. F. "Willie" Walker
  G. F. Zeimer

Page P. Stephens
  A. Beard

Vernon A. Landre
  A. "Tony" DeCenso

Gerald W. "Jerry" Thomas
  Don H. Gress

Strike Alpha -- January 22, 1945 (continued)

R. M. "Hoppy" Hopfinger
  A. W. Yarman

W. H. Cannady, Jr.
  J. C. Gerke

"…VT went up the east side of Kikai Jima and made approach from the north. The first division proceeded southward to attack the airstrip, while the second division dropped on the harbor facilities at On-otsu in the northwestern part of the island. Bad visibility hampered selection of targets and observation of damage inflicted."

"The runway at Kikai was cratered at the northern end by a few bombs and numerous unidentified buildings adjoining the airfield were fired. The apparent absence of military activity other than anti-aircraft fire suggests that the field may not have been operational."

"…During the attack, Ens Bissell made a shallow glide over the airstrip, descending below 1000 feet. As he retired, his plane was burning. The plane continued low across the island and appeared to be gliding for a water landing. The plane, however, crashed into the sea and sank instantly at a point approximately 5 miles southeast of Kikai airstrip or 28-15N; 129-59E. The time was 0856(I). VT circled the spot but saw no survivors. Only a large oil slick was observed." [1]

I was flying with the second division of VT-4, led by Page Stephens. Since the weather was bad and the AA fire increasing, he chose not to take us through the same hole in the clouds that the first

Reconnaissance photo of bombed airfield. Okinawa. 1945.

Reconnaissance photo of ruins Naha City, capital of Okinawa. 1945.

division dived through. Rather, we spotted another opening and dropped on shore facilities thought to be a PT boat base. Several buildings were fired.

This was one of the few times that I chose to strafe and went on down to near-ground level. As I flew across the island, I observed many individuals with rifles firing at me. About this time, I also heard the radio call indicating that Bissell had gone down. Neither Bissell nor his crewman, W. H. Moore, ARM3c, survived the crash.

Ens Frank H. Bissell, Jr. was a new transfer to Torpedo 4. He and Ens Keith Gardner came aboard as replacement pilots from Torpedo Squadron 13 in early January of 1945. Keith Gardner tells the story this way.[2]

"Bissell and I were ordered off the Ben Franklin at Pearl Harbor because she was heavily damaged by a Kamikaze. The Franklin was hit off the Philippines and sent back to Washington for repairs. We were all reassigned to different units, and Bissell and I were given orders to report aboard the ESSEX. We hitchhiked all over the Pacific trying to find her. They wouldn't tell us where the ESSEX was or help us find her. We were on Mog Mog Island on Christmas Day. Bissell and I went into the Officers' Club on Mog Mog and had a few drinks. Bissell had the blues and started to cry while others were singing, 'I'll Be Home For Christmas.' I asked what was the matter, and he said he felt he would never make it home. I tried to cheer him up, but he really had the blues that day -- and he never made it, either."

"Bissell usually went out on the morning flights, and I went out on the afternoon flights. I took the same plane as he did, spotted at the same place on the flight deck. The third flight out... the plane didn't come back. He crashed in the water."

"When I went up with the afternoon flight, the plane I was assigned was spot-

ted in the same place. I vowed then that I wasn't going to go anywhere in that damn plane if it had any trouble. That morning Bissell had trouble with the flaps, unfolding the wings, and other problems. I wasn't going to go up that day if there was one thing wrong with that plane, but everything went click, click, click. It was a milk run for me that day."

"Later, I had to survey all his goods, separate them all out, and send them home."

Tokuno Shima -- January 22, 1945

At 1300, 9 VF and 7 VT took off from the *ESSEX* to hit enemy air facilities, shipping, and targets of opportunity in Amami Gunto.[1]

"...Attack was initiated at approximately 1430(I) against Tokuno Shima airfield. Because of 8-9/10 cloud cover at 6000 feet and absence of aerial or AA opposition, runs were made at a low level and pilots believed their bombs, rockets, and m/g fire caused substantial damage to revetments, taxiways, hangars, barracks, and other installations. Particularly hard hit were buildings along the western and southwestern borders of the landing area. Five to seven aircraft were observed on the field and attacked, probably were destroyed. It is the opinion of all pilots, however, that the a/c were dummies or had been wrecked prior to this attack...."

The Torpedo 4 tactical organization consisted of:[1]

Strike Baker -- January 22, 1945

Lee L. "Ham" Hamrick (pilot)
  W. M. Hardin (crew)

Keith Gardner
  P. J. Wilson

Will S. Souza
  D. L. Huston

Strike Baker -- January 22, 1945 (continued)

J. E. Hewitt
  L. P. Shuman

L. C. Gray
  J. E. Ganley

Robert F. "Bob" Ruth
  C. L. McConnell

H. J. Deimel
  L. S. Leach

Seven torpedo planes took off, rendezvoused with their VF escort, and set course for Tokuno Shima in the Amami Gunto sector of the Nansei Shoto. The flight, led by Lt Hamrick, proceeded to target area, "on the deck" at 145 knots true airspeed. VT went up the east side of Tokuno Shima, climbing to 7000 feet, and cut back at the northern end of the island to initiate their attack.[1]

"Attacking from north to south, VT pushed over from 7000 feet and employing glides of 30 to 40 degrees acquired an average speed of 300 knots indicated. Practically all of the bombs dropped hit the runway, cratering it the full length. Pilots were of the opinion that the runway was left temporarily unserviceable."

"After the attack on the runway, the flight circled the island. Four barges were spotted off the east coast of Tokuno Shima. These barges were heavily strafed by VT, but none were observed to burn or sink."

VF also attacked some ships and shore installations near Agpogi and Yamma and burned two Sugar Charlie-type ships near Kaitsu Saki.

During the day Lt Col Millington led 15 VMF Corsairs on an effective bombing and strafing run against Ie Shima airfield, Nansei Shoto. In addition, the Marines flew CAP, while the second major strike group was being assembled.

Capt Bedford recorded: [3]

*"Took off on early hop, routine patrol -- no bogeys -- **TICONDEROGA** left us during night with several CL and DD, she suffered heavy casualties and damage. But is repairable. Had about 10 deg. list to port when I saw her from air."*

"We had 16-plane strike to Ie Shima.... Saw no planes, light flak, bombed airfield and strafed some small boats.... Tomorrow we refuel."

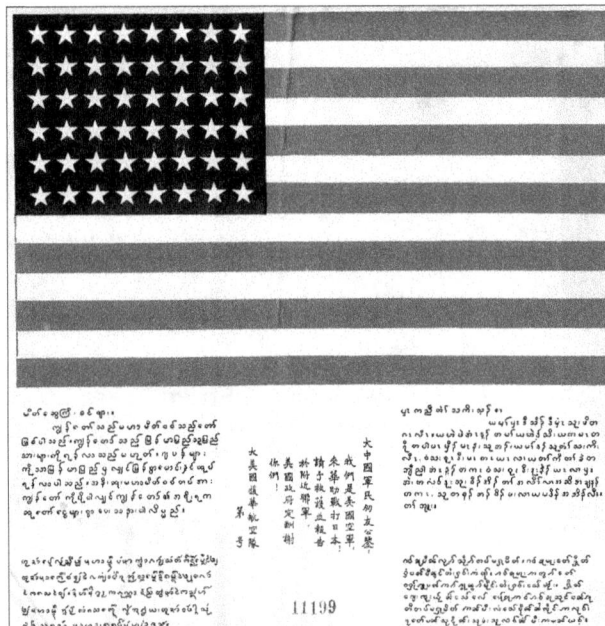

"Blood Chit" carried by **ESSEX** Marines -- It promises a reward for the safety of a downed airman. This one belonged to Capt Wilbur Thomas, VMF-213.

Chapter 29 | En Route to Tokyo

"I was shaking so badly..., that I barely had command of the controls."

On January 23, 1945, the ***ESSEX*** retired from the battle front to rendezvous with a tanker for refueling. The next day, the entire Task Group steamed toward Ulithi. Strikes and fighter sweeps were discontinued, but we launched the usual Combat Air Patrols and antisub searches. We dropped anchor on January 26 and remained in the lagoon until February 10, "replenishing in Berth 25." [1]

This replenishment was more than routine. Admiral Raymond A. Spruance, with his staff, was waiting in Ulithi to replace Admiral Halsey as Fleet Commander. The Third Fleet would now become the Fifth Fleet once more -- and our Task Force would change from 38.3 to 58.3. [2]

Most of us liked being under the command of "Bull" Halsey -- even though history shows that he made some mistakes -- including leading us into that disastrous typhoon. As one historian stated: [2]

"Admiral Halsey, despite his shortcomings, which were few compared to his virtues, was liked by all and revered by the enlisted men of his fleet. Always approachable, always solicitous, always daring, he operated not in the spirit of 'Go!' but of 'Let's go!' He asked no man to face dangers that he would not face himself."

The change in the higher levels of command was not as important to me as the mail call with letters from home. Mother wrote that my brother Byron may now be in the Pacific. That was exciting news. My letter of January 31 provides the details of our reunion in Ulithi Lagoon:

"Dear Mother, Dad, and Walter,"

"...a few hours after your letter arrived, I saw a Baby Flat Top pull up and *anchor beside our ship.... My hopes were confirmed by the Signal Bridge....It sure enough was the Kasaan Bay."*

"I bummed a ride on a guard mail boat over to her and went aboard. Golly it was good to see Byron again. We talked for hours, exchanging sea stories and finally ended up in a discussion of ranches, horses, and future plans...."

"Byron and I together can, by selling our war bonds and using my bank account, rustle up close to $2000 cash. With our present sea duty we can set aside $200 per month. We want to invest in land... maybe put some kind of a deal together to buy Lidy Hot Springs. Or, as a second choice, Blue Creek."

"Byron sure looks good since he made Chief. He really has a good deal now, even if he does kick a little... good food, good quarters.... Write soon."

"Lots of Love,
Gerald"

My flight log shows an 18-day break from flying duty -- the longest since we joined fleet operations in the Pacific. This break gave us a chance to get in some wonderful R&R on Mog Mog.

Capt Bedford recorded that he and several fellow Marines, including Millington: [3]

Jan 31, 1945 -- *"...went to Falalop Is. to visit Marine Group there. Had the big party at 'O' Club. Missed our boat back to the ship -- spent the night on the beach. Same old scene, these advance base strips.*

Marine Corsair taking off. *USS ESSEX*. January 25, 1945.

Seaplanes and fuel tanks on the beach, Mog Mog, Ulithi. February 7, 1945.

Could have been Espiritie, Guadalcanal, Russela, or Munda in the old days. Blazing white coral strips -- tattered coconut palms -- bulldozers -- jeeps -- half naked marines -- beards -- mustaches -- water trailers -- buckets and gas drums under tent flaps to catch water -- home made box furniture. One thing conspicuous by its absence -- mosquitoes. Spent night on cot -- not covers, my clothes still wet from the dousing we got in boat on way over from ship.

"Native cemeteries reminiscent of New Orleans -- crypts above ground made of coral rock slabs. One elaborate memorial smeared with pink plaster and by way of adornment -- a big green glass bottle stuck on top. Many crosses evident, with dates in English with Arabic numerals -- then an epitaph in Japanese. Houses of thatch and palm lobs. Look more like New Guinea design. Differ from Solomon structures. All built on two level platforms made of rock slabs. Gravel (coral) floors. No natives present."

Being in port made it easy to stir up some new scuttlebutt. The latest rumor was, *"We are headed for Tokyo!"* Someone painted a sign on one of the gun mounts, "Tokyo or Bust," and we took some casual photos around the sign. Each of us had high hopes that, someday, these photos, showing "intrepid airmen" on the way to Japan to avenge our losses at Pearl Harbor would reach wives and sweethearts back home.

Lt Col Millington, taking seriously his assignment as Commander of Air Group 4, prepared an analysis of our operations for the period December 30, 1944, to January 26, 1945. He commented on the high number of operational losses for the Marines flying F4Us and made some specific recommendations to reduce these losses. He mentioned the serious weather problems. He recommended refinements in the positioning and communications system used by the Picket Destroyer. He suggested measures to minimize ship losses to Kamikazes.

Millington also emphasized to the higher levels of command that our fighters should cease carrying bombs because of their vulnerability to Japanese fighters and because of the lack of training in glide-bombing tactics by fighter pilots. This concern was probably related to the fact that he and his fellow Marines flew F4Us, whereas the F6Fs were better adapted to a joint bomber/fighter mission. Another important recommendation was to eliminate "pre-dawn" launches. Millington's report states: [4]

"...this group experienced considerable trouble with pre-dawn launches, and it is highly recommended that pre-dawn flights be cut down to only absolute requirements, if not eliminated entirely. In most cases pre-dawn rendezvous were rendered very difficult due to poor weather conditions, the fact that task groups were so close together as to make ship's lights confusing, and that mixed flights (VF and VT) have too high a speed differential. The majority of pre-dawn flights failed to accomplish more than they could have had they launched at dawn, and the attendant risks and pilot strain is not compensated for."

The rumors about Tokyo were soon verified. On February 10, the Task Force raised anchor and steamed out of Ulithi Lagoon. We were now under a new Commander, Vice Admiral Mark Mitscher. Under Mitscher, the Task Force was labeled TG 58.3 instead of 38.3, which was Admiral Halsey's command. Our carrier task group (CTG) consisted of the ***ESSEX, BUNKER HILL, COWPENS, NEW JERSEY, SOUTH DAKOTA, PASADENA, ASTORIA, WILKES BARRE***, and 12 destroyers.

The day we raised anchor for Japan (Feb. 10), *"A severe earthquake rocked Tokyo, followed almost immediately by a devastating raid by 90 B-29 bombers."* [5] These B-29 raids were now occurring on a fairly regular basis, and the damage was extensive -- mostly from the fires that followed the bomb blasts.

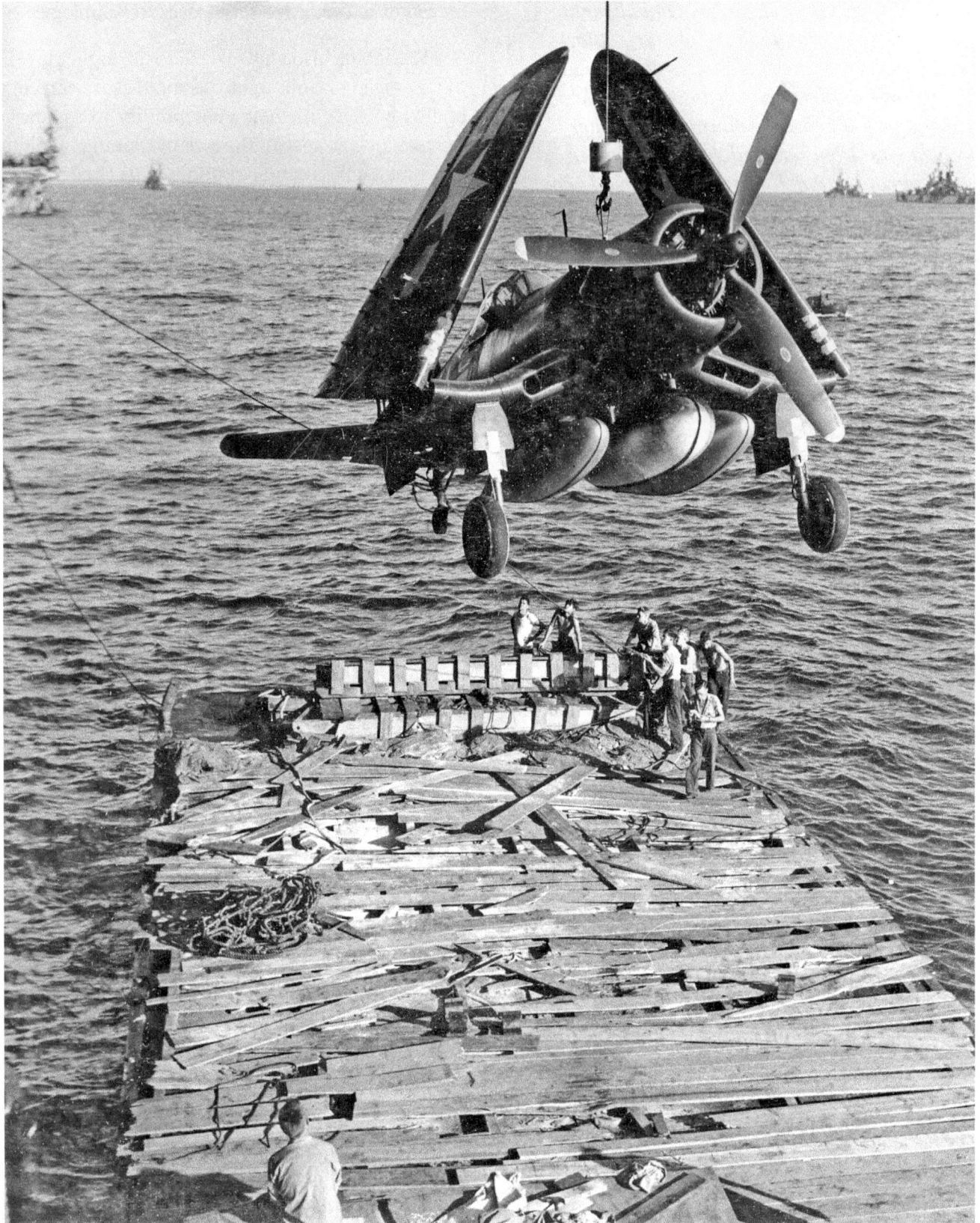

New replacement Corsair being loaded onto the **USS ESSEX**. Ulithi. February 5, 1945.

But B-29s could not do the same job as the Navy or Marine planes. These big bombers came in high, made the drop based upon bomb sight readings, and turned around for home. Our Avengers could pinpoint a target and hold into the dive until we were fairly sure of a hit or at least a destructive near-miss. The big guns fired at the B-29s -- our nemesis was the 20s and 40s at close range.

In the next few days, as TG 58.3 moved into position for the Navy's first carrier-based strikes on the Japanese mainland since the Doolittle Raid, our air group was launched for practice coordinated attacks, antisub patrols and CAPs. One of our Marines made a hard landing and wiped out another Corsair during these practices. By dawn of February 16, the *ESSEX* was approximately 125 miles southeast of Tokyo and ready for one of the most exciting Naval Air attacks of WWII.

For our first strikes on the Japanese homeland, Cdr F. K. Upham moved into position as air group CO, replacing Marine Col Millington. Cdr Upham would serve as CAG-4 for the remainder of our time on the *ESSEX*.

Mawatari, Japan -- February 16, 1945

The *ESSEX* launched Corsair and Hellcat fighter sweeps on the morning of February 16. But it was not until 1407 hours that the major strike group got off the flight deck. This group, under the leadership of Major Marshall of VMF 213, consisted of 8 F6Fs, 11 F4Us, and 13 TBMs. We carried 18 100-pound GP bombs in each of the Avengers.[5]

Lt P. J. Davis was scheduled to lead VT-4 on this strike. He reported electrical trouble on the flight deck and turned the leadership over to Lt Trexler. The Torpedo 4 tactical organization was: [6]

Strike -- February 16, 1945

P. J. Davis, Jr. (pilot) (downed, electrical trouble)
N. J. Schmolke (crew)

C. N. W. "Scott" Vogt
R. E. Kelly

G. M. "Buck" Barnett
C. Christopher

Strike -- February 16, 1945 (continued)

W. F. "Willie" Walker
S. A. Hastings

Page P. Stephens (downed, engine problems)
Andy "Marge" Mocsary

Vernon A. Landre
Charlie C. Statler

R. M. "Hoppy" Hopfinger
M. V. Wilson

Gerald W. "Jerry" Thomas
J. E. Holloman

B. R. "Trex" Trexler
C. W. Barr

G. M. Bell
R. R. Pittman

Robert F. "Bob" Ruth
C. L. McConnell

L. C. Gray
H. R. Green

Ed S. Binder
W. D. Jenkins

G. D. "Mak" Makibbin
R. Campbell

W. H. Cannady, Jr.
J. C. Gerke

We rendezvoused with 4 F6Fs and 9 TBMs from the *USS COWPENS* and proceeded toward Honshu, Japan -- climbing at 140 knots indicated to 13,500 feet.[6]

"The late launch, and instructions from base to return by 1730(K) made impractical the flight to Ota, and upon request the base gave permission for the flight to attack an alternate target."

"Mawatari airfield was selected and F6Fs with rockets were ordered to precede VT in the attack and F4Us to remain above as high cover, and go down in a strafing run after F6Fs had recovered. Undoubtedly considerable damage was done to the

VT-4 pilots ready for strike on Tokyo. Thomas at right. ***USS ESSEX***. February 15, 1945.

VT-4 Avenger gets ready to take off on first strike on Tokyo from an aircraft carrier
since Doolittle's Raid (April 18, 1942). ***USS ESSEX***. February 16, 1945.

hangars and other installations, as well as aircraft and equipment in the hangars."

"The bomb hits by the torpedo planes, observed by several of our fighters, were very accurate...."

Anti-aircraft fire was extremely heavy during the attack. I saw many tracers floating harmlessly by my cockpit while I was in the run. I purposely went in hot, pushing over until I saw the needle go past the red mark. At this speed no Grumman or General Motors guarantees were in effect. Just as I pulled out of the dive, I heard an explosion. My hatch had been sucked out by an AA burst or from the high-G pullout. I tested the controls gingerly and found no damage. My crewman, Holloman, looked relieved when I glanced in the mirror.

But the flight was far from over. With no cockpit cover, we felt a new kind of chill, this one from the Japanese winter weather. I was shaking so badly by the time we made the 150-mile return trip to the **ESSEX**, that I barely had command of the controls.

Bill Cannady also lost a cockpit hatch in the Tokyo strike. *"We pushed over at 12-13,000 feet. I threw the throttle to the fire wall and pulled rich mixture. I was the last guy down in the dive but that blast of cold air sure hastened my join up and return."* [7]

Meanwhile our fighter squadrons had run into plenty of excitement with Japanese planes.[5]

"...while the VF and VT were attacking the field, they were jumped by 2 TOJOS which attacked from a slightly higher altitude. In the ensuing brief dog fight, Ensign Fewell skillfully diverted one TOJO from his wingman's tail and got in two effective bursts which sent the enemy tumbling toward earth trailing heavy black smoke...."

"Ens Dailey engaged the other TOJO and succeeded in putting a burst into the ventral fuselage just abaft the cockpit before the enemy broke off the attack."

"...Lt Hendricks and Lt Barnett each flamed a ZEKE at the airfield. Ens Peters probably destroyed an unidentified twin-engine aircraft and Ens Zdancewicz probably destroyed a TOJO...."

During the various flights throughout the day, VF-4 pilots claimed 15 enemy plane kills, 3 probables, and 2 damaged. Confirmed kills were credited to C. J. Nicolini, J. P. Sikors, D. S. "Diz" Laird, Hal H. Avants, C. L. Martin, W. W. "Dub" Taylor, P. H. Gordon, T. J. Graham, W. C. Guyles, J. F. "Raider" Radford, W. C. "Dusty" Rhodes, W. G. Schulden, and Kinsey K. "KK" Fewell.[7]

The report on the loss of Dusty Rhodes is brief: [5]

"Taylor, Schulden, and Rhodes fell behind due to engine trouble in Rhodes' plane, and were attacked by about ten planes. In the ensuing scrap, Taylor downed three, and Schulden and Rhodes one each, but [Rhodes'] plane was smoking. As the three retired, Taylor and Schulden were kept busy by the harassing Zekes... and Dusty Rhodes disappeared. Nothing is known of his whereabouts."

Marine squadrons VMF-124 and VMF-213 were kept busy on this first day of strikes against Tokyo. The Corsairs flew CAP and combat sweeps over Japanese airfields. In the numerous dog fights with Japanese pilots, confirmed kills were credited as follows:

- Major J. M. Johnson - 1 Myrt
- Capt Wilbur J. Thomas - 2 Zekes
- 2nd Lt W. A. Dahl - 1 Val
- 1st Lt George B. Parker - 1 Zeke
- George B. Parker, W. A. Dahl, and Wilbur J. Thomas joined in a "probable"

At noon, 8 Marines joined with a VF4 flight to attack a Japanese destroyer, leaving it dead in the water. This group also strafed an SO and an FTO. It was a busy day for the **ESSEX** air group.

The Navy made the headlines back in the States with these strikes on the Japanese homeland. ***"Tokyo Attacked By Fleet Planes; Navy's Might Is Thrown At Tokyo For First Time; Mitscher Directs History's Boldest Naval Operations."*** [9]

As might be expected, this great publicity for the Navy was partially countered by MacArthur's headquarters. On the same day we hit Tokyo, *"American paratroopers landed on Corregidor Island, followed by the 34th Division infantrymen."* But, it was not until March 2 that MacArthur himself returned to Corregidor.[5]

C. C. Statler, VT-4 crewman manning the turret for Vernon Landre, summarized the day's activities in his journal.[10]

"...Today we hit an airfield near Tokyo. I saw airborne enemy planes today for the first time -- 3 Zekes over the target. Sure was awful cold. Temperature on the ground was 23 degrees. 'Dusty' Rhodes went down today. 245 planes shot down and 160 destroyed on ground by whole task force. Our losses -- 32 planes."

VOL. CLX. NO. 47.   SIXTEEN PAGES TODAY   RALEIGH, N. C., FRIDAY]

TOKYO ATTACKED BY FLEET PLANES

Navy's Might Is Thrown At Tokyo for First Time

Headline announcing Task Force 58.3's strike on Tokyo. February 16, 1945.

Chapter 30 | Window and Jammers over Japan

"Dahl, guns frozen, found an Oscar on his tail."

To inflict the maximum damage to Tokyo aircraft factories and production facilities at Nakajima Tama, two other air groups were ordered to join Air Group 4. Due to bad weather we did not get off the flight deck until 0845. The rendezvous brought together.[1]

- 22 F6Fs, 7 F4Us, and 13 TBMs from AG-4
- 12 F4Us, 15 SB2Cs, and 15 TBMs from AG-84
- 8 F6Fs and 9 TBMs from AG-46

Lt Lykes Boykin from Fighting 4 was in command. He ordered VT-4 to take position as the base element, with AG-46 next, and AG-84 in the rear. Our **ESSEX** Marines were stationed as high cover for the flight to Japan, with Hellcats as intermediate cover on both sides.

"The coast of Honshu was crossed between Oiso and Opowara. The flight passed west of the north-south line of airfields until east of Takahagi airfield. Two groups of enemy VF attempted passes at the flight that were effectively dealt with by the escort."

"West of Takahagi airfield the flight turned eastward and passed between Takahagi airfield and Sakato airfield, and then turned southward between Tokorozawa airfield and Narimasu airfield, in order to attack the target from north to south. Enemy VF heckled the flight throughout the approach attack and retirement."

"A well coordinated and effective attack was delivered on the target, bombing was accurate and undoubtedly caused considerable damage." [1]

Our Torpedo 4 Exec Lt Hamrick, led the TBMs on this strike. The tactical organization was: [1]

Strike Baker -- February 17, 1945

Lee L. "Ham" Hamrick (pilot)
R. A. Trembley (crew)

Keith Gardner
W. A. DeYoung

Felix E. Ward, Jr.
Don M. Applegate

J. E. Hewitt
L. P. Shuman

E. A. "Ted" Newell
W. J. Lace

W. J. Hopkins, Jr. (returned to base)
R. E. Simendinger, Jr.

Will S. Souza
D. L. Huston

L. A. "Cozy" Cole
N. L. Shiverdecker

B. R. "Trex" Trexler
J. W. Aldrich

G. M. Bell
A. J. Tankard

Robert F. "Bob" Ruth
J. F. "Forrest" Ballard

L. C. Gray
J. E. Ganley

Ed S. Binder
W. D. Jenkins

H. J. Deimel
C. L. Ely, Jr.

W. H. Cannady, Jr. (downed, tail damaged)
A. G. Schiesz

Cannady aborted after damaging his empennage while taxiing into take-off position. Hopkins

Captured "Zeke" (Mitsubishi A6M fighter), also known as a "Zero," being flown
by an American pilot. October 12, 1942.

Captured "Oscar" (Nakajima Ki-43 fighter). Undated photo.

had engine troubles and landed shortly after take-off on the **USS HANCOCK**.

Ham reported that *"near the town of Yoshimo, four Tojos intercepted the formation, making one pass from 180 degrees. They were engaged by fighter escort."* Three Oscars came up from behind the formation as it reached the target and two of these enemy planes fired on the Avengers as they went into their bombing runs.

"In a well coordinated attack from north to south VT, preceded by one division of VFB, pushed over from 14,000 feet. In steep glides of 45 to 55 degrees, an average speed of 355 knots indicated was acquired. Average altitude of release was 3500 feet. Interrogation of air crewmen and VMF pilots who were flying high cover indicates that VT bombing was highly accurate. As far as can be determined, all bombs dropped by VT struck within the 'vital area' of the target (north wings) or on the two southern wings housing administration and laboratories and research. No misses were observed. The exact nature of the damage could not immediately be observed because of smoke and flying debris rising from the target. VT were followed in the attack by VFB and by aircraft of the COWPENS and BUNKER HILL groups."

"Retirement was made as planned, southward 'on the deck' and giving wide margin to heavily defended Chofu airfield to the west. Once Chofu was passed, aircraft turned westward toward their rendezvous point over the town of Kawajiri, staying clear of Shimonizo and Haramachida airfields to the south." [1]

Keith Gardner, who was flying wing on Ham, described the strike in these words: *"We dove on the Nakajima Tama Engine Plant from about 13-15,000 feet. I kept pushing over until my airspeed passed the red mark. I still hung in on the dive. Just as I dropped my bombs, the hatch blew in on my shoulder. My turret gunman spotted this glass going by. He grabbed the intercom to see if I was OK. I couldn't answer, since I was still in the dive. I hoped he wouldn't panic and jump because he didn't know whether I was dead or alive."* [2]

During this second day of attacks on the Japanese homeland, our torpedo bombers were protected with excellent fighter cover by Hellcats and Corsairs. [3]

"Northeast of Fujiyama, 4 Tojos dived on the formation from 12 o'clock above. Lt Hendricks' division at 16,500 feet pulled up into the attack. Lt Hendricks gave one of the Tonys a good burst which started it smoking and caused large pieces of cowling to tear off. This plane was last seen in a steep dive and smoking. Unfortunately the kill could not be confirmed by others and is scored as a probable. Lt Burnett met another of the Tonys head on and two or three pieces of metal were ripped from the Tony's engine area by his fire. This plane was not smoked and only damaged, it is claimed. The aggressive action on the part of the top cover probably accounts for the complete failure of the enemy to inflict any damage to any plane in the flight."

"As the flight approached the target from the northeast 4 Tonys dived on the formation from 12 o'clock above. Lt(jg) Peabody pulled up slightly as the rats shallowed out in their dives and got in a long burst into the engine of one of the Tonys. This Tony was smoking heavily as it passed beneath Peabody and was observed by others in the flight as it spiraled downward and crashed."

As the fighters and bombers pushed over in their attack on the Nakajima Tama factories, 5 Tonys made a run on the base element of VT-4. Our Hellcats followed these Tonys down. Peabody smoked one of these planes, and it nosed over into a very steep dive. *"Laird shot down a Tony on the tail of a Torpecker, and while he was so engaged, an Oscar got on his tail. Avants came to Laird's*

Captured "Tony" (Kawasaki Ki-61 fighter). Undated photo.

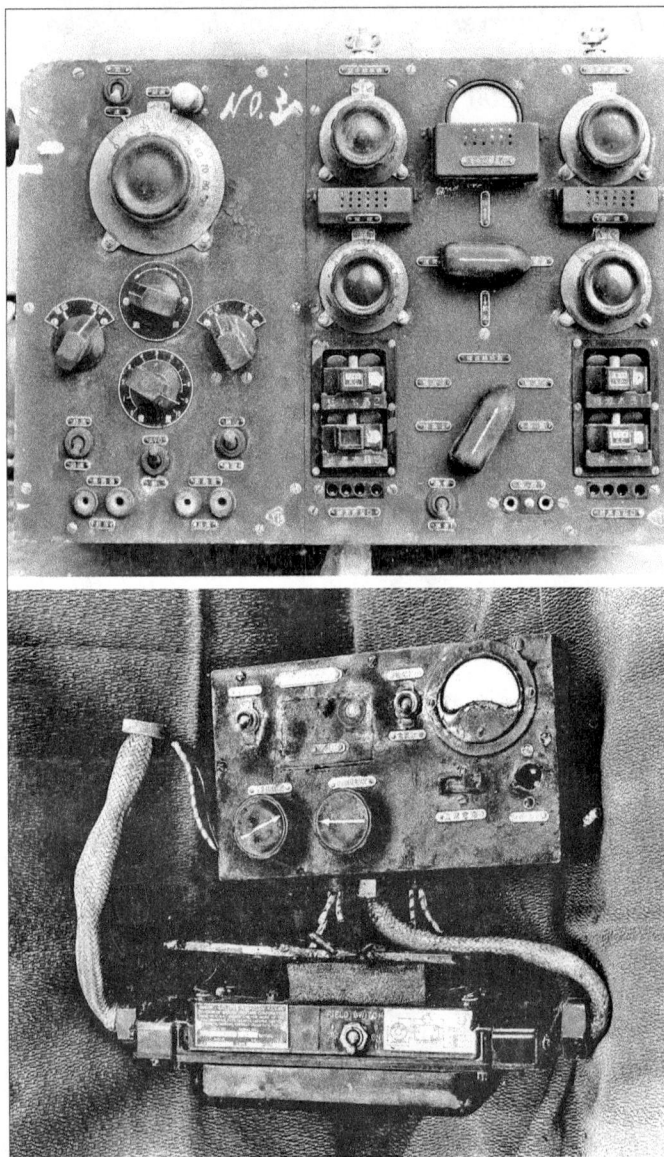

Instrument panels from an unidentified captured Japanese fighter. The bottom panel contains parts purchased from an American company.

rescue and exploded the Oscar."

"Ens K. Peters sighted an Oscar at 10 o'clock level near Tachikawa airfield on a converging course. Peters closed rapidly with the tremendous speed from his dive and just had time to get in a short burst before overshooting the enemy. His fire must have killed the Jap pilot because the Oscar nosed over sharply and crashed."

"Lt(jg) Avants found an F4U bracketed at 500 feet by two Oscars. Avants made a pass at one of the rats and they started working on him. Just as one Oscar was in the act of making a run on Avants from 8 o'clock level the F4U returned the favor by engaging this Oscar in a head-on run and smoked him. This Oscar was not seen again. During these maneuvers Avants got in a burst from head on, a deflection shot from 10 o'clock level and one last pass from head-on which caused the Oscar to nose over and crash."

"Lt Laird had jumped a Tojo near the rendezvous point and followed him on the deck through gullies and around hills northeastward toward Tokyo. He fired about 6 separate bursts one of which started the enemy a/c smoking. During the chase the Tojo flew under a high-tension line and finally spun in attempting to climb over a hill near the outskirts of Tokyo." [1]

Fighter Sweeps--February 17, 1945

In addition to the main strike group, several fighter sweeps were sent over Japan.[3]

"At 0645 a VF-4 search was launched under the leadership of Lt Keers. This flight encountered enemy planes and Lt(jg) Kelley shot down a Jill."

"At 0708 hours, Hartsock led a Marine Corsair group from VMF-124 in an attack on Teteyama airfield."

*"At 0730 Cdr Upham took a division of 4 Hellcats '**to reconnoiter the Tokyo area, photograph fields, and assess strike damage.**'"*

"At 0755 another VMF search group under Major Marshall attacked shipping along the coast and 2nd Lt Green destroyed a Judy."

"At 1030 a Combat Air Patrol of 4 Hellcats over the Picket Destroyer made strafing attacks on some Jap ships."

On one of the early Hellcat flights, *"Ens Gustafson was forced to make a water landing because of a serious hydraulic leak and electrical failure."* He made contact with the rescue picket and was picked up by the **USS CALLAHAN**.

The Marines flew high cover for the major strike group, which was launched at 0845 for Nakajima Tama. After we completed our attacks, the VMF squadrons hung around to engage more enemy aircraft. Their action reports present another perspective on the Tokyo strikes.

"First to attack were 4 Zekes, reddish-brown with big red meatballs. Making an opposite pass outside the fighter cover, they slow-rolled as they went by. Our flight was high cover, at about 17,000 feet and had just crossed the coastline. They made stab passes, possibly trying to force our cover off after them. Five Oscars then appeared above and at 10 o'clock, and followed the planes into the target area, where two more appeared. Four Oscars followed the VT down, but could not get through the fighter cover."

"Dahl, guns frozen, found an Oscar on his tail and executed a 360 degree turn, with Goetz sticking by. The maneuver relieved Dahl's situation, but put the Jap on Goetz's tail. Doing a wingover, Dahl sliced toward the Oscar, relieving Goetz's tail position (the Jap got one hit in his wing),

and the section rejoined. Falling on Oscar's tail, the old weave when he turned did the trick, and Goetz got a burst in from 11 o'clock at the Jap's engine, flaming it. Capt Thomas saw it hit the deck in flames, and the kill goes to Goetz."

"Capt Thomas and Reynolds found themselves attacked by four Oscars, and in the ensuing melee, Reynolds flames one when he turned into Reynolds' guns to get away from Thomas. A second Oscar made the mistake of getting in front of Thomas's guns for a brief instant, and was last seen smoking around the engine nacelle. A fourth, intent on getting in position to fire at Reynolds, came under Thomas's guns and fell away with 'probables' to Thomas, one destroyed for Reynolds."

"While proceeding to the rendezvous area, two Oscars came down through astern of Kercoude's 3-plane division above. The division immediately went into a defensive weave. A 20-mm shell exploded in Deboeuf's cockpit. A piece of shrapnel entered his shoulder and minute fragments splattered into his face." [3]

After these high altitude encounters with Japanese fighters, Col William Millington reported some problems with the Corsair, *"In recent operations over Japan, serious trouble was experienced with guns freezing on the F4U-1D. We lost 40 percent of the firepower above 16,000 feet at 30 degrees F.".* Millington recommended that the ship's plane mechanics install gun heaters to prevent this problem.

Returning pilots from these Tokyo raids reported that anti-aircraft fire over the target and at points along the flight path was most intense, but that *"bursts from heavy batteries en route to target were off altitude, an unusual error factor in Japanese heavy antiaircraft firing."* [1]

The reports indicated that no planes from the **ESSEX** were shot down by Ack Ack on this strike.

This was probably related to the fact that 5 of the Avengers were now equipped with a new radar jamming device. In addition, all of the VTs and some of the fighters made extensive use of "window" on the strike.

The "window" we carried in the TBMs consisted of strips of tinfoil laminated to paper. *"The strips were about 18-inches long and carried by the turret gunner in a quiver. As soon as we spotted AA bursts, or if we were over gun emplacements, we would push 5 or 6 of these strips of foil through the air control vent in the turret."* [4] Thus, the "window" would simulate several planes and tend to confuse the radar-controlled guns.

When all planes were back aboard the **ESSEX**, and we had secured "flight quarters" for the night, there were many exciting stories of dogfights, close calls, and first impressions of the snow-covered Mt. Fujiyama.

On February 17, the Fighting 4 Red Rippers reported 8 confirmed kills, and the Marines were credited with seven.

Hellcats (VF-4)

- D. S. "Diz" Laird -- 1 Tony and 1 Tojo
- Hal H. Avants -- 2 Oscars
- G. A. Peabody - -2 Tonys
- K. Peters -- 1 Oscar
- R. S. Kelley -- 1 Jill

Corsairs (VMF)

- Robert D. Green -- 1 Judy
- C. G. Hendricks -- 1 Tony
- J. H. Burnett -- 1 Tony
- W. E. Reynolds -- 1 Oscar
- F. J. Goetz, Jr. -- 1 Oscar
- Wilbur J. Thomas -- 2 Oscars

Cozy Cole sort of summarized many of our feelings. *"One of my most satisfying moments of the war was that first strike on Tokyo! I had saved up for the occasion, and when we flew over Japan, I used the 'relief tube' with pleasure."* [5]

Chapter 31 | Iwo Jima

"Millington led a flight of 24 F4Us to support the landings on Iwo Jima."

Frustration on D-Day -- February 19, 1945

Immediately after the Tokyo strikes, Task Force 58.3 moved south to support the invasion of Iwo Jima. We used the time en route for refueling the destroyers. Routine anti-sub and combat air patrols were launched for daytime fleet coverage.

In keeping with the new security policy, most of us were not informed of the date and time for the invasion of Iwo Jima. However, we had practiced close support tactics in anticipation of any scheduled assault. Complete briefings on Iwo were provided on the evening of February 18. Before dawn on D-Day, the **ESSEX** had moved into position -- about 75 miles NW of Iwo -- for our support assignment.[1]

As luck would have it, the weather turned foul. It was so bad that our torpedo planes could not be launched. The best we could do was to provide fighter coverage.

At H-Hour minus 45 minutes, one close support mission was finally able to take off in spite of the treacherous weather, and dispatched to Iwo. This flight, led by Lt Col Millington, consisted of 24 F4Us and 24 F6Fs. (Lt L. M. Boykin was the leader for the VF-4 Hellcats.) The assignment was to *"attack flanks and high ground along the flank of the landing beaches from H-45 to H-35 with Napalm, rockets and strafing."* In addition, the support group was to strafe the beaches just ahead of the landings from H-5 to H-2. A portion of the strike report follows: [2]

"The flight was split into two elements for the flank attacks with 12 F4Us with Napalm and 12 F6Fs with Napalm and rockets on each flank. The attacks were delivered from a double column approach with divisions breaking to port and starboard as assigned dropping Napalms on the first run, pulling out to seaward and repeating attacks with rockets and strafing until the time limit expired."

The Corsairs and Hellcats were then rendezvoused at Point William at 9000 feet to await orders for the H-5 strafing attack along the landing beaches.[2]

"These attacks were delivered (at 0845) from south to north in steep dives, all planes pulling up sharply to the right to rejoin the tail element for repeated runs. The attack was moved landward as the landing craft approached the beach in order to maintain the bullet impact area 200 yards from the boats. The bullet impact area was shifted 500 yards inland as the boats hit the beach. Naval and other gunfire in the same area necessitated pull-outs at 600 feet."

Capt Bedford in his journal observed: [3]

"Landing boats in 6 long waves began churning for shore, by this time the whole south side of the island was hidden in smoke from the terrific shelling. At 0855, we started our strafing, the first wave of boats about 700 yds. from the beach. 48 planes kept the beach under constant machine gun fire. Our orders were to stay above 600 feet, to keep out of our own shell fire, so we all pressed it down on the deck."

Millington reported that the coordination was excellent and timing right on: *"Only minimum small arms and machine-gun tracers could be seen emanating from the base of Mt. Suribachi, and from the higher ground on the starboard flank."*

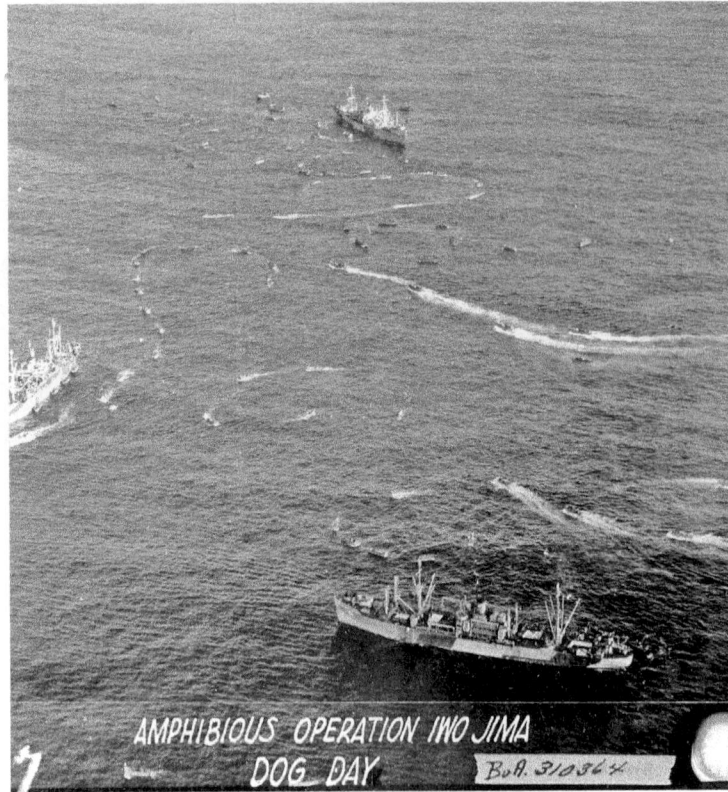

Marines in landing crafts and transports prepare to make landing on Iwo Jima.
February 19, 1945.

Five waves of landing craft stream toward Iwo Jima beach. February 19, 1945.

Millington also reported in the debriefing that: [2]

"Ships gunfire was extremely accurate and effective as to full coverage. One machine gun position on Mt. Suribachi and one automatic or dual-purpose gun were seen to receive direct hits from large naval shells."

The returning VF group stated that about 50 percent of the Napalm bombs failed to explode and burn. Also, there were hangups with some of the rockets. But, all-in-all, the pilots were pleased with the apparent effectiveness of the support mission.

"The attack had been carefully planned and rehearsed once at sea, and again at Guam on the way to Iwo Jima. The briefing of the group by the Command Air Support Control Unit while at Ulithi was excellent. It impressed upon pilots the importance of their mission in supporting the landing forces, and inspired them with a determination to carry out missions well. Coordination and timing were excellent, and no difficulty was encountered in using the two type VF in the strafing attacks." [2]

After the VF and VMF planes returned to the **ESSEX** the bad weather prevented further launches. The Marines were now battling for every inch of land on Iwo. We could do no more to help them on this first day. Kyle Palmer, a **NY Times** correspondent, who was riding in one of our VT-4 Avengers, described the situation on D-day in his article under the headline: ***"MARINES` FLAMING HELL ON IWO DESCRIBED BY `TIMES` WRITER:"***

"For three hours today, as Lt P. P. Stephens of Springfield, Ill. piloted our plane around and across the fiery hell below, we watched an endless stream of landing craft rush up reinforcements and supplies. Landing was difficult, and the black sand under the pounding preinvasion shelling was soft and spongy.... Nevertheless, without hesitation, men, guns, ammunition and supplies were moved ashore"

That night Charlie Statler recorded in his journal: [4]

"Tonight at 1920, the ship went to GQ; 9 enemy planes were approaching at 14-20 miles; 2 were shot down; others returned. GQ over at 2050."

Continued Support for the Invasion

On February 20, the ship was *"refueling, rearming, and receiving replacement aircraft in area about 100 miles SW of Iwo Jima."* [1] On the 21st, we again launched strikes against Iwo Jima, Haha Jima, and Chichi Jima. Statler reported: [4]

"Our planes flew nite sub patrol. Very cold tonight. G.Q. sounded at 1920. We were attacked by 3 or more enemy planes. None came in closer than 6 miles. G.Q. was over at 2050. Saratoga was hit by 4 Banzi Boys. Headed south."

During the fighter sweeps on Chichi Jima, G. A. Peabody destroyed a Jill and F. J. Dailey damaged a Tojo. The VF and VMF also strafed the airfields and attacked shipping in Futami Ko.[5]

Far to the north of us, another carrier group was conducting strikes on Kobe, Japan, when the **FRANKLIN** was attacked by Kamikazes. A total of 772 men aboard the ship were killed, and the Navy awarded its first Congressional Medal of Honor for heroism to a Chaplain, Lt Cdr Joseph T. O'Callahan (who had served with us on the **RANGER**).[6]

February 22 was cool and cloudy with heavy rains. *"Eleven VT were launched at 1230 to hit Iwo Jima. Failed to hit target due to very bad visibility."* [4] I was not with the strike group, but was sent out on a 3-4 hour anti-sub patrol. My visibility was very limited, but I stayed with the search. When I returned to the fleet, I had trouble finding the **ESSEX**.

Buck Barnett was flying one of the TBMs sent out to support the Iwo Jima landings. He reported that the weather was so bad, *"We couldn't even see our wing tips. We were flying around the fleet counterclockwise trying to avoid each other and the ships. I barely got a glimpse of Mt. Suribachi."* [7]

Stan Coller was manning the turret gun for Ens W. J. Hopkins. *"Suddenly, I saw this shadow come over. I ducked as our antenna was clipped off by another plane. That was close! A few years later, back on the farm, I was plowing when a crow flew over. The shadow made me duck, and I hit the knob on the tractor steering wheel. I had a big sore lip for a few days, but the recall back to Iwo Jima was very vivid."* [8]

The next day, February 23, the Carrier Task Force left the Iwo Jima area "heading toward Tokyo."

Mount Suribachi was finally taken by the Marines on February 23, 1945, but Iwo Jima was not secured until May 16. *"The battle of Iwo Jima had cost the lives of 4,554 Marines and 363 Navy men. Of the 21,000 Japanese defenders, little more than 3000 were alive."* [9]

Our Skipper, Lt Paul J. Davis, Jr., made the 20,000 landing on the **ESSEX** on February 21, 1945 during our Iwo Jima strikes.

Chapter 32 | Bombs and Propaganda for Japan

"Oscars and Tojos harassed the formation as it proceeded westward... Carlson was forced down in enemy territory."

Japan -- Koizumi and Ota -- February 25, 1945

Task Group 58.3 left the Iwo Jima area on February 23 and steamed north toward Japan. Another diversionary strike on the enemy homeland would limit the possibilities of further support to Iwo.

As we made preparations for this next attack on Tokyo, part of the discussion in the Ready Room focused on the mechanical problems we were experiencing with the newer TBMs. We had consistent trouble with our radio compass, bomb hangups were too frequent, and cockpit hatches exploded outward in the fast dives or near-miss AA bursts.

The sudden loss of a cockpit hatch was demoralizing to our crew. As the pieces of plexiglass flew by, our turret gunners, facing backwards in the dive, never knew if AA fire had killed the pilot or if the plane was out of control. That few seconds of push-over, dive, and questionable pull-out seemed like an eternity to the crew.

"One time over Manila, I thought Scott, my pilot, had been hit. It seemed that he would never pull out -- we just kept going down. I thought he was dead, so I snapped on my parachute, kicked the hatch, but it wouldn't open. (I was too excited to pull the pin.) About that time, Scott pulled out." [1]

"I was flying with Mr. Cole on a Formosa strike. The CO found a hole in the clouds, and we went in. The first planes cleared with no problems, but we were on the tail end of the formation. The AA fire was increasing and the plexiglass was shot out of our plane. I looked at those mountains, and I didn't want to jump.... We iced up on the return trip to the ESSEX." [2]

"We were in a dive and the engine skipped. I thought 'My Gosh, here we go!' and I looked for a spot to bail out." [1]

Other examples of crew reactions are in the reports of earlier strikes. The sacrifices made by these turret and belly gunners, for the most part, were not acknowledged. Nor were there appropriate medals to partially compensate them for their bravery.

On February 25, the ESSEX was in position for aircraft attacks on Japan "about 175 miles SE of Tokyo." [3]

A VMF fighter sweep, led by Lt Col Millington, was launched at 0727 hours. The flight immediately ran into Japanese opposition and several dog fights took place. Reported enemy kills were as follows: [4]

- Col William A. Millington -- 1 Tony
- 1st Lt Chop -- 1 Zeke
- 1st Lt M. Bolger -- 1 Tony
- 1st Lt J. L. Knight -- 1 Zeke
- Capt Finn -- 1 Oscar

Capt Finn and 2nd Lt Carlson joined in damaging another Oscar, and Oscars were hit but not confirmed as kills by J. M. Johnson, Pfremer, and W. S. Todd. Unfortunately 2nd Lt Carlson was forced down in enemy territory due to a gas leak after an attack.

Capt Bedford's journal notes: [5]

"Don Carlson of St. Louis began losing gas from main, ran out before they reached the Coast. He made a wheels-up landing about 30 NE of Tokyo, near lake and near Hyakurigahara Airfield. Carlson radioed

'Good luck to you guys, say howdy to my wife!' just before he landed. Finn saw him land.... Rest returned O.K. McManus broke a sinus in a barrier crash, is in sick bay."

(Carlson became a POW of the Japanese. Six months later Carlson was liberated. *"He had lost his teeth during frequent beatings, had been starved, and put in solitary confinement for 40 days."*)

The VMF squadrons strafed Kumagaya and Matsuyama airfields, then attacked 8 picket boats along the coast.

The primary strike group was launched at 0815. This flight consisted of 36 VF and 15 VT. Cdr F. K. Upham was CO, but he was forced to turn back due to engine trouble. He released the command to Lt P. J. Davis, the Torpedo 4 Skipper.

The **ESSEX** strike group joined with planes from the **BUNKER HILL** and the **COWPENS**. Our assigned targets were the Nakajima aircraft factories at Koizumi and Ota, Honshu, Japan.

Our Fighting 4 Hellcats were loaded down with bombs and rockets. Their debriefing reports read like a novel.[6]

"...when about half way between the coast and the target area enemy fighters were tallyhoed diving out of the overcast down on, abeam and astern of the formation. There were about 8 attacking enemy aircraft, four Oscars and four Tojos, which harassed the formation as it proceeded westward. The VF and VFB increased speed and weaved violently in order to meet and discourage the attacks. The enemy pilots all employed similar tactics in that they would make high beam and storm runs on the protective screen of VF, dive past their adversaries, recover in a wide chandelle into the clouds only to repeat the process. Their attacks were not pressed close and their fire was never from effective ranges."

A second division of Hellcats sighted a FTB anchored in Naha Ko. They dropped their 1000 pounders on the ship, then returned for strafing runs. The Fox Tare Baker was left smoking after the attack.

"In these encounters three Japs were shot down. The first, when an Oscar dived from 2 o'clock above on the VFB guarding the VT starboard beam. Lt Boykin's and Lt Smith's divisions turned and pulled up into this attack, and firing from head-on, Lt Smith got in an effective burst; the Oscar smoked heavily, rolled in a dive and was observed to spin downward and crash. This kill was also confirmed by a VT crewman."

"Lt Taylor's division, in the high cover position, was weaving by sections. Four Tojos were harassing this division with timid runs from astern and above. Lt Taylor got in a good long burst at a Tojo diving from 8 o'clock above, from 12 o'clock below as the sections crossed over, and observed his tracers going into the engine which began to smoke. The Jap pilot was either killed or lost control because this Tojo spun to the earth and crashed."

"A single Oscar dived in from above and dead astern and getting hits on the empennage of Lt(jg) Lew Lepp's plane. As he overshot, Lepp nosed over after him and got in an accurate burst from 4 o'clock. Tracers entered the cockpit and engine, the Oscar began to smoke, continued in the dive, and crashed."

"Lt Taylor's division jettisoned their 500-pound bombs and squared away for additional attacks. A Tojo using the now familiar tactics dived on Lt Taylor. As he shot past, Taylor pushed over, getting in an effective burst from 8 o'clock above. The Tojo started rolling as in a barrel roll and then appeared to execute a falling leaf as he went down. Although Taylor saw his tracers hitting the Jap in the cockpit and

engine regions, the Jap's maneuvers led him to believe his fire had not been fatal. However, a VT gunner confirmed this kill reporting that the 'falling bird' terminated in a crash."

"An Oscar approached the formation from the port beam. Lt Longley's division turned and pulled up toward the Oscar as it attempted to climb over the group. Lts. Longley and Morken each got in a short burst before they nearly stalled out under the weight of their 500-pound bombs. No evidence of damage to the enemy was reported."

From the cockpit of my Avenger, I could see very little of this action. We held our formation during the attacks by the Japanese and listened to the excited voices of our Hellcat pilots as they engaged the enemy. The VT-4 group consisted of 15 TBMs led by P. J. Davis. Our tactical organization was: [6]

Strike -- February 25, 1945

P. J. Davis, Jr. (pilot)
  N. J. Schmolke (crew)

C. N. W. "Scott" Vogt
  Leo E. Halvorson

G. M. "Buck" Barnett
  Joseph C. Cohen

W. F. "Willie" Walker
  G. F. Zeimer

Page P. Stephens
  Andy "Marge" Mocsary

Vernon A. Landre
  A. "Tony" DeCenso

Gerald W. "Jerry" Thomas
  Don H. Gress

R. M. "Hoppy" Hopfinger
  A. W. Yarman

Ed S. Binder
  R. D. Biddle

Strike -- February 25, 1945 (continued)

H. J. Deimel
  L. S. Leach

G. D. "Mak" Makibbin
  R. Campbell and P. S. Rundall

W. H. Cannady, Jr.
  J. C. Gerke

E. A. "Ted" Newell
  W. B. Cook

W. J. Hopkins, Jr.
  R. E. Simendinger, Jr.

L. A. "Cozy" Cole
  N. H. Knox

Our formation rendezvoused near the water and gradually climbed to strike altitude on a westward course toward the Ota and Koizumi assembly plants. As we made landfall, P. J. had some difficulty with orientation. There was a large amount of snow on the ground.

The smaller rivers were frozen over making them practically invisible from the air. Nevertheless, we had studied the maps and been briefed on other landmarks. Before long, the cleared-off runway near the target became obvious.[6]

"VT approached slightly north of target to cut back and attack the Ota plant from west to east. Pushing over from 10,500 feet in glides of 35 to 40 degrees, VT acquired an average speed in glide of 310 knots indicated. After VT had committed themselves to the attack it was observed that portions of the plant had been gutted by previous attacks, so sections of the plant which appeared to be still undamaged were used as aiming points. Ens Walker chose as aiming point the previously undamaged row of buildings housing a trade school immediately north of and adjoining the plant."

"Medium and heavy antiaircraft fire over target was intense but inaccurate and late in opening up. VT made extensive

Koizumi airport and Ota assembly plant under attack by Torpedo 4. February 25, 1945.

Detail from top photo showing Torpedo 4 Avenger strafing airstrip. February 25, 1945.

use of window and five of the planes were equipped with radar jamming devices."

"After the attack VT effected a running rendezvous eastward. Lt Binder, flying low on retirement, spotted an IRVING before him, parked on Tatebayashi airfield. He strafed the plane and set it afire. Shortly thereafter while he was still retiring low, his gunner, Biddle, strafed with the turret gun a long building near Koga which appeared to be a warehouse. The building was set afire."

Lt Lykes Boykin's VF4 division, loaded with bombs, followed the Avengers in the attack on the Koizumi plant. Several scored hits on the plant. Two of the pilots, Lt(jg) Van Sluyters and Ens P. E. Gannon were unable to get their 1000-pound bombs to release. The ship was not happy to see them request permission to land when they returned, but it had no choice but to bring them back aboard. Theoretically, the bombs would not arm themselves until a short time after release.

After the bombing and strafing attack on the aircraft factory, Fighting 4 continued to engage Japanese planes.[6]

"...When about 5 miles east of Tatebayashi, at 2500 feet, Lt(jg) Sears tallyhoed a Tony diving down from 2 o'clock above. As Sears turned toward the Tony, the Jap turned left, which gave Sears an opportunity to get in a burst from 4 to 5 o'clock. The Tony smoked and Sears had to break off as he was getting slow. The Tony was not observed again. The flight joined up as it proceeded eastward toward the coast."

"In the meantime the photographic division had been engaged in its mission and in the vicinity of Tsukoba airfield they were engaged by two Oscars at 6000 feet. The enemy planes were first sighted 2000 feet above just as Ens Fewell was finishing a photo run. The Oscars executed an overhead on the planes and scored hits on Lt(jg)

Puryear's plane. The first Oscar pulled up in front of the formation as the Jap pilot recovered. Lt McReynolds and Ens Dailey got in good bursts which caused the Oscar to smoke heavily on fall out. Further observation was prevented by an attack by the second Oscar which continued in its dive past the planes. The F6Fs gave chase but were unable to catch the Oscar."

"The four planes joined up and when at 8000 feet encountered a mixed flight of 6 Tojos and Oscars and a general melee ensued. Ens Dailey engaged a Tojo in a head-on encounter from below. He fired two good bursts and observed his tracers entering the Tojo's engine and port wing root. A flash occurred in the wing root and the plane was smoking heavily as it passed overhead."

"The enemy planes soon broke off their attack and the photographic division joined the strike group at the coast as it was returning...."

In the various dog fights with the Japanese on February 25, five VF-4 Hellcats were hit. The Japanese pilots knew by now that our F6Fs could take a tremendous number of slugs without going down. Of course, a lucky shot that killed the pilot or a gas-tank explosion was a sure credit to the enemy. After this flight our fighters reported:[6]

"The Tojo exhibited remarkable climbing ability and maneuverability. The enemy pilots, had they been aggressive and capable, could easily have been much more effective."

"Both the Tojo and the Oscar could easily out turn the F6F but the 'protection weave' enabled our pilots to counter the enemy attacks. The Tojo does not burn easily."[7]

Something else was new on this attack on the Japanese homeland. This was the first strike dur-

The Imperial Palace in Tokyo was strictly off-limits for bombing. August, 1945.

Diet (Parliament) Building, which was also off-limits for bombing. Tokyo. August, 1945.

Burned-out section of Tokyo. August, 1945.

Destroyed plant. Tokyo. August, 1945.

ing which we dropped propaganda leaflets from the bomb bay as the bomb load was released. Two of these leaflets have been translated by Nobuko Fukunaga[9] who was in Tokyo at the time they were dropped.

Leaflet No. 407 shows the Emperor speaking to young Japanese people. It emphasizes the importance of education. *"Hard study and do good work... you must be happy to help other people."* The more subtle message is to caution the people against suicidal attacks or fanaticism. *"...Do best for Japan and don't die easy way... if stay alive best for country."*

The second leaflet (No. 519) is more direct. *"Do you know that a very powerful American Base is only 1500 miles from Tokyo. ...American Navy is operating freely in Japan Sea... Japan is entirely alone... American submarines are very fast and sink Japanese ships faster than Japan can build them... Japanese people say get rid of Japanese Military before too late so Japan don't end up like Germany."*

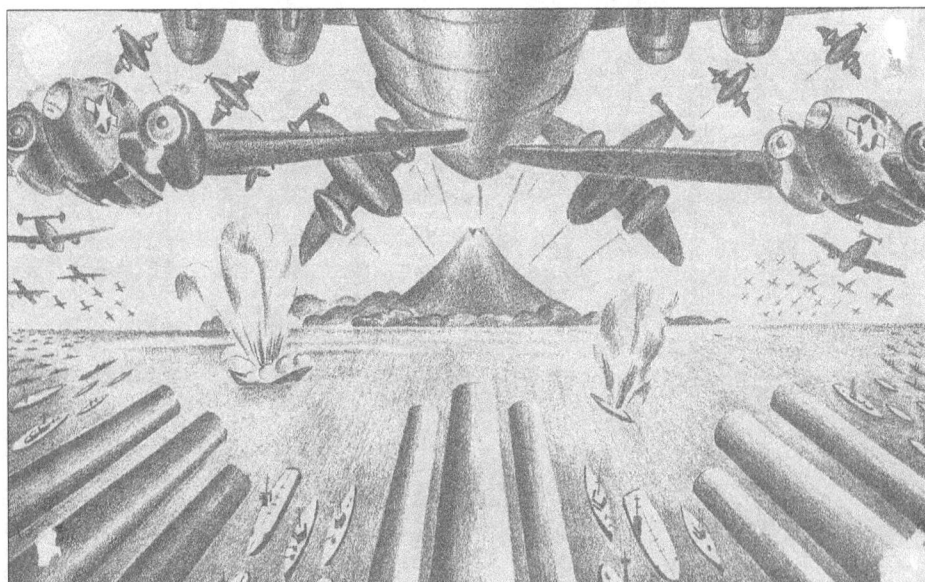

The propaganda leaflets, 407 (top) and 519, that we dropped on Tokyo. February 25, 1945.

Chapter 33 | Okinawa

"Cahoon disappeared... Vogt bailed out."

Admiral Mark Mitscher ordered Task Group 58.3 out of the Tokyo area on February 26. Records from the *ESSEX* show: [1]

Feb 26 -- *"Retiring to southward. Scheduled strikes against Nagoya, Kobe, and Osaha cancelled when high seas prevented reaching a favorable launching position."*

Feb 27 -- *"Fueling and receiving replacement aircraft in area about 100 miles SW of Iwo Jima."*

Feb 28 -- *"Steaming in TG 58.3 en route initial launching point SE of Okinawa Jima for air attacks against the same."*

Mar 1 -- *"Operating in TG 58.3 about 75 miles SE of Okinawa Jima, launching strikes against enemy installations on Okinawa Jima."*

Naha Airfield, Strike Able -- March 1, 1945

Aircraft launches began at 0715 with a major strike group under the command of Cdr F. K. Upham, CAG-4. There were 16 VT-4 pilots flying Avengers with fighter cover and strike support from 16 VMF Corsairs and 15 VT Hellcats. The target was Naha Airfield on Okinawa.[2]

"...Upon reaching the field, VMF pushed over first, followed by VF. VT dropped last. VF and VMF returned for repeated strafing runs against a/c, buildings, and AA positions."

The two Marine divisions were led by Major F. V. Domke and Capt Edward P. Hartsock. They dived through intense AA fire to strafe and bomb several planes that were on the service apron and in revetments.

The first four VF-4 fighter-bombers went in on the tails of the Marines, pushing over from 14,000 feet in 60-degree dives. One of the first four Hellcats was carrying a 1000-pound bomb and three were carrying two, 500-pound bombs each. The bombs exploded on the building and revetment area.

While the fighters were still in the dive, Lt Hamrick led the Avengers into a 35-degree dive from the strike altitude of 13,500 feet. There was a dense undercast of clouds at about 4000 feet. Ham reported that this cloud layer and the intense anti-aircraft fire forced a high pullout. Hamrick's strike group consisted of: [2]

Strike Alpha -- March 1, 1945

Lee L. "Ham" Hamrick (pilot)
   W. M. Hardin and H. L. Goodwin (crew)

Keith Gardner
   P. J. Wilson

J. E. Hewitt
   C. W. Lathrop

Felix E. Ward, Jr.
   C. J. Warrington

E. A. "Ted" Newell
   W. J. Lace

W. J. Hopkins, Jr.
   Stan W. Coller

Will S. Souza
   T. R. Sims

L. A. "Cozy" Cole
   N. L. Shiverdecker

B. R. "Trex" Trexler
   C. W. Barr

Torpedo 4 and crewmen. Thomas on wing, sixth from right. *USS ESSEX*. Februray, 1945.

Strike Alpha -- March 1, 1945 (continued)

G. M. Bell
  R. R. Pittman

Robert F. "Bob" Ruth
  J. F. "Forrest" Ballard

L. C. Gray
  H. R. Green

G. D. "Mak" Makibbin
  J. C. Gerke and P. J. Madden

Vernon A. Landre
  Charlie C. Statler

W. H. Cannady, Jr.
  A. G. Schiesz

It was hard to assess the damage from the VT bomb drops due to the scattered clouds. However all of the bombs hit the airstrip and supporting facilities.[2]

"The 8 VF armed with 6-5 inch [rockets] followed the VT in their attacks on Naha and fired 48 rockets into the revetment and building areas. The damage accomplished by these hits was unobserved."

Following the bombing and rocket attacks, the VF-4 and VMF fighters made three strafing attacks on aircraft in the revetments and along the airstrip. They also attacked antiaircraft emplacements, which were giving us plenty of trouble.[2]

"In the last attack Lt(jg) Cahoon disappeared and has not been recovered. Members of the division reported that he was with the flight just as they commenced their last strafing run of the day and failed to join up when the group rendezvoused west of the airfield over the sea."

"On return to base a special search was expedited but was in vain."

Capt Bedford was on a rescue mission that was more successful:[3]

"...we got word that a pilot was down about 8 miles from Naha, they wanted 2 F4U's to escort 2 OS2U-3 float planes to pick up swimmer."

"Gil Boyd and myself took escort. Proceeded to Naha with 2 OS's from S. Dakota, skirted S. tip of Okinawa, observed large fires in these areas."

"4 F4U's from BUNKER HILL were circling survivor who had rubber boat out, he was on tip of very small island, more of a shoal about 5 miles W. of Naha. OS landed and taxied close as possible, pilot paddled to meet him in boat. Took off."

"Boyd and I strafed rubber boat and sank it. Pilot shot down was Marine from BUNKER HILL, VMF-451, he's O.K."

Final Toll at Okinawa -- March 1, 1945

The **ESSEX** launched a photo mission and fighter sweep at 1300 under Lt P. H. Gordon. There were 15 Hellcats scheduled for this flight over Okinawa. The weather at the time of takeoff was extremely bad.[2]

"The plane piloted by Lt(jg) Puryear made a water landing off the starboard bow of the ESSEX immediately after becoming airborne.... The pilot was rescued by the destroyer, USS WALDRON."

Twenty minutes after the VF photo flight cleared the deck, the second coordinated strike group for the day was launched. While still on the flight deck one of our TBMs chewed up Dunlap's tail. He did not notice this damage and was moving into the takeoff spot when a flight-deck Chief stopped him.

It was my turn to fly with Strike Baker. We were going back to Naha -- and the stories about the intense AA defenses were not encouraging.

Our strike group consisted of 8 F6Fs, 16 F4Us, and 15 TBMs.[2]

"This flight was under the leadership of Major Marshall. Plans of approach and

Two examples of Doug Cahoon's artwork, *Attack on Luzon* (top) and *Pull Up*.

attack were made prior to takeoff, provided for 2 divisions of VMF to attack first, concentrating on AA positions, VFB and VT to follow. Adverse cloud conditions hindered the attack, and bombing results were not fully observed. Repeated strafing runs produced damage as shown."

"One division of VF attack Machiato airfield but cloud conditions were only slightly better and results unobserved."

P. J. Davis led our Torpedo 4 flight. Our tactical organization was: [2]

Strike Baker -- March 1, 1945

P. J. Davis, Jr. (pilot)
  R. F. Gray (crew)

C. N. W. "Scott" Vogt
  R. E. Kelly

G. M. "Buck" Barnett
  C. Christopher

W. F. "Willie" Walker
  S. A. Hastings

Page P. Stephens
  A. Beard

Vernon A. Landre
  A. "Tony" DeCenso

Gerald W. "Jerry" Thomas
  J. E. Holloman

R. M. "Hoppy" Hopfinger
  A. W. Yarman

Ed S. Binder
  R. D. Biddle

H. J. Deimel
  C. L. Ely, Jr.

G. D. "Mak" Makibbin
  R. Campbell

W. H. Cannady, Jr.
  A. G. Schiesz

Felix E. Ward, Jr.
  Don M. Applegate

Strike Baker -- March 1, 1945 (continued)

Will S. Souza
  D. L. Huston

J. E. Hewitt
  C. W. Lathrop

Makibbin, Cannady, Ward, Souza, and Hewitt were on their second strike for the day, as were crewmen Lathrop and Schiesz.

The debriefing report by P. J. Davis states: [2]

"The island of Okinawa was entirely obscured by clouds and had to be located by radar after the flight had passed approximately 35 miles west of target. The target, Naha airfield, could be seen through holes in the undercast only in part and from very few positions. Attack was initiated from southeast to northwest, VT pushing over from 12,000 feet and dropping through the undercast. Average speed in glide was 305 knots indicated.... Propaganda leaflets were dropped manually over target by rear seat crewmen...."

I knew we were in trouble when we approached the Naha airfield. There was only one small hole in the clouds and P. J. circled before he led the group through this opening. This gave the AA gunners plenty of time to blanket the hole. It was black with bursts of Ack Ack as I pushed over, but I followed the other planes. I saw one of the Avengers in front of me explode in the dive. This plane was piloted by Scott Vogt.[2]

"As Lt(jg) Vogt dropped his bombs, the first three or four were seen to release in train and then the remainder fell in salvo, exploding approximately 100 feet below the plane. The after part of the plane was blown off and the plane spiralled left. One parachute was observed to open over target at approximately 6000 feet."

A search was conducted since it might have been possible for the parachutist to have drifted over water. Results of the search were negative.

Most of us who saw the plane explode and someone hit the silk did not see any possibility that the parachute would drift over water. We believe that due to the nature of the explosion it was the pilot, Scott Vogt, who was able to get out of the Avenger. Furthermore, it is highly possible that, as the airman drifted down, he served as target practice for the Japanese machine guns.

"Scott Vogt's real last name was Wright. He took the name Vogt from his stepdad Bill Vogt who ran a clothing store in Danville, Illinois. Mr. Vogt put 12 other guys like Scott through college, and he wanted Scott to take over his clothing store and carry the name. Scott was married just a month before we left the States." [4]

Perhaps our strike made a small contribution to the eventual capture of Okinawa by the Americans. D-Day for the invasion of Okinawa took place on April 1, 1945, in the last -- and the bloodiest -- major amphibious operation of the Pacific War. *"In almost three months America had lost 12,520 GIs, Marines, and sailors.... The Japanese lost 110,000 troops."* [5]

This was the last combat mission for Air Group 4. The loss of Doug R. Cahoon of Fighting 4 on the morning strike and Curtis N. W. "Scott" Vogt with Robert E. Kelly of Torpedo 4 on Strike Baker was very depressing. Doug was the artist of VF-4. His combat paintings were later exhibited in Salt Lake City, Utah. Scott was the remaining transfer from the ill-fated Torpedo 8.

Lt(jg) Curtis N. W. "Scott" Vogt. **USS ESSEX**. Undated photograph.

Chapter 34 | More Kamikazes at Ulithi

"...an examination of the wreckage... showed the pilot... [was] shankled to his cockpit."

The **ESSEX** headed for Ulithi Lagoon March 2, 1945, with target practice en route. My pilot's log shows a 4.4-hour flight on March 4, 1945, as the last Pacific entry. This brought my total flight time to date at 1050.1 hours with 90 carrier landings.

The latest scuttlebutt was that our air group would finally be sent home. We could not believe this good news until orders were cut and placed in our hands. There was now jubilation to spare!

Air Group 83 was to take our place on the **ESSEX**. We did not have any opportunity to interact with the new pilots -- to tell them what we had learned about minimizing losses to Japanese planes or how to avoid anti-aircraft fire. However, Cdr F. K. Upham, CAG-4, and Lt Col W. A. Millington, Skipper of the Marine squadrons, prepared summary reports for use by Air Group 83 or the higher levels of Command.

Cdr Upham submitted several recommendations on the makeup and organization of strike groups: [1]

> *"A fighter sweep followed by a large strike group is a most effective type of attack."*

> *"A strike group composed of all VB and VT available in a Task Group with bomb-loaded VF escort can deliver an effective and destructive blow to any target.... The large number of planes not only adds to the protection against enemy aircraft but spreads antiaircraft fire over the larger group."*

Upham added a comment about operational training between strikes: *"It is believed that one day of Group Gropes is sufficient after leaving port for an operation."* The term "Group Grope" was widely used for these practice coordinated attacks and the appropriate remark as we landed back aboard, frequently with lost or damaged planes -- was "another SNAFU!"

The last several strikes certainly bore out Upham's next recommendation.

> *"The advisability of sending strikes against, or bombing airfields where no extensive facilities are located is questionable.... Results seldom seem to warrant the effort expended or the risks involved.... Pilot morale is greatly lowered by only a few losses in attacks against this type of target."*

I remember vividly the disgust I felt on the Naha airfield run as Scott Vogt's plane exploded, and I looked down at the airfield to see only dummy or damaged aircraft to decoy us from spotting the nearby gun emplacements. This strike was far from a morale booster -- it was a trap!

Both Upham and Millington[2] commented on engineering and mechanical failure -- freeze-ups of machine guns at high altitudes; altimeter and air-speed indicator problems with freezing weather; bomb hangups; poorly mixed napalm; "window" damage to tail assemblies; and the need for better radar jamming devices. CAG-4 also stated that *"Intelligence material available for Tokyo area was far superior in quality and quantity than that for Luzon-Formosa area."*

I was surprised to learn that our Air Group Commander added a final comment about our trusty Avenger. He recommended that *"The TBM-TBF be discarded when the SB2C with a similar*

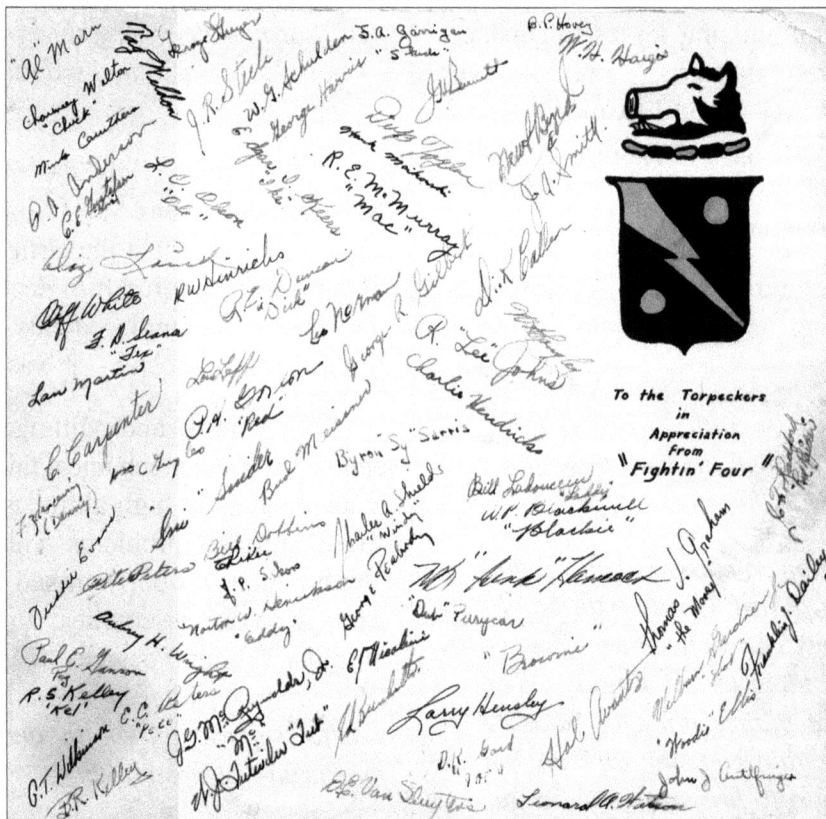

Torpedo 4 (top) and Fighting 4 signature cards signed as we prepared to leave
Ulithi for the States. March, 1945.

bomb and torpedo capacity is available." This statement would shock most torpedo pilots as well as cause concern on the part of the VB-4 pilots who labeled the SB2C a "pilot killer." Granted, our TBMs were slow, but they were far more reliable than the SB2C.

At any rate, I was no longer concerned about these "important decisions" for the fleet. As "Material Officer" in Torpedo 4, my primary assignment as we prepared to transfer off the *ESSEX* was to try to account for the various items of squadron and Navy-issued personnel gear that should remain for the next VT squadron.

Fortunately, our regulations could be loosely interpreted during wartime. I signed for most new items coming to the Squadron without too much hassle. However, new aircraft required a theoretical transfer of funds. Each new plane had a unit price of $1.00. Each new engine also required the $1.00 unit cost. Items such as wrist-watches, pistols and flight gear, including the traditional aviators' silk scarf, could stay with the pilots and crew, with a notation in their flight log book. We did not know what to do with the various war souvenirs each person had accumulated. For example, I had traded a fifth of Schenleys whiskey to a Marine on Saipan for an M-1 carbine. We were told that these items would be confiscated when we reached the States, but inspections by that time were nonexistent.

Shortly after we had transferred all AG-4 personnel to the *USS LONG ISLAND* for the trip to Pearl Harbor, I recorded the following account of a Kamikaze attack. The date shown in my journal was March 11, 1945.[3]

"Torpedo Four was finally headed for stateside -- after three tours of duty; one in the Atlantic on the RANGER with the British Home Fleet; one on the BUNKER HILL in the Pacific (starting with strikes on the Philippines); and a third on the ESSEX (ending with the invasion of Okinawa). Now we were in Ulithi Lagoon, transferred to the baby flat-top LONG ISLAND

for the trip back home."

"It was after dark. 'Mak' Makibbin and I were up on the flight deck watching the crew load damaged planes for the trip back. The flight deck of the LONG ISLAND was lit up like a Christmas tree. As a matter of fact, most of the ships in Ulithi were well lighted. After all, the war was nearly over (perhaps), Ulithi was well secured and a long, long way from the Japanese -- except for Yap Island, which was still occupied but essentially neutralized by the 'practice' bombing every week by Marines and Navy planes."

"At any rate, 'Mak' and I were talking about the trip home when we heard planes overhead -- two, at least. These planes sounded different from any we were used to hearing so we speculated out loud on the kind of plane making this new sound. Both of us finally decided the strange sound was probably the new Curtiss float plane -- recently introduced for cruiser duty. Neither of us had heard this plane, but we had seen ID pictures in ward room training sessions. About the time we reached this conclusion, there was a huge explosion on the RANDOLPH anchored next to us. Fire followed the explosion. 'Mak' and I immediately ran around the flight deck of the LONG ISLAND trying to kick out the lights -- anything to prevent a further attack by what obviously was a Kamikaze."

A few minutes after the first plane dived into the flight deck of the *RANDOLPH*, a second plane flew into the ground on Mog Mog Island -- probably mistaking the lights for an aircraft carrier. We learned later that the second plane didn't do much damage but did make a sizable hole in the ground.

The *RANDOLPH* was burning, more explosions followed the hit, sirens started, and GQ sounded. Fortunately, most of the crew of the *RANDOLPH* were up forward watching a movie on the hangar deck when the Kamikaze hit. Pawloski described the events this way.[4]

"Weary sailors were searching for good seats at the movie.... Suddenly, at 8:07, a Kamikaze took precedence over the entertainment by crashing into the starboard side of the ship, below the flight deck. The twin-engine Japanese bomber exploded, instantly erupting fires everywhere."

"Fire fighters leaped into action impulsively while damage control parties applied their valuable training. The flames were under control at midnight and completely extinguished by 6:00 a.m."

"Twenty-five men had been killed and 106 wounded from the Kamikaze visit. The sultry yet annoying voice of Tokyo Rose poured out loud and clear over the ship's radio. Japan's lady broadcaster announced

*that the prearranged attack had been planned for the **USS YORKTOWN** CV-10 and added:* **'Think you're nice and safe at Ulithi don't you? Well, we're fixing a little surprise for YORKTOWN.'"**

Navy records show that the **RANDOLPH** was repaired and returned to duty in less than three weeks. Later research indicated that the Kamikaze was a Japanese "Frances," a twin-engine bomber. W. E. Reynolds[5] reports that:

"...the Japanese sent two dozen of these suiciders all the way from Minami Daito Shima, 800 miles to the north. Apparently, only two or three of their pilots had known how to navigate. And an examination of the wreckage of the one on the Randolph showed the pilot to have been shankled [sic] to his cockpit!"

VMF-124 and VMF-213 signatures. Ulithi. March, 1945.

Chapter 35 | Torpedo Four Heads Stateside

"Don't even mention the word 'Kamikaze.'"

After recovering from the surprise Kamikaze attack at Ulithi, the **LONG ISLAND** completed loading damaged planes and raised anchor for the trip to the States. The ship's log shows that we departed Ulithi on March 12 and reached Pearl Harbor March 23.[1] We were then transferred to the **USS ALTAMAHA**, which departed Pearl on March 24 and docked in San Diego on April 1, 1945.

This trip on two baby flat-tops was more like a pleasure cruise for Torpedo 4 than a wartime assignment. It provided the last opportunity for the losers at poker or craps to try to recover. It was a time for sharing the limited beer and hard liquor supplies. It was also a time for reflection on our combat losses and successes.

We were still bitter about the last strike on Naha, Okinawa. The loss of Scott Vogt and Doug Cahoon seemed so unnecessary. Then, too, there were some guilt feelings. One of the fighter pilots took on a crying jag related to his combat role. He was being accused of purposely "downing" his aircraft, returning to the carrier with "engine trouble," taxiing into parked planes on deck, and otherwise avoiding strikes over enemy territory. This pilot talked to me, but I did not know the circumstances, so I was not much help. I do not intend to check the actual flight records to clarify this situation because I understand of the pressures he was under. Also, partial responsibility may rest with the leaders in the squadron, who could have removed him from combat flight status if they had doubts about his stability.

As the **LONG ISLAND** slowly pushed through the Pacific waves taking us out of the war zone, we talked about the role of those left fighting the Japanese. There was increasing evidence that the Japanese would not capitulate without an invasion of the mainland. The fanaticism of the Japanese troops, the willingness of young men to join the Kamikazes, and other evidence of suicidal stands meant that the Japanese homeland would not fall without extremely heavy losses of Allied forces. The firm orders that we were given, "Don't even mention the word 'Kamikaze,'" when we arrived stateside was further evidence that the war was far from over.

Regardless of the status of the war, it was unlikely that those of us in Torpedo 4 would be assigned another combat tour. We had served in both the European and the Pacific theaters. The squadron, and our associates in Fighting 4, Bombing 4, and Marine squadrons VMF-124 and 213 had made a fair contribution to the total war effort. Two of our fighters, D. S. "Diz" Laird and H. T. "Hubbie" Houston attained the status of "ACE." There were no identifiable heroes in Torpedo 4, but, we could carry with pride the decorations attained as individuals and the recognition that went with our three aircraft carriers.[2]

Note: Most Torpedo 4 personnel are eligible for the citations shown in italic print.

USS RANGER (CV-4)

- *American Defense Service Medal with bronze "A"*
- *American Area Campaign Service Medal*
- *European-African-Middle Eastern Campaign Medal with two battle stars*
- *World War II Victory Medal*

USS BUNKER HILL (CV-17)

- *Presidential Unit Citation*
- *American Area Campaign Service Medal*
- *Asiatic-Pacific Campaign Service Medal with eleven battle stars*
- *World War II Victory Medal*
- *Philippine Liberation Campaign Ribbon*
- *Republic of the Philippines Presidential Unit Citation Badge*

USS ESSEX (CV-9)

- *Presidential Unit Citation*
- *Navy Unit Citation*
- *American Area Campaign Service Medal*
- *Asiatic-Pacific Area Campaign Service Medal with 13 battle stars*
- *World War II Victory Medal*
- Navy Occupation Service Medal
- China Service (extended) Medal
- Korean Service Medal with 4 battle stars
- United Nations Service Medal
- National Defense Service Medal
- Armed Forces Expeditionary Medal
- Navy Expeditionary Medal
- *Philippean Liberation Campaign Service Ribbon with 2 stars*
- *Republic of Philippines Presidential Unit Citation Badge*
- Republic of Korea Presidential Unit Citation Badge

The *ESSEX* was labeled the "fightin'est Ship in the Fleet."

Until I researched the archives, I, like most of the members of Torpedo 4, had very little knowledge about ribbons or citations appropriate to our service in WWII. Nor did we realize that we had flown some joint missions with a torpedo pilot who later gained national and international renown.

George H. W. Bush, who was elected President of the United States in 1988, was one of the pilots of VT-51, operating from the aircraft carrier, *USS SAN JACINTO*. VT-4 and VT-51 had some parallel activities, including several strikes on Japanese shipping and shore facilities. Bush's Avenger was

shot down over Chichi Jima on September 2, 1944. A part of the combat report from the Navy Operational Archives follows: [3]

> *"Lt(jg) Bush, was piloting the third plane over the target. Bush's plane was hit in the engine shortly after final push over at 8000 ft. In spite of this hit which caused his engine to smoke and catch on fire, Lt(jg) Bush continued in his dive, releasing his bombs on the radio station at 85.6-50.6 to score damaging hits."*

> *"After releasing his bombs, Lt(jg) Bush turned sharply to the east to clear the island..., smoke and flames enveloping his engine and spreading aft as he did so, and his plane losing altitude.... At a point approximately 9 miles bearing 045° T from Minami Jima, Bush and one other person were seen to bail out from about 3000 ft. Bush's chute opened and he landed safely in water, inflated his raft and paddled farther away from Chichi Jima. The chute of the other person (either Lt(jg) [W. G.] White or J. L. Delaney, ARM 2/c) who bailed out did not open."*

> *"The rescue sub, **USS FINBACK** promptly effected rescue of Lt(jg) Bush, who was unhurt, planes of VF-20 remaining over Bush's raft to protect him. While Lt(jg) White and J. L. Delaney are reported missing in action, it is believed that both were killed as a result of action above described."*

This report on Lt(jg) Bush serves as a reminder that, while VT-4 was en route to the States, other Navy airmen were still in the combat zone flying into AA fire while ships crews were defending their home base against Kamikazes.

The *ALTAMAHA* pulled into San Diego Harbor on April 1, 1945 -- D-Day for Okinawa. Air Group 4 had arrived stateside after more than 8 months in the Pacific.

World Again at Peace

"...that a better world will emerge... a world dedicated to the dignity of man and the fulfillment of his most cherished wish for freedom, tolerance and justice."

The arrival of the ***ALTAMAHA*** in San Diego meant the end of a long and close association for the pilots and crew of Torpedo 4. Some of us had been together since February, 1943 -- much of the time confined to the Ready Room or to limited ships quarters. We had become as close as members of the same family.

New orders for all hands were issued before we dispersed from San Diego. After a 30-day leave, Bob Ruth, Will Souza, Felix Ward, and I were to report to the Naval Air Station, Corpus Christi, Texas, as flight instructors. We were glad to stay together, but we would have preferred a west coast assignment.

The authorized 30-day leave -- the longest I had received since joining the Navy -- was filled with exciting events. The war was obviously winding down. This gave everyone a feeling of elation -- a sense of buoyancy. In addition, as returning service men, we were welcomed everywhere as heroes.

I was anxious to get back to Idaho and Montana to see my parents and relatives. But, of much more importance, I wanted to follow-up on the occasional correspondence I had received in the Pacific from a beautiful young schoolteacher named Jean Ellis. She was originally from a ranch in Clark County and was now teaching grade school in Pocatello, Idaho.

While on the ***ESSEX***, I had fantasized that my periodic correspondence with Jean might lead to a deeper relationship. So I called her up as soon as I reached Idaho. We dated in Pocatello and went on horseback rides in the hills above Lidy Hot Springs. Before my 30-day leave was up, we were engaged to be married. I was now flying high -- and not even in the cockpit of my trusty Avenger.

We encountered one serious problem with our marriage plans. Jean had joined the WAVES and was awaiting orders. I couldn't stand a forced separation, so we contacted everyone we could think of in the Navy with an outline of the situation. The higher echelons of the Navy knew that the war was about over and, unbelievably, they authorized an Honorable Discharge for Jean "without any active duty."

I was still on leave when Franklin Delano Roosevelt, 32nd President of the United States, died. The date was April 12, 1945. This announcement sent shock waves through our military establishment. For nearly four years in the Navy, I had felt secure in knowing that America was in the good hands of a knowledgeable Commander-in-Chief. The deep sense of loss was not mitigated as a relative unknown, Vice President Harry S. Truman, took over our supreme command. Fortunately, American military momentum did not falter, and Truman was prepared to face some difficult decisions, including the use of the atomic bomb and the future of the Japanese Empire.

I reported for duty at NAS, Corpus Christi, on schedule and was back in the cockpit of an SNJ on May 17. I was preoccupied with my upcoming marriage, but I still tried to keep abreast of the blur of changes sweeping through both theaters of war.[1]

April 5, 1945 -- The Japanese Imperial Navy commanded its remaining men-of-war to engage the Americans in a final banzai. *"Second Fleet is to charge the enemy anchorage of Kadena off Okinawa Island... fuel only a one-way passage will be supplied."*

Pilot's license obtained by Jean while teaching school in Pocatello, Idaho.

Jean and I standing in front of my old 1939 Nash, which I had purchased before the war. My Mother volunteered to help Jean drive it to Corpus Christi so we could get married. The trip took five, very difficult days.

April 6 -- Kamikaze attacks off Okinawa sank two US destroyers, *BUSH* and *CAL-HOUN*.

April 7 -- TF 58 planes, with repeated attacks, sank the Japanese battleship *Yamato*, the cruiser *Yahagi*, and 4 destroyers. The US lost 10 planes and shot down 54 enemy aircraft.

April 12 -- The US destroyer *MANNER L. ABELE* was sunk by a Japanese "Baka" -- a piloted bomb.

News hit the States on April 18 that Ernie Pyle, American war correspondent, was killed by a sniper on Okinawa. Everyone seemed to know and respect Ernie for his courageous reporting of the war. Two more deaths of famous people soon followed.

April 28 -- Benito Mussolini was shot by Italian partisans while attempting to flee Italy.

April 30 -- Adolf Hitler shot himself, and his new bride, Eva Braun, committed suicide with cyanide capsules.

The German High Command surrendered unconditionally 7 days after Hitler's death. Churchill and Truman proclaimed May 8, 1945, as VE-Day. There was a great celebration all over the Allied world. I was in Corpus Christi and was not caught up in the mass excitement that was reported in most American cities. And, fresh from the Pacific, I knew that the world was still not at peace.

During the month of April, 30 US ships were hit by bombs or Kamikazes. The suicide attacks continued into May and June. Seventeen ships were hit in one day -- May 5 -- off Okinawa.[1]

Our former home at sea, the *BUNKER HILL*, was hit by two Kamikazes on May 11, resulting in a death toll of 346.[2]

Okinawa was finally captured on June 22, and General Douglas MacArthur announced that the Philippines had been liberated on July 5, 1945.[1]

Another important event took place in June -- Jean and I set June 2 as our wedding date. I was so excited I could hardly keep track of the "Flight" of French cadets assigned to my care at the Naval Air Base. These "Frogs," as they were called, were carefree but dangerous flyers. I worried about getting my wings or tail chewed up by their props as we flew haphazard close formation. And the inverted-spin check-outs for the cadets left me in a daze for several hours after the ride. The only plane that we had on the base that could take the rigors of the inverted-spin check was the old N2S biplane. This Stearman, with the open cockpit, was really a joy to fly -- particularly for aerobatics.

Between flights, I made arrangements for our wedding ceremony at the Naval Air Station Chapel. My worst problem was finding a place to live. The housing situation in Corpus was critical -- and most of the empty apartments were filthy and roach infested. I rented one, found another a little better, rented it, and finally rented a third -- the top floor of a small house. No money back on the first two rentals. I became so well acquainted with the lady real estate agent that she set up a reception for us following the wedding ceremony.

In a letter home dated May 20, I stated my frustration with the Navy because they would not allow time-off for my wedding, *"Here is the sad news. I've been to see every big shot on the base with this result. It is impossible for me to get over one day off to get married regardless of the circumstances. I've checked every possibility. That settles that matter."* It was obvious that the Naval aviation program was still under pressure from the Pacific war.

My mother and Jean drove my 1938 Nash from Idaho to Corpus Christi for the wedding. The tires on the car were retreads, but rationing prevented the purchase of new ones. Consequently, it wasn't long before the tires started throwing rubber and more old retreads had to be located. Add a few mechanical problems and the trip to Corpus took 5 days. Jean called periodically to report the circumstances slowing progress toward our reunion. The

Jean and Gerald, wedding photo. Corpus Christi, Texas. June 2, 1945.

Bob Ruth was my "Best Man."

Felix Ward "gave Jean away."

wedding date was still firm for June 2.

Jean's sister, Lois, came over from Louisiana for the ceremony. My Navy buddies filled in the other slots to complete the wedding party. Jean asked Felix Ward to go down the isle with her to "give her away." Bob Ruth served as Best Man. Other pilots provided moral support.

With so much help from the Navy at the ceremony, I knew it would be wise to leave town after the reception. We chose the most unlikely town close to Corpus Christi. No one would expect anyone to go to Beeville for a 1-day honeymoon -- and sure enough we were not followed. I picked out the only hotel in downtown Beeville -- small, old, rundown, no bridal suite, and without air conditioning. The Texas heat -- and the overhead fan -- really made an impression on my new bride.

I reported back to the flight line on schedule a day after our honeymoon in Beeville. Only now, I was a married man, and consequently, a more cautious pilot.

My log book shows 2-4 hops every day except Sunday through June, July, and August. We heard nothing about the experimental explosion of the first atomic bomb at the test facility near Alamogordo, New Mexico, on July 16. Then the big news came on August 6!

"A 9000-pound atomic bomb with destructive power previously unimagined was dropped by the US B-29 Enola Gay on Hiroshima at 8:15 a.m. It seared the center of the city for a fraction of a second with a heat of 300,000° centigrade. It is still not clear how many people died. Official US estimates of the dead were placed as high as 78,000. Japanese sources place the figure as high as 240,000 (about half the people in Hiroshima at the time)." [1]

The second atomic bomb was dropped on Nagasaki on August 9. Casualties from this explosion were estimated at 35,000.

Those of us fresh from the Pacific War -- and, probably those still in the Pacific -- applauded President Truman's decision to release these two bombs. We wanted the war to end without a costly invasion of the Japanese homeland. The tens of thousands of casualties produced by the atom bombs in these two Japanese cities could not compare with the estimates that, *"There will be more than a million casualties if an invasion of Japan becomes necessary."* At the time of the first atom bomb drop, only a few scientists and military leaders had any concept of the more indirect and more lasting implications of this unprecedented use of an atomic weapon. The threat of a "nuclear holocaust" did not emerge until the world was well into the Cold War.

My pleasure with the recent turn of events in Japan is reflected in a letter to my parents.

"August 13, 1945"
"Dear Mother and Dad,"

"I find it hard to concentrate with the radio full on, but Jean and I do not wish to miss the first flash of the impending Japanese surrender. Golly, this last week has been eventful from the war standpoint. It is hard for me to realize that the war may soon be over. I am so happy about the latest developments that I can hardly control my emotions. I sincerely hope that today may be VJ day."

"With the end of the war in sight we begin to wonder what will happen to those of us in the service. The Navy has given us no hint as to what may become of Naval aviators. However, I believe that the majority of us will stay on active duty for about a year. Whether I will be held in Corpus Christi as an instructor I do not know. I may be called on to serve another period of overseas duty during the period of occupation but I rather think some of these fellows who have had continuous state-side duty will go first.

In any event I'm looking forward to returning to college for further Forestry work...."

"We are still enjoying married life. Wouldn't be surprised if we tried another two months."

"Love,"
"Gerald and Jean"

VJ-Day was proclaimed by the Allied powers on August 15, 1945. While there had been wild celebrations as the European war ended, this was the big day for those of us who had experienced a touch of the Pacific. Corpus Christi was jubilant. Church bells rang, horns blared, and people took to the streets. I was out at the Naval Base, and Jean was taking a course at the beauty school when we heard the news. All duty was cancelled. We called Bob and Clara Mae Ruth and joined them in a big celebration -- **unconditional surrender by the Japanese!** The world was again at peace!

World War II had cost the lives of 14,904,000 men in battle and 38,573,000 civilians. In addition 25,218,000 individuals had been wounded -- many now unable to return to a productive post-war occupation. Surely, the cost of this war, and the lessons learned, would always remain with mankind to guide our future interrelationships.

The official signing of the surrender documents took place aboard the ***USS MISSOURI*** in Tokyo Bay on September 2, 1945. Among the dignitaries present were three of our previous commanders: Admiral Sir Bruce Fraser, Admiral Chester W. Nimitz, and Admiral William F. Halsey. General Douglas MacArthur signed for the Allied Powers. In his concluding remarks, General MacArthur stated: [1]

"It is my earnest hope -- indeed the hope of all mankind -- that from this solemn occasion a better world shall emerge out of the blood and carnage of the past, a world founded upon faith and understanding, a world dedicated to the dignity of man and the fulfillment of his most cherished wish for freedom, tolerance, and justice."

Jean and Gerald celebrate the end of WWII. Riviera Dinner Club,
Corpus Christi, Texas. August 15, 1945.

Chapter 37 | Readjustment

"But World War II Vets were supposed to be different. After all, this was a 'justified' war."

Three days after VJ-Day, I was back to my flight instructor duties. My Flight of French cadets had finally graduated. I was now trying desperately to get a new group -- this time they were English cadets -- through the final aerobatic, navigation, and ground training. These "Limeys," as they were called, were also wild flyers, but they, too, fought hard to keep from washing out.

Then the war ended! In a few days, my Limey cadets came in to see me with very sad news. They were ordered to report back to England "immediately." With only two weeks to go before receiving their "Wings of Gold," they were ordered home. I couldn't believe it!

I solicited the help of our CO and others, to see if we could get England to extend the time -- to allow the Flight to finish -- to let them get their wings. Our attempts failed. Their country was economically drained. There was no time and no money for an orderly phase down.

My life also changed rapidly, as did that of my old Torpedo buddies. Felix Ward was "Regular Navy," so there was no question that he would stay in the Service. But Will Souza and I were ready to go back to civilian life. Bob Ruth stayed with the Navy for a year, then headed for the family machine shop business in Deadwood, South Dakota. Will wanted to return to vegetable production in California. I still had aspirations for graduate school or ranching in Idaho.

The schedule for discharge from the military was set up on the basis of earned "points," giving credit for length of service, overseas assignments, and so on. However, there was a simpler way to qualify for release. Any person with a DFC or better was eligible for immediate discharge regardless of accumulated points.

Several of us took advantage of this regulation based upon citations and applied for inactive duty. Of course we had to agree to stay in the Reserves -- and perhaps become "Week-end Warriors" -- just in case the vision of a peaceful world might fade.

The last view I had from the cockpit of my SNJ was of Corpus Christi, Texas, on September 6, 1945. I flew solo for 2.5 hours -- with a happy but nostalgic feeling. I slow-rolled a couple of times -- just for fun. The world was at peace, I was happily married, and Idaho was a logical destination to start a new professional career.

It was soon evident, after the exhilaration of war's end faded, that the dream of a peaceful world was not to be. The seeds of a new confrontation were already sown during the last stages of the European occupation. The final agreement among the Big Three -- Stalin, Churchill, and Truman -- at the July 16, 1945, Potsdam Conference (code name TERMINAL) created some questionable country and political boundaries that could not last. This new world geography and the wide differences in concepts of government, economic development, and individual freedom between the Soviet Union and the Western World led to the so-called "Cold War." This new Cold War was destined to shape military and economic strategy for the next 44 years -- ending only with the collapse of the Berlin Wall in 1989.

But something unique in the history of world conflicts did emerge out of the devastation of World War II. That was a commitment on the part of the United States to assist very directly with economic recovery for Allies and enemies alike through the adoption of the "Marshall Plan." This

Torpedo Four aboard the "Essex" — Ulithi Lagoon — December 1944

front row: J.E.Gonley, T.W.Frost, A.J.Tonkard, R.R.Pittman, C.L.Ely, J.W.Aldrich, J.F.Ballard, S.A.Hastings, T.R.Sims, H.L.Blalock, G.J.Rauch, R.A.Trembley, E.A.Shirley, D.L.King, R.E.Simindinger, N.J.Schmolke, D.H.Gress, W.T.Lundry, W.S.Loce, H.R.Green.

second row: G.D.Makibbin, L.A.Cole, R.B.Cline, G.M.Barnett, B.R.Trexler, E.S.Binder, Scott Vogt, P.J.Davis, L.L.Hamrick, J.W.Harriss, G.W.Thomas, L.C.Gay, R.M.Hopfinger, J.E.Hewitt, L.G.Gardemal, P.P.Stephens.

third row: A.Beard, D.E.Venderville, L.S.Leach, J.J.Pinkney, L.E.Halverson, E.A.Newell, V.A.Landre, W.H.Gannady, D.A.Henry, J.D.Clemenson, H.J.Deimel, R.F.Ruth, W.F.Walker, F.E.Ward, W.J.Hopkins, G.M.Bell, W.S.Souza, C.Christopher, W.D.Jenkins, A.P.Robistow, C.J.Galeano, J.S.Serafin, N.L.Shivardecker.

back row: M.A.Clark, F.W.Wilson, S.W.Coller, A.DeCenso, J.C.Gerke, C.J.Warrington, G.F.Zeimer, R.E.Kelly, J.E.Holloman, D.L.Huston, N.H.Knox, A.Mocsary, C.L.McConnell, D.M.Applegate, R.C.Campbell, C.C.Slatter, L.P.Shuman, A.G.Schiesz.

The men of Torpedo Four (VT-4). These men have been called *"the Greatest Generation."*
It was the most honored privilege of my life to serve with them.
ESSEX. December, 1944.

approach and the various follow-up foreign economic assistance plans, including Food For Peace, helped bring about a miraculous recovery for many countries severely damaged by the war. Thanks largely to US policies (and support from the Allies) our two greatest enemies during WWII -- Japan and Germany -- emerged as the world's two great economic giants after the war. In the meantime, population growth and poverty problems of the so-called "Third World" became more visible -- while the solutions remained complex and frustrating.

As countries adjusted to the realities of war's end so did individuals. Some Torpedo 4 personnel remained in the Navy but most returned to civilian life a few months after war's end. Many took advantage of the GI training program to study for professional or vocational careers. Our postwar roster shows farmers, lawyers, doctors, teachers, postmasters, and mechanics -- the complete range of job classifications. While there were readjustment problems with individuals, most former VT-4 members have stated that they were thankful for a "busy" job and an understanding family.

Leo Halvorson stated that, *"I had a difficult time because some things that didn't bother me at all when I was in the Service became problems after the discharge. It took about 5 years before I got leveled out."* [1] Bob Ruth said he was phasing back to civilian life by flying as a "Week-end Warrior," when the Navy called him back for the Korean War. Thus, the stories vary.

After the war, I lost contact with my first two crew members, S. E. Garner and C. P. Jackson. One of my Pacific crewmen, John Holloman turned up at a cotton ginners conference in Lubbock, Texas, about 20 years after our return to the States. I was one of the speakers at the meeting. At that time Holloman was operating a cotton gin in New Mexico. He later died of a brain tumor -- supposedly brought on by a plane crash while he was in the Navy. Don Gress, my turret gunner, and his wife have attended most of the Torpedo 4 reunions. These informal reunions have provided an opportunity for pilots and crew to interact on a first-name basis without the restrictions of rank.

We hear so much about the lingering psychological problems associated with our men and women returning from Vietnam. We now know about -- and partially understand -- these lasting impacts. But WWII vets were supposed to be different. After all that was a "justified" war -- an all-out effort to save our freedoms and protect democracy from the horrors of Hitler and dictatorship. But, were WWII vets that different from those who fought in Vietnam? We all carry some scars. One of the worst is the guilt associated with your own survival when many more deserving buddies, particularly those with families back home, did not make it.

Like many WWII veterans, I was raised during the Great Depression. I was taught to respond to the directions of older adults -- to practice a certain level of self-discipline -- to respect the chain of command. During the war, I often felt like an inanimate weapon to be maneuvered at someone's command, rather than an individual who had some control of the situation.

I learned to take the strikes over enemy territory one at a time and to find diversions such as reading, shooting craps, or playing poker to keep my mind away from any events which might lie ahead. For this same reason I did not listen to Tokyo Rose or seek a pre-briefing until called to flight quarters for the next operation. I tried to think of the war as a game removed from realism. And I tried to discipline myself to forget the sad moments. Learning to forget was one key to survival. I was partially successful with this objective -- and part of my past did slip away. Right after the war, I found difficulty recalling the details of my years at the University of Idaho. The memories returned gradually, but I believe the self-training "to forget" helped with readjustment. In addition, my own adjustment was made easier by an understanding and supporting wife, a challenging profession, and the passage of time.

For several years after WWII, on the rare occasions when I flew as a passenger on a commercial DC-3, I re-experienced some wartime feelings. I felt very uncomfortable if we hit bad weather -- I "sweated through" the flight as if I was in the cockpit with the pilot -- always wondering if the pilot had adequate instrument training and if he could "find the flight deck."

I sympathized with the passengers -- particularly those who were experiencing their first few commercial flights. But most of all I had trouble separating each flight from the combat sensations of the war. As I looked out of the small DC-3 windows at the ground, I immediately spotted potential targets and anti-aircraft gun emplacements. I was tense and ready for the glide-bombing run or the masthead attack. I had to purposely remind myself that the war was over, this was the United States and not Japanese-occupied territory. I have talked with other combat pilots who have had similar overwhelming impressions.

Many of us went through another significant adjustment to stateside duty. This might be called the "move back to materialism." On my return to the US, I could not understand why the civilian population was so enamored with food stamps or gas rations. How could these things have such high priority compared with the real issues of life and death? Survival was important, but surely not tires for the car or sugar for the cereal.

A few weeks after my return to the States I changed my mind. I saw the problems my folks were facing back on the farm with the shortages of fuel and farm supplies. I saw the maneuvering that went on to combine gas rations for a trip to visit the relatives. I saw the value in obtaining additional sugar rations to bake a cake for the returning veteran. In a very brief period of time, I, too, began to place high priority on material goods. Perhaps human nature has not changed in spite of the pressures of periodic wars.

My tour of duty with Torpedo 4 took me to places in the world that I could not have visualized from my rural parochial background in Idaho. Many of those "far away places with the strange sounding names" became identifiable locations on the map. My Navy experience helped me to develop a better concept of our interdependent world and a strong conviction that the ultimate road to world peace lies in education and improved communication and not in confrontation and conflict.

Thomas receives the Distinguished Flying Cross with two Gold Stars from Capt John G. Crommelin, Jr. Others unidentified. NAS, Corpus Christi, Texas. May 1945.

Appendix A | Ship and Aircraft Abbreviations

Combat Ships or Fleet Units

BB -- Battleship
CL -- Cruiser
CV -- ESSEX Class Aircraft Carrier
CVE -- Escort Carrier
CVL -- INDEPENDENCE Class Aircraft Carrier
DD -- Destroyer
DE -- Destroyer Escort
TF or TG -- Task Force or Task Group
UB or U/B -- Submarine or U-Boat

Auxillary Ships or Transports

AK, AO, AP, FTB, FTC, LSM

Air Units or Aircraft

CAG -- Carrier Air Group
CASU -- Carrier Aircraft Service Unit
VB -- Bomber Group or Aircraft
VF -- Fighter Group or Aircraft
VMF -- Marine Fighter Unit or Aircraft
VNF -- Night Fighter Group or Aircraft
VT -- Torpedo Group or Aircraft

U.S. Aircraft Cited

B-24 -- Consolidated-Vultee "Liberator"
B-25 -- North American "Mitchell"
B-29 -- Boeing "Superfortress"
F4F -- Grumman "Wildcat"
F4U -- Chance-Vought "Corsair"
F6F -- Grumman "Hellcat"
J2F -- Grumman "Duck"
N3N -- Navy "Yellow Peril"
N2S -- Stearman Trainer
OS2U -- Vought-Sikorsky "Kingfisher"
P-38 -- Lockheed "Lightning"
P-40 -- Curtiss-Wright "Warhawk"

U.S. Aircraft Cited (continued)

SBC -- Curtiss Divebomber
SBD -- Douglas "Dauntless"
SB2C -- Curtiss "Helldiver"
SNC -- Curtiss Trainer
SNJ (AT-6) -- North American Trainer
SNV -- Vultee Trainer
TBD -- Douglas "Devestator"
TBF or TBM -- Grumman "Avenger"

German Aircraft Cited

FN-190 -- Focke-Wulf Fighter
HE-111 -- Heinkel Bomber
JU-87 -- Junkers "Stuka"
JU-88 -- Junkers Bomber
ME-109 -- Messerschmitt Fighter

Japanese Aircraft Cited

Betty -- Mitsubishi G4M Medium Bomber
Emily -- Kawanishi H8K Flying-Boat
Frances -- Yokosuka P1Y Navy Bomber
Helen -- Nakajima Ki-49 Medium Bomber
Irving -- Nakajima J1N Reconnaissance Plane
Jake -- Aichi E13-A Seaplane
Jill -- Nakajima B6N Attack Bomber
Judy -- Yokosuba D4Y Bomber
Kate -- Nakajima B5N Torpedo Bomber
Lily -- Kawasaki Ki-48 Bomber
Nell -- Mitsubishi G3M Bomber
Oscar -- Nakajima Ki-43 Fighter
Sally -- Mitsubishi Ki-21 Medium Bomber
Tony -- Kawasaki Ki-61 Fighter
Tojo -- Nakajima Ki-44 Fighter
Val -- Aichi D3A Dive-Bomber
Zeke or Zero -- Mitsubishi A6M Fighter

U.S.S. ESSEX

PLAN OF THE DAY

Saturday   25 November 1944.
DUTY SECTION - 2ND   DUTY DIVISION - AIR
Sunrise 0655 (Zone minus 9).

Carry out Sea Routine.

0430 Early breakfast for 79 pilots, and 60 aircrewmen.
0535 Reveille.
0555 General Quarters.
0655 Secure from General Quarters.
0710 Breakfast.
0730 Group "E" air bedding.
1300 Pipe down aired bedding.

GENERAL PLAN: Strikes on North Central and Northern Luzon.

NOTES: 1. The following battle zone rules are effective at reveille:

        (a) Have helmets, flash proof clothing and live
            jackets instantly ready at battle stations.
        (b) Put fire retardant bunk covers on at reveille,
            and leave o n until further orders.
        (c) Wear dog tags.
        (d) Uniform shall include shirts with long sleeves,
            (sleeves may be rolled up until further orders).
        (e) No sunbathing.
            (If conditions permit, the word will be passed
            permitting removal of shirts and sunbathing).

       2. All hands are advised that smoking is prohibited on all
exposed portions of the ship, such as fantail, forecastle, etc.,
after darken ship has been executed.

                        DUTY LIST

        Duty Commander - Lt.Comdr. O.R. Adams (298).

        Air Department - Lt. G. Donnelley (258).
        Gunnery Department - Lt. E.L. Andronik (450).
        Duty Gunner - Ch.Gunner F. Brophy (480).
        Hull Department - Lt. D.G. Saunders (407).
        Duty Boatswain - Bosn. G.L. Parker (624).
        Engineering Department - Lt(jg) L.L. Herzig (200).
        Communication Department - Lt. R.C. Baxter (427).
        Navigation Department - McLaughlin, Q2c (221).
        Supply Department - Lt. G.E. Horne (527).
        Medical Department - Lt. R.V. Bachman (999).

        O.O.D.   J.O.O.D.   T.B.S.

08-12 Lt(jg) Spencer   Ens. Kribs   Lt(jg) Kalczynski
12-16 Lt. Cauffman   Ens. Cooke   Ens. Wyman
16-18 (Lt. Montgomery   Ens. Lucas   Ens. Woolf
      (Lt. DeRosa
18-20 Lt. McDonald   Ens. Hastings   Ens. Phillips
20-24 Lt. Czarniecki   Lt(jg) Miller   Ens. Teschner
                         26 November 1944
00-04 Lt. Poucher   Ens. Martin   Lt(jg) Kalczynski
04-08 Lt(jg) Spencer   Ens. Kribs   Ens. Wyman

                                    D. L. McDONALD,
                                    Commander, U.S. Navy,
                                    Executive Officer.

Plan of the Day - November 25, 1944. The day the *ESSEX* was hit by a Kamikaze.

References

1. Operation Leader: Initiation Over Norway

1. German News Release, July 1943.
2. Cressman, Robert J. 2003. *USS Ranger: The Navy's First Flat-top from Keel to Mask*. Brassey's Inc, Washington, D. C.

2. OPERATION LEADER: The Historical Record

1. Combat Reports, AG-4. U.S. Navy Operational Archives, Naval Historical Center, Washington, D.C.
2. USS RANGER Ship's Log. U.S. Navy Operational Archives, Naval Historical Center, Washington, D.C.
3. During a visit to Bodø, Norway, in May 1990, Will Souza, VT-4 pilot, discovered that the Norwegians had located Lt(jg) Tucker's SBD and planned a salvage operation. Underwater photos indicate skeletal remains in the cockpit.
4. Correspondence from D. W. Taylor to Reginald Miller family, October 17, 1943.
5. German Report on OPERATION LEADER, provided by Steinbjorn Mentzoni, Sandnessjøen, Norway.
6. Interview with John Palmer, VT-4, November 1988.
7. Palmer Interrogation by Germans, provided by Alf Larssturold, Norway.
8. Interview with Odd Karlsen, October 4, 1993.
9. USS RANGER (CV-4) News, September 26, 1993.
10. Complete names with appropriate ranks for all combat flights are shown in the Index.

3. Origins of Torpedo Four

1. Navy Department. 1946. History of the USS Ranger. Stencilled.
2. Taped Interview with George Cuhna, VT-4 Pilot.
3. Taped Interview with Whitey Muller, VT-4 Ranger Reunion Historian.
4. Taped Interview with Charlie Barr, VT-4 Crewman.
5. Taped Interview with W. S. Souza, VT-4 Pilot.
6. Taped Interview with A. DeCenso, VT-4 Crewman.
7. Thomas, Gerald W., VT-4 Pilot. Personal Journal.
8. Tillman, Barrett. 1980. *Avenger at War*. Charles Scribner & Sons, New York.
9. Taped Interview with Homer H. Hamrick, VT-4 Executive Officer.
10. Taped Interview with G. M. Barnett, VT-4 Pilot, 1989.

4. The North Atlantic

1. Von der Porten, Edward P. 1969. *The German Navy in World War II*. Galahad Books, New York.
2. Churchill, Winston S. 1975. *The Second World War*. (Vol. IV). Library of Imperial History, London.
3. USS RANGER (CV-4) News, September 26, 1993.
4. Transcript, radio broadcast by Rowe, February 15, 1944.

5. USS RANGER Ship's Log.
6. Nelson, Roy. USS Ranger Newsletter, April 1990.
7. Tillman, Barrett. *Avenger at War*.
8. Correspondence with Charlie Barr, VT-4 Crewman.
9. Combat Reports, AG-4.
10. Correspondence with P. P. Stephens, VT-4 Pilot.
11. Taped interview with W. S. Souza, VT-4 Pilot.
12. Gunn, J. 1932. *Orkney: The Magnetic North*. Nelson & Sons, London.
13. Thomas, Gerald W. Letter home, January 28, 1944.
14. VT-4 Squadron Records, U.S. Navy Operational Archives, Naval Historical Center, Washington, D.C.
15. Thomas, Gerald W. Personal Journal.
16. USS Ranger Newsletter, 1988.
17. Goralski, Robert. 1981. *World War II Almanac, 1931-1945*. Perigee Books.

5. Change in Command

1. Thomas, Gerald W. Personal Journal.
2. Goralski, Robert. *World War II Almanac, 1931-1945*.
3. Chace, Capt William B. 1980. "The Cheap Seats" In Avenger At War by Barrett Tillman.

6. Tragedy Strikes Night Operations

1. Correspondence with P. P. Stephens, VT-4 Pilot.
2. Taped Interview with Mrs. June (Hutcheson) DeDakis.

7. The Pacific Theater

1. Goralski, Robert. *World War II Almanac, 1931-1945*.
2. USS BUNKER HILL Operational Records. U.S. Navy Operational Archives, Naval Historical Center, Washington, D.C.
3. Combat Reports, AG-4.
4. Taped Interview with Lloyd Cole, VT-4 Pilot.
5. Records from Admiral Nimitz Museum, Fredericksburg, Texas.

8. Introduction to the Philippines

1. Goralski, Robert. *World War II Almanac, 1931-1945*.
2. Combat Reports, AG-4.
3. USS BUNKER HILL Operational Records.

9. Cavite and Manila Harbor

1. Goralski, Robert. *World War II Almanac, 1931-1945*.
2. Statler, C. C., VT-4 Crewman. Personal Journal.
3. Combat Reports, AG-4.
4. Taped Interview with G. M. Barnett, VT-4 Pilot.
5. Taped Interview with L. A. Cole, VT-4 Pilot.
6. Taped Interview with N. L. Shiverdecker, VT-4 Crewman.
7. Taped Interview with Norm Applegate, VT-4 Crewman.

8. Taped Interview with Bob Ruth, VT-4 Pilot.

9. Taped Interview with Forrest Ballard, VT-4 Crewman.

10. Taped Interview with Stan Coller, VT-4 Crewman.

11. Vogt and his other crewman, R. E. Kelly, were shot down later over Naha, Okinawa, and reported missing in action.

12. Taped Interview with Leo Halvorson, VT-4 Crewman.

13. Both Lt(jg) Donald Dondero and his gunner Chester Knozek survived.

14. USS BUNKER HILL Operational Records.

10. Bunker Hill: Recap and Critique

1. Declassified Memo from C.O., USS BUNKER HILL to the Commander-in-Chief, Pacific Fleet. U.S. Navy Operational Archives, Naval Historical Center, Washington, D.C.

2. Confidential Memo from Commander, Air Group Four, to C.O., USS Bunker Hill. U.S. Navy Operational Archives, Naval Historical Center, Washington, D.C.

11. Phylogeny of a Torpedo Pilot

1. Thomas, Gerald W. Personal Journal.

2. Thomas, Gerald W. Correspondence.

3. Goralski, Robert. *World War II Almanac, 1931-1945*.

4. The US Government carried no insurance on us while we were in "Elimination Base" training.

12. Shakedown on the Essex

1. The USS ESSEX: CV-9, U.S. Navy Publication.

2. VF-4, *The Red Rippers. A History of Fighting Four*.

3. Taped Interview with Lloyd Cole, VT-4 Pilot.

4. Thomas, Gerald W. Personal Journal.

5. Combat Reports, VB-4.

6. Combat Reports, VT-4.

13. Essex Takes a Kamikaze

1. Thomas, Gerald W. Personal Journal.

2. Toland, John. 1971. *The Rising Sun: The Decline and Fall of the Japanese Empire*. Bantam Books.

3. Taped Interview with W. S. Souza, VT-4 Pilot.

4. Taped Interview with Andy Marge, VT-4 Crewman.

5. Taped Interview with Don Gress, VT-4 Crewman.

6. Taped Interview with Tony Schiesz, VT-4 Crewman.

7. Taped Interview with J. F. Ballard, VT-4 Crewman.

8. Taped Interview with Page Stephens, VT-4 Pilot.

9. The USS Essex: CV-9, U.S. Navy Publication.

10. Combat Reports, AG-4.

11. Goralski, Robert. *World War II Almanac, 1931-1945*.

14. San Fernando Harbor

1. Combat Reports, VF-4.

2. Combat Reports, VB-4.

3. Taped Interview with W. S. Souza, VT-4 Pilot.

4. Combat Reports, VT-4.

15. Meanwhile, Back on the Ranch

1. Thomas, Gerald W. 1982. *Food and Fiber for a Changing World*. (Second Edition). Interstate Printers.

2. Genung, A. B. 1940. "Agriculture in the World War Period." In Farmers In a Changing World. USDA Yearbook of Agriculture.

3. White, Theodore. 1978. *In Search of History*. Harper and Row, New York.

4. Goralski, Robert. *World War II Almanac, 1931-1945*.

5. Wilcox, Walter W. 1947. *The Farmer in the Second World War*. Iowa State College Press, Ames, Iowa.

6. Eskew, R. K. and Paul Edwards. 1950 - 1951. "Food and Feed from White Potatos." In Crops in Peace and War. USDA Yearbook of Agriculture.

7. I applied for a discharge on the basis of points in September, 1945, and my wife and I returned to Idaho. I still believed that there must be some way to get into the ranching business. An inventory of my assets revealed that I had no cattle that could be clearly identified as mine, and only 2 or 3 horses. My saddle was worn out and I owed 3 years of back income taxes.

    As a WWII veteran I was invited to participate in a random drawing for sagebrush land in southern Idaho. The size of these blocks ranged from 40-80 acres -- supposedly with underground water for potential irrigation. I was lucky. My name was not drawn. These parcels of land, that seemed to promise immediate wealth for the lucky vets after the war, provided only hard work and poverty-level living a few years later. I decided to accept an offer to work for the US Soil Conservation Service -- an outdoor job as close to farming and ranching as I could find. This decision shaped my future professional career.

8. Freeman, Orville L. 1940. "The Development of Agricultural Policy Since the End of the World War." In Farmers in a Changing World. USDA Yearbook of Agriculture.

16. A Question of Security

1. Goralski, Robert. *World War II Almanac, 1931-1945*.

2. Sherrod, Robert Lee. 1952. *History of Marine Corps Aviation in World War II*. Combat Forces Press.

17. Support for Mindoro Occupation

1. Combat Reports, CAG-4. Comments and Recommendations on Air Operations for the Period 22 Nov-2 Dec, 1944.

2. The USS Essex: CV-9, U.S. Navy Publication.

3. Taped Interview with Bill Cannady, VT-4 Pilot.

4. Potter, E. B. 1976. "Nimitz." Naval Institute Press.

5. Combat Reports, VF-4.

6. VF-4, *The Red Rippers. A History of Fighting Four*

7. Combat Reports, VT-4.

8. Combat Reports, VB-4.

18. Flying Conditions Average

1   Calhoun, Capt C. Raymond. 1981. *Typhoon: The Other Enemy*. Naval Institute Press.

2   Pemsel, Helmut. 1977. *Atlas of Naval Warfare*. Arms and Armour. Press, London.

3   The USS Essex: CV-9, U.S. Navy Publication.

4   Potter, E.B. 1985. *Bull Halsey*. U.S. Naval Institute Press.

5   Taped Interview with L. L. Hamrick, VT-4 Pilot.

6   Goralski, Robert. World War II Almanac, 1931-1945.

19. Marines Replace Dive Bombers

1. Sherrod, Robert Lee. 1952. *History of Marine Corps Aviation in World War II*. Combat Forces Press.

2. "War Diary of Two Marine Squadrons -- VMF-124 and VMF-213 Aboard the USS Essex." Airgroup4.com.

3. War Diary, VMF 124 and VMF 213. U.S. Navy Operational Archives, Naval Historical Center, Washington, D.C.

4. USS Essex. "Report of Circumstances Surrounding Shooting Down of Friendly B-24 Over Camranh Bay." U.S. Navy Operational Archives, Naval Historical Center, Washington, D.C.

20. Forbidding Formosa

1. USS Essex Ship's Log. U.S. Navy Operational Archives, Naval Historical Center, Washington, D.C.

2. Sherrod, Robert Lee. *History of Marine Corps Aviation in World War II*.

3. CAG-4 Report on Air Operations 30 Dec-26 Jan, 1945. U.S. Navy Operational Archives, Naval Historical Center, Washington, D.C.

4. Combat Reports, VF-4 and VT-4.

5. VF-4, *The Red Rippers. A History of Fighting Four*.

6. War Diary, VMF 124 and VMF 213.

7. Bedford, Capt William J., VMF-124 pilot. War Journal, *Aboard the Essex*. Courtesy of W. J. Bedford IV. Capt Bedford died in a bombing practice mission in 1951 while on a tour of duty aboard the USS Oriskany.

21. More Strikes on Philippines

1. Statler, C. C., VT-4 Crewman. Personal Journal.

2. Sherrod, Robert Lee. *History of Marine Corps Aviation in World War II*.

3. Toland, John F. 1971. *The Rising Sun: The Decline and Fall of the Japanese Empire*. Bantam Books.

4. Combat Reports, VF-4 and VT-4.

5. Taped Interview with W. H. Cannady, Jr., VT-4 Pilot.

6. War Diary, VMF 124 and VMF 213.

22. US Landings on Luzon

1. Sulzberger, C. L. 1966. *The American Heritage Picture History of World War II*. Crown Publishers.

2. Combat Reports, VF-4 and VT-4.

3. War Diary, VMF 124 and VMF 213.

4. Taped Interview with Noel Shiverdecker, VT-4 Crewman.

5. VF-4, *The Red Rippers: A History of Fighting Four*.

23. South China Sea

1. Sherrod, Robert Lee. *History of Marine Corps Aviation in World War II*.

2. Admiral Halsey's Story. Cited by Sherrod.

3. Combat Reports, AG-4.

4. Combat Reports, VF-4 and VT-4.

24. Saigon Takes Its Toll

1. Combat Reports, VF-4.

2. War Diary, VMF 213 and VMF 214.

3. Sherrod, Robert Lee. *History of Marine Corps Aviation in World War II*.

4. Correspondence from Martin L. Mickelsen, 1989.

5. Taped Interview with L. L. Hamrick, VT-4 Pilot.

6. Taped Interview with T. R. Sims, VT-4 Crewman.

7. News Release, Idaho Falls Post-Register. Dec, 1945.

8. Interview with Leo S. Leach, VF-4 pilot.

25. Air Group Commander Lost: Pescadores

1. Combat Reports, AG-4.

2. Taped Interview with John Selka, CAG-4 Plane Captain.

3. Taped Interview with Don Alexander, CAG-4 Chief Yeoman.

26. In the Drink

1. Combat Reports, VT-4.

2. War Diary, VMF 213 and VMF 124.

3. Taped interview with Don Gress, VT-4 Crewman.

4. Taped interview with Willie Walker, VT-4 Pilot.

5. Bedford, Capt William J., VMF-124 pilot. War Journal, *Aboard the Essex*.

6. USS SULLIVANS Ship's Log. U.S. Navy Operational Archives, Naval Historical Center, Washington, D.C.

7. Statler, C. C., VT-4 Crewman. Personal Journal.

8. The USS Essex: CV-9, U.S. Navy Publication.

9. Taped Interview with Dan Jenkins, VT-4 Crewman.

10. Taped Interview with L. L. Hamrick, VT-4 Pilot.

11. Combat Reports, VF-4.

27. From the China Sea to Formosa

1. USS ESSEX Ship's Log. U.S. Navy Operational Archives, Naval Historical Center, Washington, D.C.

2. Statler, C. C., VT-4 Crewman. Personal Journal.

3. VF-4, *The Red Rippers. A History of Fighting Four*.

4. War Diary, VMF 124 and VMF 213.

5. Combat Reports, VF-4, and VT-4.

6. Bedford, Capt William J., VMF-124 pilot. War Journal, *Aboard the Essex*.

28. Premonition at Amami O Shima

1. Combat Reports, VF-4, VB-4, and VT-4.

2. Taped interview with Keith Gardner, VT-4 Pilot.

3. Bedford, Capt William J., VMF-124 pilot. War Journal, *Aboard the Essex*.

29. En Route to Tokyo

1. USS ESSEX Ship's Log.

2. Potter, E.B. 1976. "Nimitz.". Naval Institute Press.

3. Bedford, Capt William J., VMF-124. War Journal, *Aboard the Essex*.

4. CAG-4. 1944. Comments and Recommendations on Air Operations for the Period 30 Dec. 1944 to 26 Jan. 1945. U.S. Navy Operational Archives, Naval Historical Center, Washington, D.C.

5. Goralski, Robert. *World War II Almanac, 1931-1945*.

6. Combat Reports, VF-4 and VT-4.

7. Taped Interview with Bill Cannady, VT-4 Pilot.

8. VF-4, *The Red Rippers. A History of Fighting Four*.

9. News Release, Raleigh, N.C. (no date established).

10. Statler, C. C., VT-4 Crewman. Personal Journal.

30. Window and Jammers over Japan

1. Combat Reports, VF-4 and VT-4.

2. Taped Interview with Keith Gardner, VT-4 Pilot.

3. War Diary, VMF 124 and VMF 213.

4. Taped Interview with Bob Campbell, VT-4 Crewman.

5. Taped Interview with Lloyd Cole, VT-4 Pilot.

31. Iwo Jima

1. USS ESSEX Ship's Log.

2. Combat Reports, VF-4, VMF 124, and VMF 213.

3. Bedford, Capt William J., VMF-124 pilot. War Journal, *Aboard the Essex*.

4. Statler, C. C., VT-4 Crewman. Personal Journal.

5. VF-4. *The Red Rippers. A History of Fighting Four*.

6. Goralski, Robert. *World War II Almanac, 1931-1945*.

7. Taped Interview with G. M. Barnett, VT-4 Crewman.

8. Taped Interview with Stan Coller, VT-4 Crewman.

9. Toland, J. *The Rising Sun: The Decline and Fall of the Japanese Empire*.

32. Bombs and Propaganda for Japan

1. Taped Interview with Leo Halvorson, VT-4 Crewman.

2. Taped Interview with Noel Shiverdecker, VT-4 Crewman.

3. USS ESSEX Ship's Log.

4. War Diary, VMF 124 and VMF 213.

5. Bedford, Capt William J., VMF-124 pilot. War Journal, *Aboard the Essex*.

6. Combat Reports, VF-4 and VT-4.

7. Nine Japanese "Aces" shot down over 50 Allied planes. The leading Ace was Hiroyishi Nishizawa with 87 credited kills. The leading Navy Ace, Capt David McCampbell scored 34 kills. The top Marine Ace, Lt Col Gregory (Pappy) Gregory Boyington was credited with 28 planes destroyed in the air. Air Force Major Richard Bong shot down 40 enemy aircraft. Ten German pilots were credited with more than 200 planes each, with the top world Ace being Major Erich Hartmann--352 confirmed kills.

8. Goralski, Robert. *World War II Almanac, 1931-1945*.

9. Nobuko Fukunaga, now Mrs. Bassett, was not only in Tokyo at the time of this propaganda drop, but she also was in Hiroshima on August 6, 1945, when the US B-29 "Enola Gay" released the atomic bomb.

33. Okinawa

1. USS ESSEX Ship's Log.

2. Combat Reports, VF-4, VT-4, VMF 124, and VMF 213.

3. Bedford, Capt William J., VMF-124 pilot. War Journal, *Aboard the Essex*.

4. Taped Interview with Leo Halvorson, VT-4 Crewman.

5. Toland, John. *The Rising Sun: The Decline and Fall of the Japanese Empire*.

34. More Kamikazes at Ulithi

1. Upham, F. K. Action Reports CAG-4. U.S. Navy Operational Archives, Naval Historical Center, Washington, D.C.

2. Millington, W. A. Operations Report VMF 124 and 213.

3. Thomas, Gerald W., VT-4 Pilot. Personal Journal.

4. Pawlowski, Gareth L. 1971. *Flat Tops and Fledgings: A History of American Aircraft Carriers*. Castle Books, New York.

5. Reynolds, Clark G. 1976. *The Fighting Lady: The New Yorktown in the Pacific War*. Pictorial Histories Publishing Co., Missoula, Montana.

35. Torpedo Four Heads Stateside

1. USS LONG ISLAND Ship's Log. U.S. Navy Operational Archives, Naval Historical Center, Washington, D.C.

2. Pawlowski, Gareth L. *Flat Tops and Fledgings: A History of American Aircraft Carriers*.

3. Combat Reports, VT-51. U.S. Navy Operational Archives, Naval Historical Center, Washington, D.C.

36. World Again at Peace

1. Goralski, Robert. *World War II Almanac, 1931-1945*.

2. Pawlowski, Gareth L. *Flat Tops and Fledgings: A History of American Aircraft Carriers*.

37. Readjustment

1. Taped Interview with Leo Halvorson, VT-4 Crewman.

Index of Names

L

Labyak, R. W. [AP], 33, 46
Lace, W. J. [ARM3c], 167, 185, 211, 227, 245
Lacy, C. J. [ARM1c], 23, 33
Laird, Dean S. "Diz" [Lt], 23, 169, 225, 229, 231-232, 255
Landre, Vernon A. [Ens], 75, 80, 83, 110-112, 145, 171, 173, 181, 185, 189, 197, 213, 215, 223, 226, 239, 247, 249
Lathrop, C. W. [ARM3c], 76, 80, 125, 145, 170, 185, 211, 245, 249
Laws [Crewman], 33
Leach, Leo S. [AMM3c], 79, 110-111, 170, 192, 197, 218, 239
Lepp, Louis K. "Lew" [Lt(jg)], 21, 52, 111, 21, 206, 238
Libbey, Herbert L. [2nd Lt], 157-158
Longley, William H. [Lt], 21, 125, 229, 239
Lynch, Joseph G. [2nd Lt], 183, 191

M

MacArthur, Douglas [General], 32, 73, 165, 177, 226, 259, 262, 73
Madden, P. J. [PHOM1c], 247
Maikowski, Joseph Henry "Hank" [Lt(jg)], 193, 195
Makibbin, G. D. "Mak" [Lt(jg)], 19, 50, 55, 61-62, 65, 79, 83, 85, 110-112, 145, 161, 164, 167, 175, 181, 213, 223, 239, 247, 249, 253
Mann, R. C. [AMM2c], 79, 83, 111
Marn, A. [Ens], 107
Marshall, David E. [Major], 157
Martin, C. L. [Lt(jg)], 80, 83, 191, 193, 195, 225
Mayhew, Boyd N. [Lt(jg)], 21, 23
McBee, C. R. [Ens], 193
McCampbell, David [Cdr], 92, 107
McCanley, VB-20, 83
McCarley, Donald W. [ARM2c], 20-21, 23, 29, 32
McCauley, D. H. [Lt(jg)], 125
McConnell, C. L. [AMM2c], 79-80, 110-111, 145, 167, 170, 175, 181, 193, 218, 223
McGill, William G. [1st Lt], 209
McGuire, E. A. [AMM3c], 79, 111
McReynolds, John G., Jr. [Lt], 21, 241, 73, 85
Mentzoni, Steinbjorn, 20, 25, 27
Mickelsen, Martin L., 191-192
Miller, Jack, 20, 23, 27, 29

Miller, Reginald H. AMM1c], 20, 23, 29
Millington, William A. [Lt Col], 121, 153, 157, 159, 163, 185, 197, 212, 218-219, 221, 223, 232-233, 235, 237, 251
Mitscher, Mark [Admiral], 221, 226, 245
Mocsary, Andy "Marge" [AOM1c], 46, 75, 80, 83, 110-111, 115, 145, 161, 173, 175, 197, 223, 239
Molan, John T. [2nd Lt], 212
Montague, Robert B. [PhoM3c], 111, 125, 145, 161, 164, 167, 170, 173, 175, 178, 181, 193, 197, 199-202, 205
Moore, William H. [ARM3c], 21, 185, 213, 215, 217
Morken, D. A. [Lt], 239
Morris, Wayne [Lt], 91-92
Mortag, Daniel K. [1st Lt], 170
Mullins, 163-164
Mullins, Robert W. "Moon" [1st Lt], 163
Mussolini, Benito, 259, 54

N

Newell, E. A. "Ted" [Lt], 61, 76, 80, 110, 123, 125-126, 164, 167, 171, 176, 185, 189, 193, 211, 227, 239, 245
Nicholson, R. G. [Lt(jg)], 107
Nicolini, C. J. [Ens], 225

O

Olson, L. O. [Ens], 123, 193, 195
Ostlund, William N. [Ens], 85
O'Brien, B. O. [Ens], 125, 141, 80-81
O'Callahan, Chaplain Joseph T. [Lt Cdr], 23, 235

P

Palmer, John H. [Lt(jg)], 8, 13, 16, 21, 23, 27, 32, 43
Parker, George G. [1st Lt], 157-158, 225
Peabody, George A. [Lt(jg)], 123, 229, 232, 235, 76, 79
Peters, K [Ens], 125, 215, 225, 231-232
Pfremer [1st Lt], 237
Pletts, D. C. [Ens], 111, 141, 79
Puryear, W. R. [Lt(jg)], 241, 247
Pyle, Ernie, 259

Q

Quinn, William A. [Ens], 190-191

R

Radford, J. F. "Raider" [Lt(jg)], 55, 225
Reynolds, William E. [1st Lt], 207, 232, 254
Rhodes, William C. "Dusty" [Lt(jg)], 206, 215, 225-226
Rice, Delbert, 91, 139
Roosevelt, President Franklin D., 45, 89, 137, 257
Rowe, Gordon [Capt], 5, 25, 43-44, 51, 59, 194
Ruddy, Joseph A., Jr. [Cdr], 9, 23, 25, 31, 41, 59
Ruth, Clara Mae, 262
Ruth, Robert F. "Bob" [Lt(jg)], 8-9, 23, 31, 37-39, 42, 55, 57, 59, 67, 77, 80-81, 103, 110-111, 145, 167, 170, 175, 181, 193, 195, 211, 218, 223, 227, 247, 257, 260-263, 265

S

Sanderson, [Crewman], 33
Schiesz, A. G. [AMM2c], 80, 110, 125, 171, 227, 247, 249, 76, 80
Schmolke, N. J. [AOM1c], 75, 79, 83, 107, 110, 145, 161, 164, 169, 175, 197, 215, 223, 239
Schulden, W. G. [Ens], 225
Sears, Ferrell D. [Lt(jg)], 241
Seiler, Edward M. [Lt], 23
Selka, John, 195
Sherrod, Robert [Time correspondent], 139, 158, 177, 183-185, 189, 191
Shields, C. A. [Lt], 161
Shirley, Ellsworth A. [ARM2c], 76, 80, 110, 125, 145, 167, 173, 185, 189-193
Shiverdecker, N. L. [AOM1c], 80-81, 110, 125, 171, 176, 193, 227, 245
Shuman, L. P. [AMM2c], 76, 80, 110, 125, 161, 175, 193, 218, 227
Sikors, J. P. [Ens], 197, 225
Simendinger, Ray E., Jr. [AOM1c], 110, 125, 171, 185, 227, 239, 76, 80-81
Sims, Tom R. [AOM1c], 80, 110, 125, 164, 167, 171, 176, 185, 190, 193, 211, 245

About the Author

Gerald W. Thomas was born at home in Small, Idaho, in 1919. He grew up on a ranch during the Great Depression. His rural school went only to the 10th grade, so his Mother took his brother and him to California to finish High School and attend Junior College. He graduated from the University of Idaho just in time to volunteer for Navy service following Pearl Harbor.

Drawn to flying after seeing his first flying machine while salvaging rusty barb wire at an abandoned homestead, Thomas applied for, was accepted, and graduated from flight school.

As a Navy Cadet he was trained as a dive bomber, but his duty assignment was to Torpedo Squadron VT-4 as a carrier-based TBF torpedo bomber, serving on the *USS RANGER*, *USS BUNKER HILL*, and *USS ESSEX*, in both the Atlantic and Pacific Theaters.

While on the *RANGER*, he participated in OPERATION LEADER, the most significant attack on Northern Europe by a US carrier during the war. OPERATION LEADER was a strike against German shipping and shore installations along the fjords south of Bodo, Norway. This operation was a complete surprise to the German defensive forces and destroyed 23,000 tons of shipping, damaged 4 other ships, and killed about 200 German troops.

During LEADER, while attacking a freight barge carrying 40 tons of ammunition, Thomas' plane was hit by anti-aircraft fire. The engine began burning and it appeared the plane was going down. Thomas ordered his crew of two to bail out and had just opened the cockpit and was climbing out when his turret gunner yelled, *"Don't jump, don't jump."* The other crewman had accidentally opened his parachute in the belly of the plane. With bailing no longer possible, Thomas considered his options and decided their best chance was to fly the plane toward the carrier as far as it would go. Surprisingly, in spite of the considerable engine damage, the plane made it back to the *RANGER*, where Thomas crash-landed. That landing was his 13th official carrier landing.

In the Pacific, Thomas participated in the numerous actions against Japanese targets in the Philippines, including strikes on Ormoc Bay, Cavite, Manilla, Santa Cruz, San Fernando, Lingayen, Mindoro, Clark Field, and Aparri.

Following these actions, Thomas' squadron made strikes on Formosa, French Indo-China, Saigon, Pescadores, Hainan, Amami O Shima, Iwo Jima, Okinawa, and Japan. The attack on Japan was the first attack on Japan from an aircraft carrier since the "Doolittle Raid."

While on the *ESSEX*, just after Thomas had returned from a strike on Santa Cruz, the ship was hit by a Kamikaze piloted by Yoshinori Yamaguchi, Yoshino Special Attack Corps. Yamaguchi was flying a Yokosuba D4Y3 dive bomber. The Kamikaze attack killed 16 crewman and wounded 44.

Returning from a strike on Hainan, off the Chinese coast, Thomas' plane ran out of fuel. After a harrowing water landing, Thomas and squadron photographer Montague succeeded in inflating and launching one rubber boat and his crewman Gress another. After a long day in pre-Typhoon weather with 40 foot swells, the three were rescued by the *USS SULLIVANS*.

Following World War II, he earned a Ph.D in Range Management, and after stints as professor at Texas A&M University and Dean of Agriculture at Texas Tech University, he became president of New Mexico State University. He retired after serving as president for 14 years.

Thomas was awarded 3 Distinguished Flying Crosses, 2 Air Medals, and 2 Presidential Citations for his combat actions in WWII. He retired from the Navy Reserve with the rank of Lieutenant Commander.

Doc45 Publications

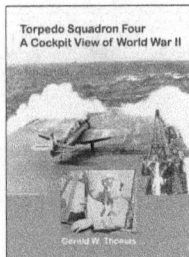

Torpedo Squadron Four – A Cockpit View of World War II, Gerald W. Thomas, paperback, 280 pages, 209 photos, e-book available.

"This book contains more first-person accounts than I have seen in several years. ...we can feel the emotion... tempered by the daily losses that characterized this final stage of the war in the Pacific. All in all, one of the best books on the Pacific War I have seen lately." – Naval Aviation News, Fall 2011.

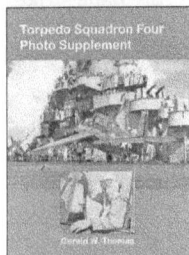

Torpedo Squadron Four – Photo Supplement, Gerald W. Thomas, e-book, 120 pages, 120 photos.

"I love authentic photographs, so this book was a huge enjoyment and a no-brainer since I already have the original book. Photos of the USS RANGER, USS BUNKERHILL, and USS ESSEX. Warbird photos I've never seen (American and Japanese) before. Also photos of Manila Harbor, Saigon, Japan, Iwo Jima and Okinawa – places the author attacked as a pilot of Torpedo Squadron 4 (VT-4)." – Amazon Reviewer

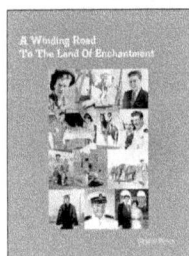

A Winding Road To The Land Of Enchantment, Gerald W. Thomas, paperback, 270 pages, 205 pictures, e-book available.

A memoir. Born in the smallest town in Idaho – aptly named Small, Idaho – in 1919, the author grew up on a ranch during the Great Depression. While in Junior College, he played baseball and tennis with Jackie Robinson. During WWII he served as an TBM Avenger pilot. Following the war, he pursued an academic career, eventually becoming president of New Mexico State University.

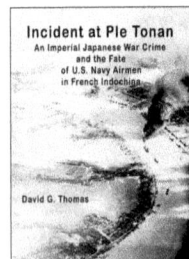

Incident at Ple Tonan, An Imperial Japanese War Crime and the Fate of U.S. Navy Airmen in French Indochina, David G. Thomas, paperback, 320 pages, 59 pictures.

This book began 33 years ago, in early 1990, with a question posed to the author by his father. The author's father was just completing his memoir of his World War II military experiences and he was greatly troubled by not knowing the fate of two of his fellow fliers in his USS ESSEX based air squadron, Torpedo Four (VT-4). The two men whose fate still haunted the author's father 45 years after the fact were shot down in an air raid on Japanese-occupied French Indochina.

The answer to this question would have remained hidden but for an Imperial Japanese war crimes trial. In this book, you will find the events, investigations, statements, related documents, and stories of the men that led to that trial - and the riveting testimony of the trial itself.

Not surprisingly, uncovering the stories of the two missing squadron members' fates also uncovered the stories of other men. Many of these others, as disclosed in this book, paid the ultimate price - some for heroism, and some for acts later judged war crimes.

The airmen killed in this incident were Lt(jg) Donald Augustus Henry, AMM2c Frederick Chester Barnes, AMM3c Thomas Joseph McGowan, AOM3c Gordon Hugh Yates, AMM3c Warren Halvor Daley, AMM3c Donald Howard Douglas, and S1c Joseph Nicholas Venditti.

The trial testimony of an Imperial Japanese war crimes trial has never been published before.